12·28·76

CHINA IN THE 1920S

A History of Modern China

CHINA IN THE 1920S

NATIONALISM AND REVOLUTION

Editors:
F. Gilbert Chan and Thomas H. Etzold

New Viewpoints
A Division of Franklin Watts / New York   London   1976

Library of Congress Cataloging in Publication Data
Main entry under title:

China in the 1920s.

(A History of modern China)
Bibliography: p.
Includes index.
1.   China—Politics and government—1912–1937—
Addresses, essays, lectures.   I.   Chan, F. Gilbert.
II.   Etzold, Thomas H.
DS777.47.C496   320.9'51'041   76–8246
ISBN 0–531–05383–0
ISBN 0–531–05589–2 pbk.

New Viewpoints
A Division of Franklin Watts
730 Fifth Avenue
New York, New York 10019

To C. Martin Wilbur
with affection and gratitude

Contents

Foreword
C. Martin Wilbur   ix

Preface
F. Gilbert Chan   xi

Introduction / A Decade of Challenge
Ssu-yü Teng   1

1
Sun Yat-sen and the Origins of the Kuomintang Reorganization
F. Gilbert Chan   15

2
Soviet Russia and Chinese Nationalism in the 1920s
Dan N. Jacobs   38

3
**From Revolutionary Iconoclasm to National Revolution:
Ch'en Tu-hsiu and the Chinese Communist Movement**
Richard C. Kagan   55

4
Training and Indoctrination at the Whampoa Academy
Richard B. Landis   73

5
**Nationalism and Revolution: The Nature and Causes of
Student Activism in the 1920s**
Ka-che Yip   **94**

6
**The Military and Nationalism: The Political Thinking
of Wu P'ei-fu**
Odoric Y. K. Wou   **108**

7
**Provincialism within the Chinese National Revolution:
The Case of Chekiang, 1926–1927**
Donald A. Jordan   **127**

8
Chiang Kai-shek's April 12th Coup of 1927
Tien-wei Wu   **147**

9
**Japanese Response to Chinese Nationalism: Naitō (Ko'nan)
Torajiro's Image of China in the 1920s**
Shumpei Okamoto   **160**

10
**In Search of Sovereignty: The Unequal Treaties in
Sino-American Relations, 1925–1930**
Thomas H. Etzold   **176**

Notes   **197**

Selected Bibliography   **232**

Contributors   **235**

Index   **239**

Foreword   C. Martin Wilbur

This volume deals with an important and exciting decade in the modern history of the Chinese nation. It was a turning point from political disintegration to reintegration. It was a time of surging nationalism. It was a period in which China's two modern political parties, the Communists and the Nationalists, cooperated in anti-imperialism and anti-warlordism, and then fell apart in a conflict that has never been healed.

The decade saw the beginnings of a number of modern institutions that have persisted, such as industrial unions, peasant associations, and other mass organizations; the politically indoctrinated national army; the hierarchical political party organized along Bolshevist lines. The new culture movement and the drive for emancipation of women flourished. It was a time of youthful idealism and activism.

The influence of revolutionary Russia was particularly strong. Its agents helped to develop the Communist movement and laid down the party's basic strategies, which were extremely successful at first but led to disaster by 1927. Soviet Russia also assisted the Kuomintang to change from a rather ineffective cluster of aging revolutionaries around Sun Yat-sen into a well-organized modern party equipped to rally the nation against China's humiliating international status and against power holders who were draining the nation's resources. Russia did not teach China anti-imperialism, yet it taught the Chinese leaders how to make that sentiment effective.

Quite a number of these matters are discussed in this exciting volume. The authors are careful scholars who have specialized in their research upon the topics that they present here in chapter form. Each takes a fresh look at subjects that previously, for the most part, have not been examined in detail. The writers are from a new generation of historians teaching in America, except for the veteran who introduces this volume, Professor Ssu-yü Teng. I know most of the writers well and several did their graduate work at Columbia. It is interesting to note that there is an equal balance between scholars of Asian and of western ancestry, an additional reason why the volume is so interesting. I am delighted to commend it.

Preface   F. Gilbert Chan

The decade of the 1920s was an epoch of cataclysmic changes in China. Ssu-yü Teng correctly labels it as "a decade of challenge." In the context of the Chinese revolution of the twentieth century, it marked an important transitional stage. Sun Yat-sen's proposals for a political solution to China's problems—the 1911 revolution, the anti-Yüan campaigns, and the so-called "constitution protection movement"—had mostly been unsuccessful. The intellectual revolution of the May Fourth period had lost much of its momentum. There was an urgent need for a new medicine to cure the national ills.

Under the tutelage of Soviet Russia, Sun collaborated with the Chinese Communists and launched a nationalist, anti-imperialist movement in the early 1920s. Thanks partly to its fresh emphasis on mass mobilization, the Kuomintang created in South China an atmosphere congenial to a social revolution. Yet, with the rise of Chiang Kai-shek in the midst of a bitter factional struggle and his subsequent purges of the Communists in 1926–1927, the party regressed "from revolution to restoration."[1] Whatever hope the radical revolutionaries may have had for social changes in China evaporated.

The two major themes of this volume are nationalism and revolution. My chapter on Sun Yat-sen and the origins of the Kuomintang reorganization provides the historical background behind his decision to collaborate with Soviet and Chinese Communists. In a complementary essay, Dan N. Jacobs examines the policy of the Kuomintang-Russian alliance with a basically Soviet orientation. Since he has completed a manuscript on Mikhail Borodin, his emphasis on the role of the Russian *sovetnik* in the execution of the policy appears reasonable. On the whole, he disagrees with Conrad Brandt and Harold R. Isaacs and gives the Soviet involvement in the Chinese revolution of the 1920s a more positive appraisal. [2]

Richard C. Kagan, Richard B. Landis, and Ka-che Yip analyze three significant aspects of the revolutionary movement of this decade: the birth of a politically indoctrinated party army, the early development of Chinese Communism under Ch'en Tu-hsiu's leadership, and the phenomenon of student activism. Tien-wei Wu's chapter on Chiang Kai-shek and the April coup of 1927 traces the events that led eventually to the collapse of the Kuomintang policy of collaboration with the Communists. The split between the two groups represented the conclusion of one important stage of the Chinese revolution. While Wu insists that the coup "was not a betrayal" of the revolutionary cause, he admits that Chiang "lost both the zeal for revolution and the trust of the masses that characterized his early success in Canton."

The remaining chapters concentrate on two principal topics of Chinese history in the 1920s. Odoric Y. K. Wou and Donald A. Jordan treat militarism with different emphases and reach different conclusions. In his study of Wu P'ei-fu's political thinking, Wou claims that the Chihli general had "genuine nationalist sentiments." According to Jordan, however, the three militarists in Chekiang defected to the Kuomintang during the Northern Expedition chiefly for provincial reasons. In the second pair of essays, Shumpei Okamoto and Thomas H. Etzold discuss the response of foreign powers to Chinese nationalism and revolution. A diplomatic historian, in particular a student of protection of citizens, Etzold focuses on legal questions and bases his study of American policy in China on government documents and consular dispatches. Okamoto breaks new ground in his examination of Sino-Japanese relations in the 1920s. Instead of evaluating the diplomacy of Shidehara Kijūrō and Tanaka Giichi, he probes into the writings of an influential Sinologist, Naitō Torajirō.

This volume is the product of the collective effort of a group of mostly young scholars, who share a common interest in a period of Chinese history that is still relatively unexplored. About half of the chapters are taken, in one form or another, from the doctoral dissertations of the contributors. Consequently, this volume does not claim to offer any definitive answer to the complicated historical problems of the era; it is rather a preliminary report on the research results of a fascinating subject in modern Chinese history.

Acknowledgments are due to Clarence K. Williamson, dean of the College of Arts and Science at Miami University, for his sponsorship of a conference on January 18–19, 1974. It provided the contributors with an opportunity to meet as a group in Oxford, Ohio. I am thankful for the participation in the conference of Samuel C. Chu of Ohio State University, Ping-leung Chan of the University of California at Los Angeles, Tsing Yüan of Wright State University, Leigh Kagan of Hamline University, and my dear friends at Miami, Richard M. Jellison, Dwight L. Smith, and Bruce W. Menning. They read some of the chapters and offered constructive suggestions for improvement. I am also grateful for the invaluable assistance— editorial and otherwise—of Jean Reynolds and Will Davison of New Viewpoints. No expression of appreciation is adequate for my wife, Rosalind, and our two children, Edmund and Sharon. The long hours I spent away from home cannot be compensated.

My association with Ssu-yü Teng dates back to 1969–1970, when he, as visiting professor, was a colleague of mine at the Chinese University of Hong Kong. Since then he has been both a teacher and a friend to me, always generous in helping me with my problems. With his introductory chapter, he brings respectability to the volume. To him, I am deeply indebted.

It is my personal privilege to have been a student of C. Martin Wilbur's; his knowledge of the period of Chinese history covered by this volume is unsurpassed. He is primarily responsible for directing my research interest to the decade of the 1920s. As a token of my appreciation, I dedicate this work to him with affection and gratitude.

CHINA IN THE 1920S

Introduction / A Decade of Challenge

Ssu-yü Teng

The Chinese in the period from 1910 to 1919 were at the crossroads between monarchism and republicanism; there were several years of indecision at this intersection. The first president of the Republic of China (established in 1912), Yüan Shih-k'ai, made himself emperor in 1916, but was forced to end his rule after eighty-three days and soon met a melancholy death. The following July, General Chang Hsün restored the abdicated Manchu emperor to the throne, but his rule lasted for only thirteen days. After these two unsuccessful attempts to restore the monarchy, people realized that its time was past.

The Japanese Twenty-one Demands imposed on Yüan Shih-k'ai, the new literature movement (both occurred in 1915), and the Soviet Russian revolutions spurred the Chinese intelligentsia to explore new directions. Some intellectuals believed in anarchy, nationalism, or socialism; others took interest in Mohandas K. Gandhi's passive resistance, Rabindranath Tagore's eastern civilization, Bertrand Russell's western philosophy, or John Dewey's pragmatic education. The May Fourth Movement in 1919 ushered in a new generation of revolution.

The first ten years of this revolutionary generation seem to have been a decade of challenge. The new challenged the old, the subordinate challenged the superior, the poor challenged the rich, the weak challenged the strong, and the East challenged the West.

Student Challenges Teacher; Modern, Old

In intellectual circles, students dared to challenge their teachers and questioned everything, including classroom assignments. The new vernacular expression *(pai-hua)* opposed the flowery classical style, paving the way for popular propaganda and mass movement. Ku Chieh-kang's study of history refuted the authenticity of the ancient King Yü, thus shortening Chinese written history by some fifteen hundred years. A Hunan scholar, Wu Yü, attacked the Chinese family and clan system, calling it the basis of despotism, while Fu Ssu-nien (later director of the Academia Sinica) criticized the Chinese family system as the source of all evils. Students challenged their teacher of teachers, Confucius; an anti-Confucian movement evolved, leading to serious doubts of Confucian ethics, moral standards, traditional human relationships, and old customs. The movement expanded to oppose Christianity and missionary schools, other religions, and superstitions.

In Chow Tse-tsung's words, the years following the May Fourth Incident witnessed "an era of mingled skepticism, romanticism, liberalism, realism, and anarchism in the thought of the new Chinese intellectuals. Traditional thought and institutions were criticized and attacked from every side." [1]

Subordinate Challenges Superior in the North

In political and military circles, there was a disjunction of leadership following the death of Yüan Shih-k'ai. No one was of the same caliber, enjoyed the same prestige, or commanded the same loyalty as the former "strong man" had. Yüan's demise, happening as it did during the loosening of ancient Confucian ties, permitted a series of complicated political and military problems to arise. Vice President Li Yüan-hung moved into the presidency and Feng Kuo-chang, a Chihli general, took over the vice presidency. President Li was soon challenged by his premier, Tuan Ch'i-jui, an Anhwei senior general of the Peiyang military clique, and was compelled to resign. In August 1917, Feng Kuo-chang became acting president

and, in agreement with Premier Tuan, declared war against Austria
and Hungary. On October 10, 1918, Feng turned over the acting presidency to his elected successor, Hsü Shih-ch'ang, a civilian proté-
gé of Yüan Shih-k'ai. Hsü, the fourth president of the republic, managed to remain in office for nearly four years. The first Chihli-Fengtien war broke out in May 1922. The Fengtien forces were defeated
near Peking, leaving Wu P'ei-fu, a general with a *hsiu-ts'ai* degree
in classical education, dominant in North China. The Chihli clique,
led by Ts'ao K'un and Wu P'ei-fu, demanded the resignation of
President Hsü Shih-ch'ang, who complied in June 1922. Li Yüan-
hung was again made president by the Chihli militarists, who dominated both the cabinet and the national assembly. After a year,
however, the president's former supporter, Ts'ao K'un, forced Li to
retire.

Ts'ao managed by bribery to be elected and was inaugurated as
the fifth president of the republic in October 1923. But he, too, was
challenged by a subordinate, Wu P'ei-fu, the powerful general of
the Peiyang military clique. Wu advocated the unification of China
by force, and this resulted in the second Chihli war, September-Oc-
tober 1924, with the Fengtien clique led by Chang Tso-lin, a warlord
of ignominious origins. As Wu's forces fought victoriously at the
border of Fengtien, Wu's junior general, Feng Yü-hsiang, suddenly
revolted against his superior. Feng engineered a coup in Peking
and, forcing President Ts'ao K'un to resign on November 2, 1924,
held him under house arrest until April 1926. General Wu P'ei-fu
was forced to flee to the Wuhan area where he gradually reestab-
lished and expanded his military power.

Feng Yü-hsiang also ousted the last Manchu emperor from the Peking palace; the emperor became a refugee resident in the Japanese
concession in Tientsin. The adroit Tuan Ch'i-jui was invited by
Feng, Chang Tso-lin, and Lu Yung-hsiang, the *tuchün*, or military
governor, of Chekiang, to serve as the provisional chief executive of
the Peking government in November 1924. After killing forty students in a public deomonstration on March 18, 1926, however, Tuan
Ch'i-jui was compelled to retire to the Tientsin Japanese concession
for the rest of his life.

For several months there was neither a president nor a chief executive in the Peking government; a few cabinet ministers, including V. K. Wellington Koo, stayed to look after the palace and
government buildings. In 1927 Chang Tso-lin, who had defeated

Feng Yü-hsiang, entered Peking and headed a military government
under the title of generalissimo. On June 3, 1928, he was forced by
the Nationalist army under Commander-in-Chief Chiang Kai-shek
to leave Peking for Mukden. As Chang Tso-lin's train approached its
destination, he was killed by a time bomb planted by the Japanese
Colonel Komoto Daisaku. There was evidence that a Japanese officer defied the order from the chief of the general staff in Tōkyō pro-
hibiting the disarming of the retreating forces of Chang Tso-lin. [2]

Subordinate Challenges Superior in the South

This was indeed an era when betrayal was the order of the day. The
Fengtien warlord Chang Tso-lin was betrayed by his subordinate,
Kuo Sung-ling, in December 1925, but this attempt failed. Chao
Heng-t'i (of the Hunan government) was driven away by his junior
officer, T'ang Sheng-chih, who took over the governorship.

Sun Yat-sen in the south was also betrayed by his subordinates.
Frustrated by the political swirl in the north, Sun in 1917 formed a
dissident government in Canton, a federation of six of the southern
provinces, with the intention of launching a campaign against the
northern warlords. He was elected generalissimo *(ta-yüan-shuai)*
of the military government in Canton and appointed Ch'en Chiung-
ming commander of the first Kwangtung army. Being a non-military
man and an unskilled politician, Sun was deprived of his authority
as generalissimo in 1918 by his inferiors, T'ang Chi-yao, Lu Jung-
t'ing, and other southern warlords. He was obliged to return to
Shanghai where he stayed for more than two and a half years, reading and writing. In November 1920, when the situation had stabi-
lized, he returned to Canton, and the following April he organized
the Government of the Republic of China, of which he was then
elected extraordinary president. He ordered Ch'en Chiung-ming,
army commander and governor of Kwangtung, to lead his army
against the Yünnan and Kwangsi militarists, T'ang Chi-yao and Lu
Jung-t'ing. After victory against Lu, Ch'en rebelled against Sun,
bombarding the Canton presidential headquarters. Sun fled aboard
the gunboat *Yung-feng*, and Chiang Kai-shek rushed from Chekiang
to join him. After undergoing an ordeal of sixty-two days, Sun managed to return in August 1922 to Shanghai, living again in the French
concession, where he received the Soviet representative, Adolph
Joffe.

On January 26, 1923, Sun and Joffe signed a manifesto, in which the Soviet emissary assured the Kuomintang leader of the "willingness" of the Russian people "to lend support."[3] While denying the suitability of Communism in China, Sun welcomed Soviet Russia's offer of money, arms, and advisers, which he had failed to obtain from democratic nations. The program of Kuomintang-Soviet collaboration was further discussed between Joffe and Liao Chung-k'ai, Sun's liberal-minded lieutenant, and was carried out by Mikhail Borodin, Sun's important political adviser from Moscow.

Meanwhile, the Yünnan and Kwangsi troops had driven Ch'en Chiung-ming out of Canton, making room for Sun's return in February 1923 to head the Canton government again. With the assistance of Borodin, Sun reorganized the Kuomintang—patterned after the Russian Communist Party and stressing iron discipline—and founded the Whampoa Military Academy. In November 1924, Sun Yat-sen went to Peking to negotiate a peaceful unification of China with Tuan Ch'i-jui, but on March 12, 1925, Sun died of cancer of the liver before any real progress had been made.

The Weak Challenge the Strong; the Minority, the Majority

It was an era when the weak challenged the strong, the minority the majority. For instance, when Chiang Kai-shek launched the Northern Expedition in July 1926, his seven army corps, including many Whampoa cadres, totaled about 85,000, with Kwangtung as his major base. On the other side, Wu P'ei-fu, Sun Ch'uan-fang, Chang Tso-lin, and others controlled a much larger territory with more than 500,000 soldiers. Yet, the unification of the Chinese republic by force of arms was completed in 1928, only two years after the launching of the expedition from Canton.

Meanwhile, in August 1927, the Kwangsi militarists successfully pressed for Chiang Kai-shek's resignation. During his compulsory retirement, Chiang married Soong Mei-ling, a sister of T. V. Soong, who came from one of the richest families in China. At the request of his allies, Chiang resumed his former authority in January 1928 to continue the Northern Expedition.

Laborer Challenges Employer

In the socioeconomic field, laborers challenged their employers and peasants challenged landlords; women challenged men against oppression, unequal treatment, and unilateral chastity.

The labor movement gained momentum in the 1920s. Previous laws concerning working conditions and management-labor relations were no more than window dressing to give China the appearance of keeping pace with other nations. The May Fourth Incident galvanized industrial workers and businessmen into striking and demonstrating in many cities in support of the student movement in Peking. The immediate results included the Peking government's release of the students who had been imprisoned and removal from office of the three state ministers who had been attacked as traitors to China's national interests for promising privileges to Japan; their dismissal had been demanded by the May Fourth demonstrators.

The birth of the Chinese Communist Party in 1921 strengthened the labor organizations. In 1922 the First National Labor Congress convened in Canton, representing some three hundred labor unions. With the help of the Communist Party, the Federation of Han-yeh-p'ing Labor Unions and that of the Canton-Hankow Railway Workers Unions were established. In January 1922 the Canton and Hong Kong seamen went on strike for higher wages, a strike that ended victoriously in March. The workers of the Han-yeh-p'ing mines followed suit and were also successful. But the railway workers' strike in 1923 was mercilessly suppressed by Wu P'ei-fu, even though one of the labor leaders said, "Of all the unions, the Peking-Hankow Railway Workers Union was the best organized." [4] The laborers' activities made great progress after the May Thirtieth Incident in 1925, when a British police officer ordered his men to open fire on a demonstration, thus killing eleven and wounding scores of students and workers in the Shanghai foreign settlement, and provoking widespread strikes and boycotts from Shanghai to Canton and Hong Kong. Industrial workers in China totaled only 1,489,000 in 1919, and yet they bravely challenged Chinese and British capitalists with truly proletarian victories. [5]

Peasant Challenges Landlord

Throughout most of Chinese history, peasants were silent toilers and silent supporters of the empire and its ruling class; lacking good education and able leadership, they were silent rebels without much articulation against the government. Even when their burdens were unbearable they were timid and slow in taking revolutionary action, because some 40 million peasants lost their lives during the Taiping, Nien, and Moslem rebellions in the latter half of the nineteenth century. Peasants were the oppressed, despised, and neglected.

Mao Tse-tung may be considered one revolutionary leader who paid peasants serious attention and recognized them as a major force in Chinese revolution. At the time of the May Fourth Movement, the impoverished peasants were resentful of the restrictions of the traditional way of life but lacked the courage to do anything.

In 1925 Mao undertook to promote the peasant movement in Hunan. As a result of his organization of formidable peasant associations, he was threatened with arrest by the Hunan governor and obliged to flee to Canton. In 1926 he became principal of the Kuomintang Peasant Movement Training Institute. In August he returned to Hunan to lead the peasants' activities and began confiscation of land. He made a social survey of many peasant families and published the "Report on an Investigation of the Peasant Movement in Hunan" in 1927. He headed a Peasant Movement Training Institute in Hankow and gave the students actual military drill. Excessive attacks against landlords by these student Communist leaders caused retaliatory measures against Communists and their party cells in Changsha on May 21, 1927.

Meanwhile, Chiang Kai-shek had launched a great coup in Shanghai on April 12, killing thousands of real or alleged Communist students and workers. The ensuing Communist actions of the Nanchang Uprising on August 1, 1927, and the Autumn Harvest Uprising in Hunan and Hupeh, failed; so, too, did the Chinese Soviet government in Hailufeng and the Canton Commune. By the end of 1927, the Communists were nearly annihilated. Yet, it was characteristic in the 1920s that the weak challenged the strong.

Woman Challenges Man

Women also had a weak position in Chinese society. They challenged the special privileges of men and demanded equal opportunities of education, vocation, suffrage, and right of divorce. They objected to the three obediences—to the father while young, to the husband after marriage, and to the son when widowed. They opposed sex segregation, the concubinage system, one-sided observation of chastity, and restrictive Confucian moral principles.

As a result of a decade of challenge against old traditions, a Civil Code was proclaimed in 1931 that incorporated many new ideas from western social and legal systems. In this code sexual equality was maintained, and a woman was legally allowed to select her own mate, to seek a divorce and remarry, and to inherit property. Childhood betrothal and marriage by purchase were forbidden. The new code, though quite radical in concept and revolutionary in its provisions, remained to a great extent just words on paper. The government made little effort to advertise and enforce the new laws among the people, and the lives of only a very small portion of educated urban citizens were affected.

China Challenges Foreign Powers

The most daring challenge of the period was the revision or abolition of the unequal treaties by which the dreadful foreign powers had reduced China to the level of a subcolony since the Opium Wars. The Twenty-one Demands of 1915 and the failure to annul them at the Paris Conference following the end of the war led directly to the May Fourth Movement. China's continued requests for the elimination of special privileges at the Washington Conference of 1921–1922 obtained the promise of a Tariff Conference, which was held in Peking from October 1925 to the following July; the session of the Extraterritorial Commission, to prepare for the relinquishment of the privileges, met also in Peking, from January to September 1926. During the two meetings, China achieved none of its expectations; it witnessed, instead, only a number of shiny black automobiles, carrying foreign flags of specific nationalities, maneuvering in the dusty streets, rushing to banquets and sight-seeing trips.

The Chinese learned the lesson that it was impossible to persuade a tiger to give away its skin. The only method was to rely on the power of the people: The general strike and boycott had forced the Hong Kong government to concede to the laborers' demands, and it had been the power of the masses that forced the British to return its concessions at Hankow and Kiukiang early in 1927. [6]

The warlord Chang Tso-lin lost no time in imitating his radical enemies in the Wuhan area. On April 6, 1927, he ordered a few hundred policemen and soldiers to raid the premises of the Soviet Embassy in Peking; they captured a number of Chinese and Communists, including one of the founders of the Chinese Communist Party, Li Ta-chao, who was soon put to death. Several truckloads of Communist documents were salvaged from the fire set by the Russians in the military attaché's office. This bold, unprecedented action could have been taken only with the consent of the diplomatic corps of the legation quarter. It could have been an English plot; on May 12, just over a month after the Peking raid, the British police raided the Soviet premises of Arcos Limited in London. This was followed by the breakup of diplomatic and trade relations between the United Kingdom and the Soviet Union. [7]

Actually there was little that England could do against the tide of anti-imperialism in China. It gave up its other concessions in Tientsin and Chinchiang in 1929 and relinquished its leased territory of Weihaiwei in the following year. Belgium also yielded to China its concession in Tientsin; Japan surrendered its concession in Hankow; and Mexico forfeited extraterritoriality in China. People in Shanghai defied the Mixed Court, which was replaced in 1930 by a Special Court that restored Chinese jurisdiction over its own people. Extraterritoriality was not abrogated by England and the United States, however, until 1943.

China Challenges Missionary Schools

Simultaneously, a recrudescence of anti-Christian feeling convulsed the whole country, causing the closing of many missionary schools. Chinese Christian leaders requested Chinese management of churches, missionary universities, YMCA's and YWCA's. Western missionaries were reluctant to comply, conceding in some cases, as at Yenching University, so far as to give an eminent Chinese the administrative power in name but maintaining the real authority themselves in practice.

Reasons for the Challenges

In their analyses of the ideology and motivating force behind the decade of challenges, many scholars blame Communists for all the trouble, as if to imply that without Communism the world would be orderly and peaceful. It goes without saying that this accusation cannot be entirely true, because there were wars and struggles long before the birth of Karl Marx. It appears to me that both nationalism and Communism were motivating forces behind most of the above-mentioned challenges; but nationalism played the major role, with Communism supplying the means and strategies for the struggles for national and class interests.

Nationalism

Nationalism, defying brief and logical definition, may be tentatively described as a national consciousness, a political creed, or a patriotic feeling of a people in a given territory, with a common culture, with common economic and social institutions, with loyalty and devotion to the nation-state, and with the hope of maintaining its independence, sovereignty, rights, and equality with other nations or peoples. Nationalism and patriotism are sometimes synonymous. It stimulates the nationals to strive to compete and catch up with advanced nations in cultural advancements. For instance, Chinese businessmen, previously rather inactive in politics, sympathized with the May Fourth students' boycott movement and made efforts to develop their own industry and commerce in Shanghai, Canton, and other large cities.

Militant nationalism or chauvinism was demonstrated by the masses in harassing the British to recover the concessions in Hankow and Kiukiang. Thus, nationalism moves in many directions: national unification, rights restoration, national security, production promotion, and anti-colonialism.[8] It was often utilized by militarists and politicians for a power struggle or personal greed under the guise of national salvation or national interest.

Communism

Communist discipline, die-hard spirit, propaganda technique, and the "mass line" were almost without equal in their effectiveness. Soviet Russia's material and advisory assistance to the Kuomintang and the Communist Party was instrumental in many initial struggles and triumphs. The admission of Communist members to the Kuomintang was like a transfusion of new blood to the old, enervated party. Its reorganization and reindoctrination revitalized the national army's fighting ability. While Sun Yat-sen had made several abortive northern campaigns, the 1926 expedition achieved his long-unfulfilled desire after his death.[9]

Self-interest

Besides nationalism and Communism, self-interest may be a third motive and a better explanation of the real purpose in overthrowing the senior warlords and the seizure of their positions by their junior generals in the 1920s. These militarists had neither much national consciousness nor any love of Communism; they were greedy for power and aggrandizement.

Brief Review of the Articles in the Volume

After this general introduction, let us take a look at the articles in this valuable volume on nationalism and revolution. In the first chapter Gilbert Chan succinctly presents Sun Yat-sen's political and ideological transformations from 1918 to 1923, a crucial period in his revolutionary career, and his important decision to reorganize the Kuomintang. Having made a special study on Liao Chung-K'ai, Sun's entrusted left-wing assistant, Chan's paper shows insight into Sun's mind as it shifted from indifference to the student movements and the pai-hua style to cooperation with Soviet Russia and the Chinese Communists.

Dan N. Jacobs' article is a political scientist's analysis of the Sino-Soviet relations in the mid-1920s. Using Russian and English sources, the author critically reviews the role played by Joffe, Borodin, Blyukher (Galen), Sun Yat-sen, Chiang Kai-shek, and others. He observes that Borodin "eschewed class warfare and centered instead on the twofold theme of nationalism and anti-imperialism." Richard Kagan's study on Ch'en Tu-hsiu, including the Fukien rebellion, which is not often mentioned, and some translation of Ch'en's writings is informative and interesting.

"Training and Indoctrination at the Whampoa Academy" by Richard Landis is an important topic and a well-prepared paper. One of the reasons for the success of the Kuomintang Northern Expedition was the Whampoa cadets. This military institute was patterned after the red command schools, but the Whampoa commandant, Chiang Kai-shek, incorporated into the training traditional Chinese educational concepts, Chiang's own practices, Russian revolutionary experiences, and the methods of Ch'i Chi-kuang (died 1585) and Tseng Kuo-fan (died 1872), both famous trainers of military forces. Through strict and persistent drill, Chiang fostered an esprit de corps and a strong sense of loyalty to himself. Along with the requirement that all applicants for Whampoa agree to join the Kuomintang, this training succeeded in winning the loyalty of the cadets, sought also by the Communist leaders at the academy. After the matriculation, Chiang frequently gave long speeches, inoculating such ideas as loyalty, obedience, patriotism, bravery, and self-sacrifice into the veins of students. Many of Chiang's speeches are analyzed in this chapter. Following the conceptualization, one can readily see that Whampoa cadets were Chiang's political and military investment toward the future success of his career.

In Ka-che Yip's "Nature and Causes of Student Activism," he attempts an explanation of the political behavior of students after 1919. The author examines the sociological, cultural, and political roots of Chinese student activism and finds that the movement was sustained by the common nationalistic concern for China's salvation. His other ideas and valuable data can better be appreciated by reading his chapter.

Whether or not a warlord was immune from nationalism is examined by Odoric Wou, who selects the political thinking of Wu P'ei-fu as a case study. Nearly the entire first half of the paper consists of a definition of nationalism and its characteristics. He then raises a question: Many warlords claimed that they were fighting for a national cause, but "did they actually embrace any form of nationalism?" After an attractive presentation of some facts, his answer seems to be that Wu P'ei-fu "was not anti-nationalistic." Wu's mind, however, was deeply implanted with such Confucian values as law and order, authority, hierarchy, obedience, conformity, discipline, and loyalty. This writer can attest to the truth of this by his personal experience, if he may be excused for doing so. In 1932, after Wu's defeat and retirement in Peiping (a new name for Peking after 1928), he was invited to give a lecture at Yenching University and appeared with a suite of eight assistants in Confucian robes sitting with him on the auditorium platform. As the general rose to deliver the lecture on Confucianism, all his followers rose like a fountain and remained standing until he finished his long lecture and sat down first. In this case he was not democratic, nor was he "anti-foreign" in coming to the missionary university. At any rate, Odoric Wou's paper is interesting and interpretive, written in accordance with the new historiography.

The next selection is Donald Jordan's well-researched and well-written paper based on Chinese sources and American and British diplomatic dispatches from China. It deals with the Chekiang provincialism within the Chinese national revolution during the period of the Northern Expedition in 1926 and 1927. While Wou labors on the big warlord Wu P'ei-fu, Jordan's research includes a number of lesser warlords whose names are not available in ordinary textbooks, and that is valuable information.

Another painstaking article is on Chiang Kai-shek's coup on April 12, 1927. This coup decimated the Chinese Communist Party's central organization and drove it from Shanghai to Kiangsi in the interior. It, too, consolidated Chiang's own power by mass execution. Tien-wei Wu has collected a large amount of source material, presented in a readable style; it will save other researchers a good deal of time in working on the same topic. It is not, however, a bibliographic essay, but rather a well-documented, thoughtful study delineating a broad background, tracing the progress of the coup with a critical evaluation of the leading actors, especially Chiang Kai-shek, who engineered the plot with the assistance of many secret society members.

Shumpei Okamoto's "Japanese Response to Chinese Nationalism: Naitō Torajirō's Image of China in the 1920s" interests this writer greatly. For one thing, China owes a debt of gratitude to Japan for stimulating the growth of nationalism in the family-centered Chinese society by its defeat of China in 1895 and the Twenty-one Demands. For another, Naitō Torajirō happens to be this writer's most highly respected Japanese Sinologist, whose Chinese style is considered by many to be the best of the Japanese writers, indistinguishable from that of a Chinese essayist. He is also a renowned historian. He believed that "Chinese government after the Han dynasty ceased to have any bearing upon the daily lives of the people." He repeatedly advised China to "entrust to foreigners its entire government functions." He sympathized with Japan's China policy, which is natural. In retrospect, the Chinese slogans "Down with Japanese imperialism" and "Boycott Japanese goods" were irritating to the Japanese. Okamoto has done a superb job in presenting, candidly and objectively, many interesting generalizations made by Naitō.

Thomas Etzold's "In Search of Sovereignty" reads as smoothly and delightfully as eating a banana split after a heavy meal. Readers of this chapter from the dextrous hand of an American diplomatic historian would have the same feeling.

On the whole, most of the articles in this volume seem to have been derived from monographic studies. No doubt several of these articles will appear in independent books. The strength of the collective wisdom cannot be adequately indicated in a brief summary; the best and most profitable way is for the readers to find out for themselves.

1

Sun Yat-sen and the Origins of the Kuomintang Reorganization

F. Gilbert Chan

I

When Sun Yat-sen resigned as generalissimo of the military government in Canton in May 1918 his career was at a low ebb. The Chinese Revolutionary Party (Chung-hua ke-ming-tang) existed merely in name, and his so-called "constitution protection movement" evoked little enthusiasm from either the politicians or the militarists. He had an even weaker hold on the masses. During his retirement in Shanghai, only a few of his followers remained close to him; their loyalty resulted more from personal attachment than from ideological commitment. In short, he appeared to be a political failure, whose main asset was a memorable past.

Nevertheless, with the promulgation of his joint manifesto with Adolph Joffe in January 1923, Sun reemerged as a leader of a new revolutionary movement. A month later, he returned to Canton—for the third time since July 1917—to establish a southern government. In this last bid for national prominence, he posed as a champion of intellectual radicalism, and he enlisted the assistance of Soviet and Chinese Communists in his task of Kuomintang reorganization. In the last years of his life, he was seemingly hopeful that he would eventually accomplish his revolutionary goals.

Many historians account for Sun's decision to collaborate with Communists in terms of political expediency. He was reportedly desperate for help and Soviet Russia was his only source of support. This interpretation is, at best, partially correct; it fails to take into consideration Sun's shrewd response to the political and ideological transformations of China during the critical years of 1918–1923. This chapter traces the development of these important changes and relates them to the dramatic resurgence of Sun's revolutionary career. Indeed his alliance with Soviet and Chinese Communists was largely the outcome of his realistic adjustment to the new conditions in China.

II

In spite of his unenviable predicament in 1918, Sun never wavered from his determination to reunite China under his leadership. In Shanghai he devoted much of his time to writing in order "to open up the mind of the Chinese people."[1] Yet his primary concern was to reconquer Kwangtung. To achieve this, he had to depend on Ch'en Chiung-ming's military support. Contrary to claims of Kuomintang historians, this relationship was by no means intimate. In 1914, for example, Ch'en had refused to become a member of the Chinese Revolutionary Party. Moreover, he was more interested in local reforms than in the movement of national reunification. Consequently, he did not always respond favorably to Sun's calls for aid, and this frustrated the plan for the reconquest of Kwangtung.

Meanwhile, the prospect for an amicable settlement of the difference between north and south was as remote as ever. At the beginning of 1919, President Hsü Shih-ch'ang of the Peking government initiated a conference in Shanghai to negotiate with southern leaders for a peaceful reunification of China. Sun doubted Hsü's sincerity and remained adamant in his opposition to the northern regime. As early as February he had predicted the failure of the overture and asked Ch'en Chiung-ming to prepare for the renewal of hostilities.[2] He was proved correct. The conference broke down in May, after only four months of negotiations. China reverted to a state of political anarchy.

During these years of national disunity, China underwent an intellectual revolution that brought a ray of hope to the dark age of political decadence. One of the leaders, Hu Shih, described the movement as "the Chinese Renaissance," obviously comparing it with the European experience of cultural flowering toward the end of the medieval period.[3] It began in 1915 when Ch'en Tu-hsiu published *Youth Magazine (Ch'ing-nien tsa-chih)* in Shanghai. To emphasize the new role of the young Chinese, he later renamed it *New Youth (Hsin ch'ing-nien)*. It soon emerged as one of the most widely read publications in China.

Educated in Japan, Ch'en was an ardent admirer of western democracy and science. To him, China was ripe for change. He called for a break with the past, and Confucianism, the symbol of Chinese traditionalism, was the natural target of his onslaught. With *New Youth* as his mouthpiece, he became the most influential leader of the cultural movement that was to transform drastically the intellectual climate of China.

Ch'en's endeavor was reinforced by the efforts of Hu Shih, a student of John Dewey's at Columbia University, to substitute a vernacular literature for one that was written in the classical language. Hu's article, "Some Tentative Suggestions for the Reform of Chinese Literature," in the January 1917 issue of *New Youth* heralded the advent of the literary revolution. Ch'en supported Hu's idea by writing in the next issue under a daring title, "On the Literary Revolution." Within a year, the vernacular was adopted by *New Youth* and other magazines. The introduction of this simpler yet more realistic form of writing lessened the gap between the intellectuals and the masses, and thus insured Ch'en's campaign for the ideological transformation of a larger audience.

The intellectual revolution gained momentum with Ts'ai Yüanp'ei's appointment as chancellor of the National University of Peking (Peita) in December 1916. Under his stewardship, this training ground of government officials, formerly known for its conservative tradition, became a center of liberalism. When he invited Ch'en, Hu, and other like-minded intellectuals to join the faculty, the heartland of Peiyang warlords supplanted Shanghai as the focal point of the cultural movement. The publication of *New Youth* in Peking in 1918 was symbolic of this change. These intellectuals exerted a strong influence on their students and helped to create an atmosphere in the capital that was at least partially responsible for the patriotic outburst of the Peking students on May 4, 1919.

While the May Fourth Incident was a dynamic expression of the cultural transformation, its student leaders personified Ch'en Tuhsiu's ideals of the "new youth." Through his exaltation of Chinese youth, Ch'en imparted a new sense of mission to these young intellectuals. In 1919 Fu Ssu-nien and Lo Chia-lun, both studying at Peita, published a magazine entitled *New Tide (Hsin-ch'ao)*, which inherited the anti-Confucian spirit of *New Youth*. The attacks of these students on traditional values strengthened their political consciousness. They viewed the notorious Twenty-one Demands as an emblem of foreign imperialism in China. When Woodrow Wilson failed to live up to the promises outlined in his Fourteen Points at the peace conference in Versailles and sanctioned the decision of the other powers to award the German concessions in Shanghai to Japan, student demonstrations broke out in Peking and other cities. These disturbances projected the students as a new revolutionary force. The Peking government testified to the freshly gained strength of these youthful leaders when it yielded to their demands and dismissed the three ministers accused of being pro-Japanese.[4]

The leaders of the cultural revolution were mostly intellectuals disillusioned with the political stagnation of China after 1911. Significantly, they had identified themselves with neither Sun Yat-sen nor his anti-Manchu movement. Though nominally a leading member of the Revolutionary Alliance (T'ung-meng-hui), Ts'ai Yüan-p'ei spent most of his pre-1911 years in Europe. In fact, some of Sun's followers regarded his acceptance of the university chancellorship in 1916 with disfavor.[5] Ch'en Tu-hsiu was in Japan in 1906, but he stayed away from the T'ung-meng-hui as a result of his disenchantment with Sun's revolutionary program.[6] Hu Shih, the youngest of the triumvirate, was studying at Cornell University when the Wuchang uprising took place in October 1911.[7] Instead of seeking political solutions to existing problems, as Sun and his entourage had been trying hard to do since 1905, these intellectuals stressed the need for China's emancipation from the cultural bondage of Confucianism. Imbued with a spirit of radicalism which was lacking in the leadership of the political revolution of the T'ung-meng-hui era, they demanded a large-scale adoption of western civilization. With their insistence on radical intellectual transformation, they shifted the emphasis of the Chinese revolution.

While living in Shanghai, Sun kept himself abreast of the turbulent developments in Peking. He lauded the revolutionary ideas of "the patriotic youth" and described the cultural movement as "the unprecedentedly great intellectual change of China."[8] He met occasionally with some of the young intellectuals. Chang T'ao-fan recalls that he and his friends went to pay homage to Sun in 1919 before they left to study in France.[9] Through Chiang Meng-lin (better known in the west as Monlin Chiang), an American-educated scholar, Sun also became acquainted with John Dewey. When Bertrand Russell visited China in October 1920, Sun attempted in vain to invite the western philosopher to dinner.[10]

Sun was positively impressed with the success of *New Youth* and *New Tide* in influencing student thinking. Under his tutelage, Tai Chi-t'ao and Shen Ting-yi began a new publication, *Weekly Review* (*Hsing-ch'i p'ing-lun*), in June 1919. *Reconstruction Magazine* (*Chien-she tsa-chih*), jointly edited by several of Sun's followers, appeared two months later. Both publications advocated reconstruction and concentrated on the propagation of western democratic and social theories. Sun wrote a foreword for the first issue of *Reconstruction Magazine*, in which he emphasized the importance of reconstruction in a revolutionary movement.[11] In a treatise that appeared serially in the same publication, he called for the international development of "the bast resources of China . . . under a socialistic scheme."[12] In 1920 his growing interest in the indoctrination of Chinese youth prompted him to ask his comrades to work on the revision of textbooks.[13]

Sun responded to some other facets of the intellectual revolution with intense caution, sometimes even with suspicion.[14] Although he was not blind to the spread of western ideas in China, his attachment to traditional culture prevented him from supporting wholeheartedly the program of westernization favored by the intellectual leaders of the period. As late as 1924 he still insisted that his political beliefs had originated with the teachings of the sages.[15] Since he doubted the effectiveness of the vernacular as a written language, he continued to write in classical Chinese. This conservative approach to the Chinese cultural heritage largely accounted for his failure to exert any significant ideological impact at a time when Confucianism was falling into disrepute among many young intellectuals.

In retrospect, it seems that Sun's interest in China's youth was rather superficial. He steadfastly clung to the elitist concept of revolutionary leadership and did not recognize the need for the mobilization of young intellectuals, let alone the masses. This was evident when he organized the Kuomintang (Chung-kuo kuo-min-tang) in October 1919 to replace the Chinese Revolutionary Party, which had become ineffective since 1916. Kuomintang historians exaggerate the importance of this change and hail it as a prelude to the reorganization of 1923–1924. Since the new party resembled the old one in almost every significant way, this assertion can hardly be substantiated by historical evidence. Despite the success of the students in the May Fourth Incident, Sun did not endeavor to recruit them as new members; as always, his few loyalists constituted the core of the party. Moreover, the Kuomintang continued to rely heavily on the conspiratorial strategy of revolution. While the intellectuals blamed militarism, among other evils, for China's degradation, Sun compromised his position as a revolutionary leader by seeking the help of militarists in the reconquest of Kwangtung. Principally because of his indifference to the radical aspirations of the May Fourth intellectuals, he lost an opportunity to catapult his party once more to national prominence. The Kuomintang was thus doomed, until 1923, to play only a minor role in the Chinese revolutionary movement.

III

With the militarists in South China engrossed in a power struggle, political dissension ensued within the Canton government in the beginning of 1920. Sun was eager to take advantage of this to press his campaign against Kwangtung, and he repeatedly sought Ch'en Chiung-ming's assistance. Nonetheless, the federalist movement had seemingly attracted Ch'en's attention. Busily engaged in his program of modernization in Changchow, he was not interested in aiding the Kuomintang to regain its control over Canton. On July 22 Chu Chih-hsin, Sun's emissary in Changchow, reported that he had given up all hope of enlisting Ch'en's support.[16] His pessimism was premature. Ch'en reversed his position in October, when the Canton regime was on the verge of disintegration. Shortly afterward, he routed the forces of southern militarists and entered Canton as a victorious hero.

After his triumphant return to Canton, Ch'en planned to establish an independent regional government in Kwangtung under his own leadership. His views on provincialism were "altogether incompatible" with Sun's constitutionalism, in spite of their alliance against the militarists. Besides, there was a "fundamental difference in political objectives" between the two leaders. While Ch'en labored for "the immediate welfare of Kwangtung," Sun championed "the cause of the national revolution." [17] Since the victorious general had not been a zealous supporter of Sun's anti-warlord movement, he advised Sun to stay in Shanghai. [18]

Wang Ching-wei and Liao Chung-k'ai, two of Sun's closest associates, were in the south at the time of Ch'en's reconquest of Canton. In a meeting with Ch'en on October 30, the two Kuomintang leaders sought to win his endorsement of Sun's proposal to reinstitute the military government, of which Sun had been generalissimo prior to his departure for Shanghai in May 1918. Without disclosing the details of the conference, Wang and Liao telegraphed to urge Sun to appoint Ch'en to the governorship of Kwangtung. In addition, they recommended that the new governor should concurrently serve as the commander-in-chief of the army and navy. Sun readily accepted their counsel and announced Ch'en's appointment on November 1. [19] Ch'en acceded to the compromise for the time being, although Sun's proclamation was only a recognition of the political realities of the province. It did not bestow on Ch'en any power that he had not already possessed.

Accompanied by Wu T'ing-fang and T'ang Shao-yi, Sun arrived in Canton on November 28 to revive the military government he had abandoned eighteen months before. As a conciliatory gesture, he named Ch'en minister of the army. [20] But it was apparent from the beginning that Sun's new political venture was on shaky ground. Among politicians with a national reputation, only Wu firmly supported his movement of "constitutionalism"; T'ang stayed away from Canton and lived mostly in his native district. In consequence, the success of Sun's government depended almost entirely on Ch'en's cooperation. Their alliance was, at best, a marriage of convenience, and Sun's decision to assume the presidency in Kwangtung in the early days of 1921 further impaired this fragile relationship.

Sun had always considered himself a man of destiny, genuinely concerned with the welfare of China. He was unwilling to restrict his ambitions to the provincial level. On January 1, 1921, he confessed that his "constitution protection movement" had failed "to solve the basic problems," and he proposed to establish in Kwang-

tung a "formal government" that would represent the whole of
China.[21] In a manifesto to foreign powers, he later insisted that his
opposition to Peking was "a struggle between militarism and democracy, between treason and patriotism."[22] In preparation for the
forthcoming presidential election, he invited some friendly members of the national assembly to come to Canton.

Sun's plan to reorganize the government encountered serious objection from his political associates. T'ang Shao-yi disagreed with
Sun that "the time is ripe for the election of a president." Wu T'ing-
fang, probably Sun's staunchest ally, was equally skeptical about
the desirability of government reorganization.[23] The most vigorous
opposition to Sun's presidential aspirations came from Ch'en
Chiung-ming. In February, when the election appeared imminent,
Ch'en and a few of his military comrades declared that "they would
not guarantee the peace of Kwangtung" in the event of a change in
the structure of the Canton government. Sun yielded and postponed
the election in order to avoid a confrontation.[24]

Notwithstanding the strong political opposition, Sun succeeded in
convincing about 225 members of the national assembly that it was
necessary to hold a presidential election in Canton. The group was
"composed practically completely of Sun's satellites"; those who
objected to his views were "immediately dismissed on grounds of
incompetency."[25] On April 7 the rump assembly met without a quo-
rum, and an overwhelming majority of the participants elected Sun
extraordinary president. While T'ang Shao-yi was reportedly "disappointed and displeased," other leaders who had not supported
the election left for Hong Kong for fear of being "arrested."[26] Yet
Ch'en Chiung-ming intended to give Sun "a fair trial," and his backing partially assured the survival of the new Canton government. In
return, Sun rewarded the general with the portfolio of the Ministry
of Domestic Affairs, besides his previous appointments.[27]

Shortly after his inauguration on May 5, Sun began to prepare for
a northern expedition against the Peking regime. He vowed "to
unite all provinces and territories" of China under a "progressive
and enlightened" government.[28] Thanks to this ambitious mission,
his conflict with Ch'en was most likely inevitable. Indeed, Ch'en regarded Sun's determination to reunite China by military means as
an obstacle to his federalist aspirations. In the following months,
newspapers in Shanghai rumored that the Cantonese general had

reached an agreement with Wu P'ei-fu, the powerful warlord in Peking. Similarly, the American minister in China predicted the termination of the Sun-Ch'en alliance. [29] Under these circumstances, Sun's attempt to unify the country was doomed to failure, and the persistence of his effort was, to a large extent, responsible for his ultimate expulsion from Canton.

In October, despite Ch'en's opposition, most of the members of the national assembly in Canton approved of Sun's proposal for a northern expedition. Sun implored Ch'en to lend him financial assistance, while he promised to give the general a free hand in his management of Kwangtung and Kwangsi. With only a vague commitment from Ch'en, Sun launched his northern expedition from Wuchow on November 15. He arrived in Kweilin twenty days later and established the military headquarters there. Throughout the winter of 1921–1922 Ch'en adopted an attitude of "sympathetic indifference" toward Sun's anti-warlord campaigns. He refused to supply Sun with any funds from the treasury in Canton, which was "absolutely" under his control. [30] This, in part, accounted for the stalemate of the expedition.

The assassination of Sun's chief of staff, Teng K'eng, at the railway station in Canton on March 21, 1922, brought his relationship with Ch'en close to a breaking point. Some members of the Kuomintang suspected that Ch'en had arranged for the murder, although they were unable to substantiate their accusation. They charged that Ch'en was in collaboration with Chao Heng-t'i, who had successfully obstructed the passage of Sun's troops through the province of Hunan. [31] In the midst of this hostile atmosphere, Sun was still eager to settle the dispute peacefully. He badly needed Ch'en's backing, without which his alliance with the two powerful warlords in the north, Tuan Ch'i-jui and Chang Tso-lin, would probably crumble. [32]

On March 26, owing largely to the lack of progress of the northern expedition, Sun decided to retreat from Kweilin. Thirteen days later he started back to Kwangtung. [33] When he reached Wuchow on April 16, his associates invited Ch'en to come for a conference. Ch'en declined, because his subordinates had allegedly learned that an assassin would be waiting to kill him at the proposed meeting place. [34] Sun issued orders to deprive Ch'en of his position as governor of Kwangtung and commander-in-chief of the Kwangtung army. This was merely a face-saving gesture, which did not really diminish Ch'en's influence in South China. He remained unconciliatory when Liao Chung-k'ai promised that Sun would restore him to both positions if he would apologize. Henceforth, Ch'en's "betrayal" became more and more obvious. [35]

Two days prior to Sun's arrival in Canton on April 22, Ch'en departed for Huichow "to care for his mother." [36] Apparently, Sun did not take the general's opposition seriously. He believed that Ch'en would eventually support the northern expedition, because "there is not much else for him to do." As he insisted, Ch'en "had promised me everything, he had promised me obedience." [37] As a result of this seeming confidence in his ability to sustain Ch'en's loyalty, Sun rejected Chiang Kai-shek's suggestion to destroy Ch'en's military forces in Huichow before the resumption of the northern expedition. On May 6 Sun left Canton for Shaokuan to renew his campaign against Peking.

On May 18 Yeh Chü and some other military subordinates of Ch'en's reached Canton from Kwangsi with about 12,000 soldiers. Two days afterward they telegraphed Sun to demand Ch'en's reinstatement as governor of Kwangtung and commander-in-chief of the army. They declared that it was their duty to eradicate the "evil influences" to which Sun had been exposed, and they selected Liao Chung-k'ai, who was in charge of the finances of the Canton government, as their prime target of attack. Yeh presented excessive financial demands to Liao, but he refused to accept the paper money issued by the Provincial Bank of Kwangtung. [38] On May 23 he besieged Canton with his soldiers. Liao concluded that the consolidation of the Kuomintang control in Kwangtung should have priority over the military campaigns against the north. He requested Sun to return to negotiate a settlement with Ch'en's lieutenants. Sun hurried back to Canton on June 1. Little did he realize, however, that in so doing, he precipitated a confrontation with the dissenting generals and quickened his own fall from power.

Hsü Shih-ch'ang's resignation from the presidency of the Peking government on June 2 provided Ch'en and his associates with an issue to challenge Sun's leadership in Kwangtung. In May 1921 Sun had written to ask Hsü to resign for the sake of national harmony. [39] Now that Hsü had done so, Ch'en asserted that Sun should likewise renounce his claim to the presidency. According to the general, this selfless move would guarantee a peaceful reunification of China. Ch'en's proposal received strong support from the intellectuals, including Ts'ai Yüan-p'ei who had, in past years, maintained regular contacts with Sun and his comrades. Thus, Sun's refusal to honor Ch'en's request created for him the unfavorable image of an ambitious politician with an insatiable thirst for power. The American minister in China bluntly characterized the Kuomintang leader as "the one outstanding obstacle to reunification." [40]

At a tea party given for journalists in Canton on June 12 Sun delivered an "inflammatory" address, in which he threatened to take drastic action against Yeh Chü and his troops. He urged the press to transmit his message to the militarists, who were to evacuate the city "within . . . ten days to a distance of thirty *li*." He then outlined the consequences of noncompliance in menacing terms:

> Otherwise, I have eight-inch guns with poisonous shells which are capable of entirely finishing their sixty battalions of troops in three hours.

Although Sun's subordinates later explained that this provocative speech was a "pure bluff," Ch'en's associates justified the June 16 coup as a defensive reaction to Sun's explicit intimidation. [41] In any case, the incident evidently heightened the crisis, and Liao Chung-k'ai became the first victim.

On June 14 Liao received a telegram from Ch'en asking him to go to Huichow to collect some money. He was reportedly aware of the risks involved in the trip, yet he considered this a good opportunity to soften the strained relations between Sun and Ch'en. Upon his arrival in Sheklung, Ch'en arrested him and imprisoned him for sixty-two days. [42] On June 15 Yeh Chü openly demanded Sun's resignation and on the following day bombarded his presidential palace. Sun survived by taking sanctuary on a gunboat, where he stayed until August 9. Chiang Kai-shek arrived from Shanghai on June 29 and was among the few who joined him. [43] The American minister objected to the idea of foreign mediation, because it "will dignify and magnify Sun Yat-sen and assure him of prestige in the future." [44] When Sun reached Shanghai on August 14, he was a defeated man.

To Sun, the thought of betrayal by Ch'en, "a follower of over ten years," must have been most discomforting. In a letter to his Kuomintang comrades, Sun depicted the recent debacle as his "saddest failure." Ch'en was "malignant" and "wicked-hearted." From Sun's standpoint, his expulsion from Canton was "a misfortune for the republic" and "an indication of a decline in moral integrity."[45] Despite this bitter rhetoric, he benefited from the experience. He realized that without help he could never recover Kwangtung, let alone unite the nation. Significantly, while he was eagerly seeking assistance, Adolph Joffe, who had arrived in Peking on August 12, was negotiating a treaty with the northern government for Soviet Russia.

IV

During Sun's previous sojourn in Shanghai (June 1819–November 1920), the impact of Marxism was beginning to be felt, especially by the young intellectuals who organized themselves into groups for the study of Marxist teachings. The May Fourth Movement helped to accelerate this development. In March 1920, before the excitement had subsided, the Soviet proposals, outlined in the Karakhan manifesto of July 25, 1919, to surrender voluntarily all privileges obtained from China by the Czarist predecessors became known to the Chinese populace.[46] In May 1920 *New Youth* published the Chinese translation of the document. If the Japanese victory in the Russo-Japanese War in 1905 had exerted tremendous influence on Chinese intellectuals, that influence was definitely superseded by the impact of the Soviet success in the Bolshevik revolution and the subsequent friendly attitude of the new government toward China.[47]

A number of the leaders of the cultural movement in China, hitherto fascinated with western liberalism, began to turn their eyes to Russia. By mid-1920 the two activists of the movement, Ch'en Tu-hsiu and Li Ta-chao, became converted to the Marxist philosophy. In July of the following year, the Chinese Communist Party held its first national congress in Shanghai under the supervision of two Soviet representatives, G. Maring and M. Nikolsky. Thanks to his residence in the French concession of Shanghai during most of these critical years, Sun was probably affected by the ferment of the time. To a certain degree, this accounted for his growing inclination toward Russia.

Since the beginning of his career, Sun had stressed the need of his revolutionary movement for foreign assistance. Anti-imperialism did not play a role in his early political thinking.[48] In comparing China's revolution with the American War of Independence, he maintained that much of the success of the American effort was due to the help of France. He referred, in particular, to the contributions of Marquis de Lafayette and repeatedly called upon foreign governments to emulate "the spirit of Lafayette."[49] Conditioned by his own personal background, he naturally looked to the west—especially the United States—for aid. In May 1921, when he issued a "Manifesto to the Foreign Powers" in his capacity as president of the Canton government, he asked Ma Su (Ma Soo), his representative, to make "a particular appeal" to President Warren G. Harding.[50] As a result of his advocacy of pan-Asianism, he was also interested in Japan. This was clearly shown by his dispatch of Chiang Kai-shek to Kyōtō and Tōkyō in October 1919, as well as his letter to Miyazaki Torazō, a friend of long standing, a year afterward.[51] Nonetheless, in spite of Sun's emphasis on the importance of foreign support, Russia was not an object of attraction for him before the Bolshevik revolution.

Notwithstanding his fascination with the United States and Japan, Sun's experiences with both countries during 1918–1922 had been most frustrating. They refused to take him seriously, although he had twice headed a government in Canton. In February 1921, the American minister in China described him as "at the best an unpractical idealist," whose revolutionary programs were nothing but "impractical and grandiose schemes."[52] According to Sun, Japan offered to recognize his regime in 1921 if he would acquiesce to the Twenty-one Demands of 1915, and thus strengthen Japan's position in the forthcoming Washington Conference.[53]

While the Japanese behavior was tantamount to political blackmail, the American treatment of Sun was hardly an improvement. In 1921 the Department of State declined to accept his letter to President Harding and reprimanded the vice consul in Canton for communicating with "an organization in revolt against a government with which the United States is in friendly relations."[54] This refusal to treat Sun on his own terms was one of the factors in driving him into the arms of Soviet Russia in 1923. In this way, the United States and its allies lost an opportunity to patronize the Chinese revolutionary movement.[55] When Sun made his last bid for national leadership under Soviet tutelage in 1923–1925, these powers became natural targets for his vehement attacks on imperialism—a concept he apparently borrowed from the Leninist philosophy.

Sun was interested in the success of the Bolshevik revolution in Russia. This was verified by his communications with Lenin, Chicherin, and other Soviet revolutionaries. Sometime in 1918–1920 he planned to send Liao Chung-k'ai to Russia to study. To prepare for this, he instructed Liao to attend classes in the Russian language.[56] Yet his enthusiasm should not be exaggerated. As a matter of fact, he had serious reservations about the Marxist concept of class struggle, and his later decision to accept Soviet assistance was reached only after he had been assured that Russia had no intention of introducing Communism into China.

Without question, Soviet Russia was interested in Sun, who had first attracted Lenin's attention in 1912. The revolutionary strategy of the Comintern called for a united front of the major social classes in China—the national bourgeoisie, the petty bourgeoisie, the middle and poor peasants, as well as the proletariat—to stand against imperialist exploitation. With his worldwide reputation as an experienced revolutionary, Sun seemed to be a logical leader of the Chinese "national bourgeoisie." Accordingly, in 1920, the propaganda organ of the Comintern, *Kommunisticheskii Internatsional,* extolled him as "the soul of the Chinese youth" and "the embodiment of the intellectual force of the Chinese revolutionary movement."[57]

Just as Russia was not the only foreign nation from which Sun hoped to obtain assistance, he was by no means the sole political leader in China with whom the Kremlin wanted to cultivate friendship. Aside from his strengths, he had serious shortcomings. For example, he lacked a strong military force, which was essential in a successful nationalist revolution. In consequence, Soviet leaders were simultaneously interested in Wu P'ei-fu and Ch'en Chiungming, both of whom had expressed sincere aspirations to Chinese nationalism. The ultimate decision of Russia to collaborate with the Kuomintang was the outcome of a complicated process of tactical maneuvering, dictated largely by the overall strategy of the Soviet government in China.

The first Comintern emissary to talk personally with Sun about a Canton-Moscow rapprochement was Grigorii Voitinsky, who came to China in 1920 to work for the establishment of a Chinese Communist Party. Accompanied by a "Comrade Ch." (probably Ch'en Tu-hsiu), he visited Sun in Shanghai in the autumn of the same year. Sun was very inquisitive about Russia and its revolution.

The meeting, however, failed to cement an entente between the Kuomintang and Soviet Russia. Sun was then preoccupied with campaigns against southern militarists, and he returned victorious to Kwangtung shortly afterward. Owing to "the geographical position of Canton," as he admitted to Voitinsky, he did not believe in the feasibility of setting up contacts with Russia.

Although Voitinsky commented favorably on Sun's "modesty and the cleanliness of his attire," he was still uncertain that Sun was the best leader the Comintern could support in a war against the imperialists in China. He was obviously attracted by Ch'en Chiung-ming, whom he later met in Canton and praised as "a man of great willpower and self-control." [58] This policy of expressing interest in more than one Chinese leader at about the same time was not Voitinsky's own creation; it was rather a manifestation of the Soviet dilemma.

In 1921, Maring, a Dutch Communist whose real name was Hendricus Sneevliet, followed the same strategy with enthusiasm. [59] He had reportedly read Sun's writings as early as 1912. After his participation in the first congress of the Chinese Communist Party in July 1921, he tried to arrange for a meeting with Sun, who then headed a government in Canton. [60] His mission was principally exploratory. On his way to the south, he visited Chao Heng-t'i, a Hunanese warlord, who supported the federalist movement in China. He probably conferred with Wu P'ei-fu. [61] After his meeting with Sun in Kweilin in December, he traveled to Canton and, through Ch'en Tu-hsiu's introduction, had a conference with Ch'en Chiungming "at the beginning of 1922." [62]

Maring stayed with Sun for at least three days. [63] As in his previous meeting with Voitinsky, Sun was mostly interested in the Russian revolution. During the conversation, Maring apparently brought up the subject of Kuomintang reorganization. While he emphasized the need for the mobilization of students, peasants, and workers, Sun was more receptive to the proposal of the founding of a military academy. [64] This is not surprising, considering Sun's frustrating experiences with the militarists in China. Indeed, before Maring's visit he had written to Chicherin to inquire about the organization of the Soviet army. [65]

Upon his arrival in Canton from Kweilin, Maring expressed disillusionment with Sun to both Liao Chung-k'ai and Wang Ching-wei. He found the organization of the Kuomintang and its methods of

propaganda most disappointing.[66] But there were also other causes
for his dissatisfaction. Despite Maring's insistence on a popular
base of support for the Kuomintang, Sun was still inclined to the establishment of a tightly controlled party with himself wielding dic-
tatorial power. Moreover, the Chinese revolutionary leader lacked
an adequate understanding of the Marxist philosophy. He contended that Marxism was not dissimilar to the teachings of the Chinese sages. He once asked Chang T'ai-lei, a Chinese Communist
who served as Maring's interpreter in Kweilin:

*Why should the youth look toward Marx for wisdom, while the
principles of Marxism are to be found in the Chinese classics?*[67]

Most important of all, Sun had not completely forsaken his hope
of obtaining assistance from western countries. He explained to
Maring that an alliance with Russia before he had successfully reunited China would drive Britain into the arms of northern militarists.[68] Prior to Maring's visit, he had attempted to seek help from
Britain, Canada, and the United States. He had also sent Chu Ho-
chung, a European-educated associate, to Berlin to explore the
possibility of reaching an understanding with Germany. When the
German vice consul arrived in Canton in September 1921, Sun personally negotiated with him for a workable program of mutual
cooperation.[69]

His doubts about Sun notwithstanding, Maring preferred the
Kuomintang leader to the generals. Sun was "a pure bourgeois-na-
tionalist," who was influenced to a considerable degree by "socialist ideas." Hence, he was much better equipped than either Wu
P'ei-fu or Ch'en Chiung-ming to combat the domination of capitalism.[70] On the other hand, after his conversations with the Soviet
emissary, Sun was gratified to inform Liao Chung-k'ai that Communism had failed in Russia. Maring seemed to have given him the impression that the new economic policy of the Soviet government resembled his own Principle of People's Livelihood.[71] This had the
effect of dispelling some of the suspicion that Sun had formerly harbored against Moscow. It is interesting to note that he reiterated the
same conviction in a meeting of the Provisional Central Executive
Committee of the Kuomintang on January 3, 1924. Owing to his
strong emphasis on the issue, the committee found it necessary to
record in the minutes that the Soviet economic policy had origi-

nated with Sun's beliefs in socialism. Instead of being a teacher of the Kuomintang, Russia was actually its student.[72]

The change of Sun's attitude toward the Soviet government was perhaps reflected by Chang Ch'iu-pai's participation in the First Congress of the Toilers of the Far East as a Kuomintang representative in January-February 1922.[73] Meanwhile, Sun started to cherish the idea of a triple alliance with both Germany and Russia. He lauded Germany as a nonaggression nation, and he was confident of its willingness to help China. His agent, Chu Ho-chung, had been "active" in Germany since the end of 1921.[74] On March 8, 1922, Sun wrote from his headquarters in Kweilin to ask Liao Chung-k'ai, his chief financial manager in Canton, to remit a sum of 4,200 yüan to Chu and his family. Chu was seemingly optimistic about the outcome of his mission in Berlin, when he reported to Sun that Paul von Hintze, the former German minister in Peking, would soon travel to Canton.[75]

The visit of S. A. Dalin, a Comintern representative, turned a new page in the chronicle of Sun's rapprochement with Soviet Russia. His first meeting with Sun took place on April 29, 1922, two days after his arrival in Canton. They conferred regularly at least twice a week for about two hours until either June 12 or 14.[76] While Sun expressed "sympathy" with the Soviet leadership, he was obviously anxious to obtain information about the Red Army in Russia.[77] Dalin, however, disapproved of Sun's "old methods" of revolution; he was, in particular, critical of Sun's reliance on the military support of mercenary soldiers, who would never rally faithfully under the banner of the nationalist revolution.[78]

During the initial period of Dalin's stay, Sun treated his guest with "a certain amount of distrust." He stressed the strong opposition to the Communist philosophy in China. According to him, the inhabitants of the cities—products of "modern civilization"—were "enemies of Communism." Thus, as he further argued, Marxism-Leninism would likely find a more friendly reception among the Miao people who, secluded in "wild and mountainous provinces," remained uncorrupted by the impact of modernity.[79] He confessed that many of his followers did not share his sympathy with the Soviet government and reiterated the belief that his "recognition" of Russia would so infuriate the British that they would "start to act against" him.[80]

The success of the June 16 coup resulted in Sun's expulsion from Canton. Although it interrupted his meetings with Dalin, they were able to maintain indirect contact through an intermediary, Eugene Ch'en. Thanks to his catastrophic defeat, Sun experienced a "great turning"—or, to borrow Dalin's phrase, *"velikii povorot"*—in his revolutionary career. The Soviet emissary detected a change in Sun's "outlook of the world." The political debacle had seemingly helped the Kuomintang leader to decide in favor of leaning toward Moscow for assistance. In a message delivered to Dalin through Ch'en, Sun admitted to having "thought much about the fate of the Chinese revolution." He became convinced that Russia was "the only actual and true friend." He assured Dalin that he had taken "all the documents relating to their previous discussions" aboard the gunboat on which he was seeking sanctuary. On the eve of Dalin's departure for Russia, Ch'en brought to him another letter from Sun, written "on pages torn out of a notebook." In this farewell message, Sun requested Dalin to covey his "friendly feelings" to Lenin and to acquaint Chicherin with the dismal situation in which the Kuomintang had found itself.[81]

Other sources confirm Sun's determination to solicit Soviet help after his banishment from Canton in June 1922. On August 9 he spoke approvingly of both Russia and Germany to his lieutenants on board a gunboat. He asserted that the Soviet government shared China's interests and was eager to extend a friendly hand to the Chinese people.[82] He also discussed with Chiang Kai-shek the possibility of sending him to Moscow.[83] In spite of his overtures to Germany, Sun's flight from Canton had virtually ended his hope of an entente with Berlin, and Russia became his most likely source of assistance. On September 22, when the *Hong Kong Telegraph* published three documents disclosing Chu Ho-chung's negotiations with von Hintze, the former German minister in China hastily issued a flat denial of any involvement on the part of his government.[84]

Sun arrived in Shanghai on August 14. Shortly afterward he met Maring again. He conceded that it had become "absolutely necessary" for the Kuomintang to establish closer relations with the Kremlin.[85] He even agreed to permit the Soviets to take part in the management of the Chinese Eastern Railway after his own accession to national power—a privilege that Russia had so far failed to extract from the Peking government. [86] Although Maring did not agree with Sun on the importance of a reconquest of Kwangtung, their meeting paved the way for the success of the subsequent Sun-Joffe negotiations.

On August 25, Adolph Joffe dispatched an aide to visit Sun in Shanghai. The Kuomintang leader reported this meeting to Chiang Kai-shek. He stated that he expected to discuss the military affairs of the Kuomintang with a Soviet representative soon, and he urged Chiang to travel to Shanghai to participate in this forthcoming conference. [87] It is easy to understand Sun's special interest in the improvement of the military capacity of his party, since he was then working hard to recapture Canton. To achieve this objective, he had sent a close associate, Hu Han-min, to Fukien to negotiate with the militarists there. In the following month, Wang Ching-wei went to Fengtien in an attempt to gain Chang Tso-lin's support of Sun's campaigns against Wu P'ei-fu. [88]

In addition to his preoccupation with the militarists, Sun was concerned with the reorganization of the Kuomintang. With the probable intention of broadening his base of support, he enlisted the help of the Chinese Communists, notably Ch'en Tu-hsiu and Lin Tsu-han. On September 4 he invited Ch'en to participate in a meeting to discuss the work of party reorganization. Two days later he appointed Ch'en to a nine-member committee for the same purpose. [89] The recruitment of these two leaders did not come as a surprise. While Lin's association with Sun dates from the years of the Chinese Revolutionary Party, Ch'en was on friendly terms with such Kuomintang veterans as Wang Ching-wei, especially in 1920 when he was commissioned by Ch'en Chiung-ming to reform the educational system in Kwangtung.

This intimate relationship between leaders of the two revolutionary parties was not restricted to a few individuals. Among Kuomintang members, Tai Chi-t'ao was perhaps the one most amicably associated with Chinese Communists. In fact, he might have joined the Chinese Communist Party in 1921 had his friendship with Sun not prevented him from doing so. [90] Nor is this relationship difficult to explain. Chang Kuo-t'ao, for instance, rationalized his fascination with Russia in terms of "the death of a dream," resulting from Woodrow Wilson's failure at the Paris Conference and his own disillusionment with the west. [91] On the other hand, Ch'en Tu-hsiu stressed the important role of Chinese Communists in both "the anti-warlord movement" and "the patriotic movement against Japan." [92] These nationalist sentiments were not monopolized by Communist leaders; Sun and his comrades were equally dedicated to the cause of national salvation. After all, in his Master's essay submitted to Columbia University in 1924, Ch'en Kung-po traced the origins of the Chinese Communist Party to the patriotic activities of the students in the May Fourth Movement. [93] As discussed above, this nationalist outburst also had strong impact on the Kuomintang leaders.

During the first congress of the Chinese Communist Party in July 1921, the participants deliberated upon the question of their relationship with the Kuomintang. [94] But the idea of an alliance, in one form or another, originated with Soviet Russia. The Kremlin was interested in the promotion of a nationalist revolution in China to rid the country of imperialist influences. Since the forces of the Chinese Communists were still weak, they should accept the leadership of the "national bourgeoisie" until they were strong enough to take over. In a circular to his Communist associates on December 10, 1929, Ch'en Tu-hsiu credited Dalin with being the first to suggest to Sun the formation of a united front with the Chinese Communist Party. [95] Nonetheless, in April-June 1922 the idea did not appeal to Sun, who complained that the Chinese Communists had connived with Ch'en Chiung-ming against the Canton government. [96] He was skeptical about the wisdom of a collaboration of the two parties, particularly if the Communists were to share a position of equal standing with the Kuomintang. As its leader, he was very proud of the long history of the Kuomintang in the Chinese revolutionary movement. On June 16, Ch'en Chiung-ming's coup interrupted the Sun-Dalin discussions and forced Sun to withdraw from Canton.

When Sun was taking refuge on board a gunboat, the Chinese Communist Party held its second congress in Shanghai in July 1922. As a reaction to recent political developments in China, the participants in the meeting reversed their former policy of "non-compromise" toward existing parties. For the sake of establishing "a real democratic independent nation," they resolved to cooperate with the "nationalists" in the struggle against "feudalism" and "imperialist oppression." Rather than abandoning their party's identity, they demanded that "the proletariat must not forget their own independent organization." [97] Their new position vis-à-vis the Kuo-mintang—commonly characterized as "bloc without"—signified no radical departure from the proposal Dalin had previously suggested to Sun, who had summarily rejected it.

After Maring's arrival in Shanghai, he summoned a special ple-num of the Central Committee of the Chinese Communist Party in Hangchow. At this August conference he refuted the contention that the Kuomintang was a bourgeois party. Instead, he commended it as a coalition of all classes. To substitute for the idea of a two-party al-liance, which Sun had declared unacceptable, Maring proposed the "bloc within" policy that would give the Chinese Communists dual party membership. They would join the Kuomintang as individuals, with the understanding that they would retain their Communist af-filiations. Ch'en Tu-hsiu was the principal opponent to this arrange-ment. [98] In the end, probably after Maring had invoked the author-ity of the Comintern, the Chinese Communists formally approved of a "bloc within" alliance with the Kuomintang. [99]

Despite his previous reservations, Sun, too, showed more flexibi-lity toward the Chinese Communist Party after his Canton catas-trophe. During his August meetings with Maring, the Soviet emis-sary informed him that Russia had advised the Chinese Communists to join the Kuomintang. Thereupon, Sun agreed to the admission of Communist revolutionaries into his party as individ-uals. [100] Li Ta-chao was the first Chinese Communist to become a member of the Kuomintang. Ch'en Tu-hsiu, Ts'ai Ho-sen, and Chang T'ai-lei immediately followed his example. [101] By the end of August 1922, Sun's policy of collaboration with both Soviet Russia and the Chinese Communist Party had taken definite shape. Al-though the Kuomintang leader never really terminated his effort to win help from non-Communist nations, Ch'en Tu-hsiu's participa-tion in the September 4 meeting on party reorganization symbolized the beginning of the united front. Sun's subsequent negotiations with Joffe centered more on the elaboration of policy than on its formulation.

After his conference with Joffe's aide on August 25, Sun received from the Soviet representative three letters, to which he responded favorably. In December he sent Chang Chi to Peking to discuss the details of the alliance with Joffe. [102] At that time, Joffe was having difficulties in reaching an agreement with the Peking government.

A trip to Shanghai might help to exert pressure on the Chinese ne-
gotiators. Besides, he was likely impressed with Sun and his party.
In an article sent to Moscow for publication, he praised the Kuomintang as "the meeting point for nationalism and revolution." [103]
Hence, his illness notwithstanding, he journeyed to Shanghai to
confer with Sun in the middle of January 1923, when the military efforts of Sun's allies in the south showed clear signs of success. At
the conclusion of their conference on January 26, the two leaders issued a joint declaration of cooperation. Two days later, Liao Chung-
k'ai, who had participated in the discussions, accompanied Joffe to
Japan.

V

New forces were at work in China during 1918-1923 when Sun
Yat-sen experienced a metamorphosis in his revolutionary career.
A small group of radical intellectuals emerged to lead the May
Fourth Movement. Thanks to the friendly gesture of the Karakhan
manifesto of 1919, some of them turned to the Russian mode of revolution for inspiration after they had been alienated by the western
powers at the peace conference in Paris. With their emphasis on
anti-imperialism and anti-warlordism, they provided a challenging
alternative to Sun's formula of political revolution. The founding of
the Chinese Communist Party, which insisted on a proletarian leadership, pointed the direction to a social revolution in China.

An experienced revolutionary, Sun was not immune from the influence of these developments. He had been spurned by the foreign
powers and, in June 1922, he suffered a humiliating defeat at the
hands of Ch'en Chiung-ming. His movement to "protect the constitution" had evidently foundered. The Soviet offer of assistance was
attractive, but his eventual rapprochement with Russia was not
motivated solely by material considerations. He was impressed by
the success of the Bolshevik revolution. While the June 16 coup of
1922 was indicative of the treachery of his military allies, various
Communist emissaries taught him the importance of the masses in
his struggle against warlordism. Lenin's theory of imperialism further provided a rationale for his nationalist revolution.

The Sun-Joffe manifesto was mostly of symbolic significance. Although it assured Sun, in the name of the "Russian people," of their
"warmest sympathy for China" and their "willingness to lend sup-

port," the document made no specific promise of Soviet material assistance. [104] Yet Sun's discussions with Joffe marked the beginning of months of negotiations that ultimately resulted in a Kuomintang alliance with Soviet Russia. In the last eighteen months of his life, Sun benefited from the lessons of the Bolshevik revolution, in spite of his reluctance to accept all the tenets of Marxism-Leninism. His new emphasis on mass mobilization in the nationalist movement was merely one of the many examples of his adoption of Soviet revolutionary tactics. The successful reorganization of the Kuomintang on the Russian model subsequently gave his party a fresh lease on life, and thus enabled it to launch another bid for national power.

Despite the persistent efforts of Kuomintang historians to belittle the importance of Sun's decision to admit Chinese Communists into the party as individuals, the so-called "toleration of the Communists" (jung-Kung), in fact, contributed much to his return to prominence. It was obviously a manifestation of his realistic response to the political and cultural changes in China during the May Fourth epoch. His failure to recruit the new intellectuals into his revolutionary camp prior to 1921 was partially responsible for driving some of them into the arms of Soviet Russia. This, in turn, led to the founding of the Chinese Communist Party. When he started to lean toward Russia himself, he became keenly aware of the danger that the Chinese Communists would monopolize all Soviet assistance. By offering them party membership as advised by both Dalin and Maring, he hoped to divert Russian material aid to the Kuomintang. [105] This policy would also unite the revolutionary forces under Sun's leadership. After all, his party has never been an ideologically exclusive organization. Its members had included socialists and anarchists. The admission of the Communists, therefore, did not necessarily result in any sacrifice of the Kuomintang ideals. On the contrary, by advocating a radical program for the nationalist movement, the party had a rare opportunity of achieving an attractiveness that had so far eluded it.

2

Soviet Russia and Chinese Nationalism in the 1920s

Dan N. Jacobs

At the beginning of the 1920s Chinese nationalism was a tender shoot. It seemed to have great potential, but it was still weak and indeterminable in shape. During the decade, it had a full flowering, and while its potential remained unfulfilled, its destiny was no longer in doubt. Much of this development was attributable to China's contact with Soviet Russian internationalism.

Chinese disillusionment in 1919–1920 was intense. The failure of the 1911 revolution had been a source of frustration for the intellectuals and their middle-class urban allies. The monarchy had at least maintained an illusion of unity and strength, yet the political power during the republican years deteriorated instead of showing signs of improvement. In the eyes of many Chinese, the way in which the powers treated China's claims at Versailles in 1919 was indicative of the depth to which it had fallen in world esteem. China's weakness was in glaring display for all to see.

The humiliation and degradation of the country profoundly affected tens of thousands of Chinese, particularly the students. Nevertheless, few of them were yet prepared to dedicate their lives to China's regeneration. One of the exceptions was Sun Yat-sen, a revolutionary from South China.

Sun had been a leader in the struggle against the Manchus, but his image was tarnished in the decade after the Wuchang uprising in October 1911. He had argued that the Manchus were at the root of Chinese degeneration; their elimination would permit China to resume its place among the powers. The overthrow of the Manchu dynasty, however, had not led to the revivification of China. In a decade of effort, the Chinese failed to make any significant progress toward national unification; they had seemingly slipped backward. The removal of the Manchus had thus proved inadequate to strengthen China. Some other elements were required, and one of these, according to Sun Yat-sen, was foreign assistance.

Even the United States, which Sun had repeatedly visited in order to seek support for his revolutionary movement, had not established itself without outside aid. To George Washington's side had come the French and their Marquis de Lafayette. Popularly referred to in the west as the "Chinese Washington," Sun was eager to find his own Lafayette.

The decision to embark on such a course was not sudden. Indeed, Sun had emphasized the importance of foreign support in his earlier anti-Manchu revolution. Moreover, he had long learned to respect western ways, thanks to his residence, education, and experience abroad. He had, too, recognized the necessity for modernization. In the early 1920s he was becoming desperate. The revolution of 1911 had not revitalized China, and there was almost daily evidence of the increasing corruption and dismemberment of the country. On the personal level, Sun's attempts to seize power had led him into alliances with the militarists, who turned against him at whim and used him as a front man for their own ambitions.

There was no strong force in China that appreciated Sun's vision and was willing to share its power with him. Its sizable membership notwithstanding, his own party, the Kuomintang, had an amorphous organization, and its principal focus was fund-raising through voluntary contributions. Already in his fifties, Sun realized that if his revolution was to have any chance of success, it had to come soon. Hence, at the dawn of the 1920s, he conducted his search for the Chinese Lafayette with increasing determination. During these same years, China came into contact with the Russian revolution.

At the time of Lenin's successful coup in late 1917, the Bolsheviks believed that their revolution must spread quickly throughout war-ravaged Europe. As Karl Marx had insisted, a socialist revolution would first break out in the most highly developed capitalist nation, and then spread to other countries in descending order of their level of capitalist development. Yet, it had taken place in Russia, which was hardly a capitalist nation. Therefore, to follow the Marxist formula, the revolution should spread to a leading capitalist country as soon as possible, if it was to succeed at all. Otherwise, when the capitalist powers unleashed their forces, it would end in the bloodbath of the Russian proletariat.

Nevertheless, the major concern of the Bolshevik leaders in 1918–1919 was their own political survival at home. Besides, there was little that they could do to hasten the revolution in the west, and the large-scale capitalist intervention of which they were so afraid had failed to develop. After four years of destructive warfare, the Europeans wanted no more bloodshed, and they certainly would not support any military action to defend the corrupt and oppressive Romanov regime. Thus, unless its threat to western stability became great enough to arouse opposition on nationalistic grounds, Russia would be left alone by the powers to settle its domestic affairs.

In the last part of 1920, as the turmoil of the civil war had largely subsided, Lenin abandoned the idea of spreading the revolution to the west. Instead, he concentrated his work on the development of a peacetime government and a stable economy. He had not, however, forsaken the principle of international revolution; he merely put it aside for the time being.

For Lenin, this was not a serious deflection, since he had been concerned with the international movement mostly as a means to quicken the Russian revolution. But there were other leaders who were attracted to Marxism by its ideals of internationalism and universal brotherhood. In their opinion, the only important revolution was the international revolution. Many of them worked in the Comintern, which, established in 1919, was involved in the promotion of revolutionary movement outside Russia. It soon became the vehicle through which the Russian leaders controlled other Communist parties. Yet, in the early 1920s, they were more interested in seeking revolutionary opportunity than in extending Bolshevik organizational control.

In 1920 Lenin began to suggest that the internationalists should look to Asia and Africa for the revolutionary opportunity they had failed to find in Europe. As he conceded, countries like India and China were not ready for a socialist revolution. Their economy was either feudal or, at best, in the early stage of capitalist development. Nonetheless, they were smarting under foreign domination and exploitation and were thus susceptible to a "national" revolution. By supporting their nationalist aspirations, the Comintern could weaken the capitalist powers, whose economic prosperity was founded on wealth extracted from the colonies.

Even prior to Lenin's suggestion, some Comintern leaders had already turned their attention to Asia. In 1920 one of their representatives, G. N. Voitinsky, came to China in search of potential revolutionary elements. Instead of promoting revolution, his principal objective was to assess the Chinese situation and establish contacts for the future. One of the several leaders he met was Sun Yat-sen. [1]

In the next few years a number of other Muscovites visited China. Some of them sought to establish diplomatic relations with the Peking regime, while others laid the groundwork for a Chinese Communist movement and then served as midwife at its birth. The latter group, too, maintained connections with Sun and other leaders in China. During 1921–1922 the two groups remained separate from one another and pursued their different ends independently.

The importance of these operations in Moscow's eyes needs to be kept in perspective. They were not given a high order of priority by either the Comintern or the Politburo. The leadership of the former was primarily interested in promoting revolution in the west. It was western-oriented; it knew little about the east and cared hardly more. The Ministry of Foreign Affairs was similarly oriented. But in view of the limited revolutionary and diplomatic opportunity in Europe, both bodies started to turn to the east at Lenin's order. They did so with little determination and enthusiasm.

In order to protect its interests in East Asia, Moscow sent to China in late 1922 one of its top diplomats, A. A. Joffe, who had been involved in the negotiations at Brest Litovsk and later at Rapallo. His major duty was to pressure Peking into establishing relations with the Russian government. He was a difficult person, and he did not know how to deal with the Chinese. He also had his share of bad luck. The mission failed, however, mostly because Moscow did not have much to offer to Peking. [2] Yet, since he had come so far and had, in the process of his negotiation, exposed the weakness of Soviet Russia, it was decided that he should not return home empty-handed.

Accordingly, in January 1923, Joffe conferred with Sun Yat-sen in Shanghai. Prior to their meeting, at least three Soviet agents had visited, interviewed, and evaluated the Chinese leader. In spite of their relatively negative judgment of him, Moscow was convinced that Sun could be useful to the revolution in China. [3] Besides, the pressure on the Comintern to become involved in the east had grown. Hence, if Joffe was unable to establish diplomatic relations with Peking, he should try to reach an agreement with Sun instead.

The Sun-Joffe discussions in Shanghai were fruitful, and the two leaders issued a joint manifesto on January 26. According to a Russian source, Moscow promised to assist Sun Yat-sen with advisers, funds, and supplies, so that he could launch his "northern expedition" to liberate China. [4] As did many of his close confederates, the Chinese revolutionary had doubts about his alliance with Russia, but he saw no viable alternative. On its part, Soviet Russia did not trust the bourgeois Sun, in spite of his genuine nationalist aspirations. In January 1923, however, the agreement seemed to offer immediate advantages to both parties, and neither side saw its commitment as final.

Sun sent to Moscow—either through Joffe himself or through another emissary after Joffe's departure for Japan—a list of military equipment that he would need. In the spring of 1923 the Politburo decided to honor its commitment in a limited fashion, since its immediate objective was still to gain recognition from Peking. [5] To oversee its interests in China, Moscow dispatched a youthful yet experienced, dynamic, and personable Armenian revolutionary to Peking. Thanks to his 1919 declaration to surrender all Czarist privileges in China, the new Soviet representative, L. M. Karakhan, had endeared himself to every Chinese with even the slightest nationalist inclination.

Since Karakhan worked mostly in Peking, he needed someone to represent him in Canton after Sun Yat-sen had returned to South China in February 1923. In late spring, Moscow ordered an experienced Comintern operative, Mikhail Markovich Borodin, to travel to East Asia. As a Bolshevik, he had played a role in the 1905 revolution in the Baltic area. He had met not only Lenin but also Stalin and many other revolutionaries who were to become prominent in the formation of the Soviet government about a decade later. In 1906 he was arrested and exiled from Russia. When the revolution broke out in 1917, he had lived in Chicago for almost ten years and had ceased to be an active Bolshevik.

For Borodin and many other Russians scattered around the world, the news of the Bolshevik revolution created a longing to return to Russia and participate in the building of an ideal society. He had been the owner-director of a school that provided foreign-born adults in Chicago with skills to cope with their life in America. In 1917 he abandoned this work and smuggled back to Russia, where many Bolshevik leaders still remembered him for his services in 1905. He became a "foreign specialist" and went on missions during the next few years to the Scandinavian countries, the United States, Mexico, the Caribbean, Spain, the Netherlands, and Germany. As an "agent," he was highly regarded in some Soviet circles. In the early part of 1922 he was sent on an important assignment to reorganize the movement in Britain. Until his arrest in Glasgow in August of the same year, he enjoyed considerable success in bringing order out of the chaotic leftist politics in the British Isles. Thus, his apprehension hardly diminished his reputation in Moscow.

Borodin's six-month confinement in Glasgow's Morleybone Prison revealed his identity as a Soviet agent. His physical appearance and characteristics were carefully noted and dispatched to intelligence services throughout the world. [6] It would henceforth be difficult for Moscow to send him across international borders, particularly in the west. Yet, as the Soviet policy was beginning to look more to the east, Russia needed an experienced emissary to assist Sun Yat-sen in the reorganization of the Kuomintang. In consequence, shortly after Borodin's arrival in Moscow in February 1923, he received instructions to travel to China.

Borodin was flabbergasted. [7] He had little knowledge of either China or its revolutionary potential. Nevertheless, it was not for him to question an assignment. As one of his first acts, he asked an assistant to go to the used book marts in Moscow to purchase all available publications on China, and he then sat down to study them. In this way, he became an "expert" on the country he was about to visit. [8]

As it turned out, the selection of Borodin, like that of Karakhan, was a wise one. While he did not know Chinese, his English was virtually flawless because of his previous stay in Chicago. Without an interpreter, he could communicate with Sun Yat-sen and a number of other foreign-educated Chinese who were to work closely with him in Canton. [9] Moreover, he had obvious organizational skills, and he was gifted with the ability to get along with a wide variety of people. He emphasized what men had in common and brushed aside their differences. To a large extent, these qualities accounted for the success he later achieved in China.

Borodin arrived in Peking in the autumn of 1923. He remained in North China for several weeks, while the Chinese Communist leaders, among others, briefed him on what to expect in the south. Meanwhile, he arranged the details of his forthcoming trip to Canton with Karakhan. [10] At this point, the latter was doubtless the senior Soviet representative. Unsure of himself, Borodin probably preferred a subordinate role, at least for the time being.

In spite of his taste for luxury, Borodin arrived in Canton in a decrepit cattle scow. [11] Sun Yat-sen came to the dock to welcome him. During the next few weeks, the two leaders met on a number of occasions. It was a period of learning for the Soviet agent, and one of the first things he learned was the tenuousness of Sun's position in Canton. [12] Sun was powerless and almost bankrupt. His erstwhile allies had turned against him even before Borodin set foot on the Canton docks. When they marched toward the city, it seemed that Sun would soon have to climb aboard his "flagship" and retreat once again to his refuge in the French sector of Shanghai.

Borodin, however, had not come halfway around the world just to say "hello." After consulting with the handful of Soviet advisers who were with him in Canton, he decided to try to keep Sun Yat-sen in power. [13] They moved rapidly to bring both troops and civilians together, supplied them with ammunition and weapons, and dispatched them to strategic points to resist the enemies. [14] Borodin had perhaps hoped that the forces of the opponents would disperse if the Kuomintang could put up even a mildly spirited defense. He was proved correct. Forty-eight hours after the beginning of the "final" offensive, the opposition gave up their effort, and Sun's government was "saved."

Borodin's success in weathering the crisis strengthened his hand tremendously. Friends and diplomats had warned Sun Yat-sen—himself filled with reservations—against allying with Bolshevik Russia. [15] Now that the Soviet agent had helped to repel his enemies, the Kuomintang leader was convinced that Borodin was indeed China's Lafayette. [16] For the next four years Russia became inextricably linked with the development of Chinese nationalism. With Borodin as its *éminence grise*, the southern government emerged as the focus of nationalist aspirations in China.

Shortly after the crisis, Borodin and his small corps of advisers presented to Sun Yat-sen a blueprint for a national revolution. They called for the reorganization of the Kuomintang, the establishment of a party army, and the mobilization of mass support for the government in Canton. In many respects, their plan was attractive. But it emanated from Bolshevik sources and was heavily laden with intimations of class struggle.

Borodin often went to great length to win Sun's cooperation. He fully realized that Sun was the key to his position in South China. He could only maximize his own effectiveness with Sun's support. [17] As a result, he worked hard to cement his personal relations with the Chinese leader. He treated the latter with deference, and he indicated to visitors that Sun was a great man. When he drafted a new constitution for Sun's party, he made the Kuomintang revolutionary *tsung-li* (director-general) for life.

During this early period of their collaboration, Borodin and Sun spent long hours together in the latter's garden. [18] They conversed on such topics as the Russian revolution and the civil war. Borodin stressed both the need for the adoption of the Soviet style of organization and the importance of mass support. He, too, elaborated on the greatness of V. I. Lenin. Thanks to his proselytizing talent, the Bolshevik adviser gained a powerful influence on Sun, sometimes even in the area of ideology.

Sun had developed his Three Principles of the People over the past decades. In the last two years of his life, he adjusted his thought in order to bring it into greater conformity with the ideas advocated by Borodin. He accepted, in particular, the Soviet revolutionary tactics. In the first half of 1924 he delivered a series of lec-

tures on his principles, and he argued that there was "no real difference" between Communism and his Principle of People's
Livelihood. [19]

Nonetheless, his public statements notwithstanding, Sun frequently demurred when Borodin tried to persuade him to carry out
proposals that would truly advance the concept of social revolution.
He questioned, for example, the wisdom of repeated reference to
the masses as the driving force of his revolutionary movement. [20]
The two leaders were clearly aware of their differences on certain
important issues, but they were willing to compromise. Hence, Sun
insisted that Borodin enjoyed his complete confidence, and he ordered his comrades to follow Borodin's instructions as if they had
come directly from him.

The first Kuomintang congress of January 1924 endorsed Sun's
policy of allying with the Communists. It also sanctioned Borodin's
proposals for the development of nationalist forces in China. A significant part of its work was the reorganization of the amorphous
party, which had hitherto been Sun's personal operation, devoted
principally to supplying funds for his attempts to gain power. Prior
to the congress, Borodin and a few like-minded Chinese leaders had
already labored to model the new organization of the Kuomintang
on that of the Russian Communist Party, which was closely knit and
centrally controlled. Although the revitalized Kuomintang might
still not be so tightly organized as its Soviet prototype, they hoped
that the product of their work would be a strong party with an in-
tegrated and responsive structure.

As both Sun Yat-sen and Borodin realized, the Chinese revolution
would never succeed if it had to rely, as Sun himself had previously
done, on the militarists, who had to be sufficiently paid. These mercenary troops had no sense of commitment either to Sun personally
or to the cause of Chinese nationalism. A successful revolution required its own dedicated forces. To meet this need, the Kuomintang
established a military academy in the spring of 1924 on the sight of
an old fort at Whampoa on the Pearl River, some ten miles south of
Canton.

The idea of founding an academy to train able leadership for the
new revolutionary army was undoubtedly sound. Yet it was difficult to select an appropriate student body. The Whampoa Military
Academy was to resemble an institute of higher education, and its

students had, at least, to be able to read. This requirement for an already educated student body almost assured that the recruits would come largely from the bourgeois class. For those who advocated a social revolution, this was a portent of catastrophe. Nevertheless, at this initial stage of their movement, they were not seriously concerned with a problem that might plague them in the future.

Despite the overwhelmingly middle-class origins of the revolutionary leadership in South China, the Bolshevik tactics called for the active involvement of the masses, who were, by Marxist definition, mainly the proletarians. Unlike Shanghai, however, Canton did not have many large factories, and its economy was mostly pre-industrial. [21] The chief form of labor organization was the guild, which was politically conservative. On the other hand, there were many people of all classes who would respond favorably to a nationalist appeal. Therefore, it soon became apparent to Borodin and his associates that the Kuomintang could not emphasize class interest in its attempt to mobilize mass support. In consequence, the party program that these advisers helped to devise eschewed class warfare and centered instead on the twofold theme of nationalism and anti-imperialism.

For the first time in Kuomintang history, propaganda played a prominent role in the revolutionary movement, and this was Borodin's particular bailiwick. Its technique was, to a great extent, alien to the Chinese leaders. Because the masses were largely illiterate, the main portion of the propaganda messages had to be pictorial. Brief written slogans were changed almost daily. Most of these assaults were directed against the British, who were the principal target of the Kuomintang campaign against foreign imperialists.

The Shanghai massacre of May 30, 1925, in which more than fifty Chinese were either killed or injured by British guns, led to widespread anti-imperialist outbursts in China. [22] Large sections of the middle class and some parts of the upper class supported the strikes and demonstrations organized by workers, students, and intellectuals. [23] Canton responded on June 23, when the bourgeois Whampoa cadets demonstrated jointly with the workers and peasants. Conflict ensued, and more than 150 people died as a result. [24] Chinese nationalist sentiments reached a height. As Karakhan claimed, the Russians did not incite the Chinese against the imperialists. It was not necessary, since the imperialists had done that themselves. [25]

The Canton-Hong Kong strike was a product of the June 23 incident, and it symbolized the victory of Chinese nationalism over the British authorities in the colony. By early 1926, trade had almost come to a standstill. Less than 20 percent of the normal tonnage was going in and out of Hong Kong harbor. Property values had plummeted, and there were daily bankruptcies of venerable business enterprises.

Thanks to its effectiveness, the strike also created problems for the Kuomintang leaders. Many of the hard-pressed merchants maintained intimate connections in Canton, and some had formerly supported the party. Moreover, tens of thousands of strikers had flocked to the city. They harassed the politically influential middle-class people, took over office buildings, and blocked streets. They even organized their own courts and levied fines. [26] Thus, the upper-class elites in Canton turned increasingly against the Kuomintang policy of collaboration with Russian and Chinese Communists. They condemned, in particular, what they considered to be the "Sovietization" of Kwangtung.

Yet when Borodin left Canton for the north in early 1926, he was convinced that the situation in the city was secure. After all, the short-term goals of the Soviet policy in South China had been accomplished. The Kuomintang had been strengthened. If it was not so tightly run as its Russian model, it was certainly a greatly improved organization. Furthermore, a military academy had been founded, and its students had proved themselves in battle. Most important of all, Kwangtung was under the control of the Kuomintang, relatively free of military opposition.

On the other hand, Borodin's success notwithstanding, the regime in Canton continued to have an obvious middle-class character. Whatever social reforms it had implemented were, at best, moderate in scope and nature. The Chinese Communist Party was weak, and the labor movement had failed to make any significant progress. In addition, there was the constant fear that the middle-class leaders would appeal to the British in Hong Kong for assistance, if Borodin became too aggressive in his advocacy of mass participation in revolution.

Accordingly, the Soviet adviser concluded that there was no future for the revolution in Canton. With its urban life dominated by guilds and merchants, the city lacked a strong industrial base for a proletariat to develop. As Borodin maintained, Canton was "a tower of Babel in which it is possible to get completely lost."[27] It would therefore be detrimental to the revolutionary movement if the Kuomintang should remain in the south. As a result, he favored the transfer of the headquarters from Canton to some other areas where the proletarians were more powerful, preferably areas farther away from the threat of imperialism.

The chief reason for Borodin to travel to the north in early 1926 was to confer with A. S. Bubnov, who headed a delegation sent to Peking by the Central Committee of the Russian Communist Party to determine the future of Soviet involvement in the Chinese revolution. In their discussions, the Soviet leaders never really considered the possibility of withdrawing from China because they had already set the national revolution in motion. They had not scored many victories outside Russia, and they were not going to abandon the battlefield after achieving an almost unique success in Kwangtung. This was simply not the Bolshevik mode of behavior.

Nevertheless, if the revolution was to succeed, it needed more backing than it had received in Canton. In the opinion of the Soviet representatives, there were two major ways through which they could gain wider support for the Chinese revolutionary movement. First, they could forsake their program for social transformation so that they would not alienate the middle-class people in the south. This, however, was unacceptable to Stalin, because his opponents in the developing struggle for Lenin's succession would surely attack such a decision as "anti-Marxist." The other alternative was for the Kuomintang to move their center of revolution to a new area where the inhabitants were more susceptible to radical changes. Borodin personally preferred the exodus from Canton, and the Bubnov delegation concurred. They believed that the Chinese leaders could conveniently leave South China under the guise of the "northern expedition," a long cherished dream of the late Sun Yatsen. [28]

While Borodin was in Peking, the situation in Canton, which he had thought secure, was deteriorating. With the deaths of Sun Yatsen and Liao Chung-k'ai, the principal Kuomintang leaders were Wang Ching-wei and Chiang Kai-shek. Wang regarded himself as Sun's prime disciple, thus having a legitimate claim to Sun's power and prestige in the party. But, known for his indecisiveness, he did not have the will to fight for the prize he desired. On the other hand, Chiang had not been, until recently, a member of the upper echelon of the Kuomintang leadership, and he was sensitive about his want of stature. Furthermore, he was never truly close to Borodin. Although willing to cooperate with the Muscovites, he was anti-Communist by inclination. As a result, he was fearful that Wang and the Communists would plot against him. In early 1926 the development in Canton seemed to substantiate his concern.

Much of Borodin's success in the south was attributable to his awareness of the sensibilities of the Chinese. He understood their emphasis on "face." In his relationship with Sun Yat-sen prior to the latter's death, he had always insisted that his policy proposals were mere "suggestions." He had treated other Kuomintang leaders in similar ways. In the early part of 1926, when he left Canton for Peking, he had planned to return to Moscow—probably for good—after his meeting with Bubnov. [29]

N. V. Kuibyshev, known in China as Kisanko, assumed most of Borodin's duties in the south. His brother, V. V. Kuibyshev, was politically powerful. A rigid ideologist, the new Soviet adviser did not possess Borodin's tact in his dealings with the Chinese. He miscalculated the situation in Canton when he "unleashed" the Chinese Communists. This frightened Chiang Kai-shek, who was suspicious of the Communists even under the best of circumstances. The arrival of the Bubnov delegation in the city at this time did not abate his misgivings. Hence, prompted by his suspicion and, not unlikely, his ambition, the general struck on March 20 to gain control of the Kuomintang government and oust both the Communists and his rival, Wang Ching-wei.

The success of Chiang's coup compelled Bubnov and his associates to reassess their situation in Canton. They had no intention of abandoning their work and recalling their advisers. Stalin had lately suffered diplomatic setbacks in Europe, and he was concerned with their effect on the contest for power in the Kremlin. For obvious political reasons, he could not afford to fail in China. [30] Chiang, too, realized that his own position was far from strong. He needed foreign help, and he could only obtain it from Russia. Therefore, he agreed to the continuation of the Kuomintang-Communist alliance if the Soviet representatives would accept his terms.

According to the new arrangement, Chiang would control both the army and the government in Canton. He also extracted a promise of military aid from Russia, which would enable him to launch an expedition against the regime in Peking. As an acknowledgment of his freshly acquired power, his main rival in the Kuomintang, Wang Ching-wei, would leave China for an unspecified period. Borodin had returned to the south in late April, yet his political authority would henceforth be significantly curtailed. As for the Chinese Communists, they would be prohibited from holding any important position in either the party or the government.

This was hardly a favorable arrangement for the Communists, but the Russians did not have much choice. To insure his own political survival at home, Stalin believed in the need for Moscow's continued involvement in the Chinese revolution. In fact, by the summer of 1926 when Chiang Kai-shek directed his Northern Expedition against Peking, the primary reason for the presence of Soviet advisers in China was no longer to help the Kuomintang develop a nationalist, anti-imperialist movement. It was rather to protect Stalin's political interests in the Kremlin. Although Moscow had not lost its concern for the Chinese revolution, even Borodin apparently admitted that he was mostly responsible for "the protection of Russian interests." [31]

For different causes, Chiang Kai-shek and the Communists were all eager to depart from Canton. Chiang wanted to demonstrate the strength of his troops and thereby improve his political status. Besides, he was hopeful that he would gain additional support once he reached the northeast. He could then be much less dependent on the Russians. The Soviet and Chinese Communists, however, would like to move to an industrial area, which was proletarian-oriented and yet far away from the threat of imperialism.

The Northern Expedition was extremely successful. By November 1926 half of China had come under the sway of the National Revolutionary Army. The triumph was brought about as much by Kuomintang military forces as by Russian planning, organization, and supply of armament. Also important was the contribution of Soviet-trained propagandists. Hundreds of them journeyed north from Canton to spread the news of the advent of the National Revolutionary Army. They publicized their concern for the political unity of the country as well as the economic well-being of the people. [32] While they welcomed local leaders to join their nationalist cause, they attacked their opponents as lackeys of imperialism. As the victorious troops entered a city, they put up anti-foreign posters along the route of the march. [33] There were, too, agitprop trains with large portraits of Sun Yat-sen and slogans that hailed the new China and excoriated the imperialists. [34]

Nonetheless, every military victory that the Kuomintang won during the expedition brought the divisiveness of the revolutionary leadership closer to the surface. As the troops approached the Yangtze, Chiang Kai-shek and his opponents clashed over the selection of their new headquarters. The Communists and their Kuomintang allies preferred the industrial Wuhan area, some 600 miles upstream from the coast. But Chiang himself favored Nanchang, which manufactured enamel ware, its only industry. The people of the city had scarcely heard of a proletariat. [35] Between late 1926 and early 1927 both sides tried to reach a compromise. In December 1926 Borodin visited Chiang in the mountain resort of Kuling, yet the meeting failed to settle their differences. [36] Similarly, Chiang's travel to Wuhan in the following month ended in a series of shouting matches. [37] Reconciliation was clearly impossible. In April 1927 Chiang moved his headquarters to Nanking. With Borodin and his like-minded comrades in Wuhan, the split of the revolutionary movement was seemingly complete.

According to many historians, the Wuhan government was "leftist," and it was under the control of the "left-wing" leaders of the Kuomintang. Nevertheless, evidences do not substantiate this assertion. Though they might be "leftist" when compared with Chiang, the Kuomintang leaders in Wuhan were actually middle-class in origin as well as in orientation. Many of them sided with Borodin because Sun Yat-sen had pursued the same course, and they were no more prepared than Sun to support radical reforms. Others joined the government out of spite against Chiang. The Chinese Communists in Wuhan were ineffective. Apparently under Borodin's instruction, they endeavored to restrict the hitherto successful activities of the workers and peasants, although to do so in the midst of a revolution seemed incongruous with Communist principles.

In spite of the March 20 coup of 1926, Moscow steadfastly maintained the myth that the Chinese revolution, as originally envisioned by Lenin and his comrades, was as "alive" as ever, and it continued to back Chiang Kai-shek as an important leader of the movement. Borodin, however, questioned the possibility of further collaboration with Chiang, especially after the general had allied with the capitalists of Shanghai and their imperialist backers. Chiang's suppression of Chinese Communists in April 1927 confirmed Borodin's skepticism. Thus, as the Soviet adviser argued, Russia should break its relations with Chiang and support only the revolution in Wuhan.

While the Chinese leadership in Wuhan was distinctly middle-class in nature, many workers and peasants were radically oriented. They had been actively involved in a mass movement that aimed at improving their livelihood. Some Russians suggested that Borodin should assist this radical element, instead of conspiring with the bourgeoisie. Indeed, the Trotskyites later blamed Borodin for his failure to have utilized the full potential of the masses in China. Yet Borodin was convinced that the workers lacked discipline and were therefore an unreliable revolutionary force. The peasants were even less prepared for the role they were expected to play. Moreover, Borodin was afraid that a turn toward radicalism would alienate the bourgeoisie and probably invite imperialist intervention. In consequence, he decided to restrain the movement of the masses in order to maintain the momentum of the national revolution. In so doing, he also tried to insure the continuation of Moscow's participation in China's struggle against imperialism.

Nonetheless, it was apparent in the spring of 1927 that Chiang Kai-shek, in the name of nationalism, had gained the backing of a significant number of militarists in Central and South China, as well as the endorsement of many Chinese and foreign capitalists. Against these odds, the Wuhan leaders could hardly emerge victorious in their political battle for supremacy. To strengthen their position, Borodin and his Soviet colleagues turned to Feng Yü-hsiang for help. Russia had recently revitalized Feng's military forces at great cost.[38] As a result, its leaders hoped that they would be able to appeal to his sense of gratitude. After all, they had no other viable alternative.

But Feng was a political realist. Under the circumstances, he could do little to change the tide that was running against Wuhan. Besides, he did not want to be a part of the movement in which Borodin and the Communists were involved. Accordingly, he negotiated an agreement with Chiang Kai-shek on June 20–21. Among other things, he yielded to Chiang's demand that Borodin and other Soviet advisers should leave China. When Borodin heard the news, he realized that this was the end of his mission. In fact, by August, virtually all the Russians who had participated in the Chinese revolution had departed from China. The Soviet involvement in the nationalist movement was over.

In the view of many historians, the Soviet experience in China in the 1920s was a failure. This seemingly supports the Trotskyite theory that Borodin and, indeed, Stalin missed an opportunity to cleanse China of its capitalists, militarists, and imperialists. The masses were eager to rise against their exploiters; all they needed was a word from Moscow. Stalin, however, did not share this optimism. The struggle for power in the Kremlin had a significant impact on his formulation of policies. In many ways, the Russian involvement in the Chinese revolution was an embarrassment for him. Because of his fear that the critics would accuse him of defeatism, he could not admit that it was probably impossible to bring about a successful Communist movement in China in the 1920s.

Nevertheless, despite their ultimate expulsion in the summer of 1927, Borodin and his Soviet comrades could legitimately be proud of their achievements in China. Thanks to their guidance, the Kuomintang was revitalized. It emerged as a tightly organized party with considerable appeal to the masses. They also helped to establish the Whampoa Military Academy. With the support of its cadets, Chiang Kai-shek launched an expedition that ended in the overthrow of the Peking government. The development of Chinese nationalism reached a height. Although imperialist influences remained strong, the national revolution was, to a large extent, a success. This was the major accomplishment of Borodin's mission in China.

Their purges in 1927 notwithstanding, even the Chinese Communists benefited from the presence of Russian advisers. There was a remarkable increase in party membership in the years of their collaboration with the Kuomintang. Most important of all, the Communist leaders, including Mao Tse-tung himself, gained an invaluable experience in mass mobilization, which must have proved helpful in their rocky road to power. In short, the Soviet advisers were capable tutors. During their stay in China, they left indelible imprints on the course of the Chinese revolution.

3

From Revolutionary Iconoclasm to National Revolution: Ch'en Tu-hsiu and the Chinese Communist Movement

*Richard C. Kagan**

For the leadership of the Chinese Communist Party in the 1920s, the definitions and strategies of "nationalism" and "revolution" posed a series of contradictions. The Communist leaders included intellectuals active in the May Fourth Movement. Their advocacy of anti-Confucianism and cultural iconoclasm led them to reject a nationalism built upon an emotional appeal to the patriotic chauvinism and historical identity of the Chinese. Even a Chinese state was unacceptable to them if it did not support basic social and cultural reforms. This stand initially had limited popular appeal.

In the early 1920s Marxism provided the strategies and goals for a social revolution. The nature of the Kuomintang-Communist alliance, however, imposed united effort for a bourgeois national revolution and pinched off most social revolutionary activities. The decade witnessed an attempt by Chinese Communists to accept some form of state nationalism without fully sacrificing their support for a social revolution. The ordeal of Ch'en Tu-hsiu as secretary-general of the party in 1921–1927 presents a case study for the

*The author wishes to thank his colleagues who have worked with him on this volume, as well as Professors Leigh Kagan, Edward Farmer, and Scott Johnson for their encouragement and criticism.

analysis of the failure of Chinese Communists in the 1920s to resolve the contradiction inherent in nationalism and revolution.

As the leader of the Chinese Communist Party in its first six
years, Ch'en provided the intellectual impetus for both the attack of
the traditional order and the conception of a new one. This was the
stage of orthodox Marxism in Chinese Communism. By the end of
the 1920s its leadership was rejected in a period of extremist reaction. Not until the mid-thirties did another revolutionary leader offer a clear rationale for the destruction of the past, and a Sinified
Marxism for the future.

The Chinese Communist Party was initially composed of a loose
group of highly educated men with gentry background. To talk of a
"party" and its organization was really to engage in political "con-
ceit." [1] Only in 1925 did the Chinese Communists gain any mass con-
stituency. From 1927 to the early thirties, the party was decimated
by arrests, hampered by poor communications, and finally its leadership was forced to flee to the countryside.[2] Yet, in spite of the
weakness of the party, Ch'en Tu-hsiu played a prominent role
among the intellectuals in Peking and Shanghai, the two important
centers of China.

The purpose of this essay is to analyze Ch'en's contribution to the
concepts of nationalism and revolution in the early 1920s and to in-
dicate some of his later changes in order to highlight his thinking.
While the first stage, 1915–1922, shows the development of Ch'en's
cultural and political strategy for revolution, the second period,
1922–1931, witnesses his struggle with the Comintern over the nature of the national revolution in China. The essay concludes with a
study of Ch'en's reinterpretation of Chinese society and culture.

Literary and Political Revolution, 1915–1922

In his writings on iconoclasm and the nature of politics, Ch'en evaluated the relationship between cultural and political changes. It is
in this respect that he probably made his major contribution to the
Chinese revolution.

Iconoclasm

There were two principal elements in Ch'en's interpretation of Chinese Communist nationalism that distinguished it from the Kuomin-

tang rendition. First, he insisted that a social revolution ied by the proletariat was necessary to prevent the creation of a bourgeois state dominated by one party. Moreover, as a cultural iconoclast, he attacked Confucianism and the Chinese tradition. In view of the nature of the traditional heritage and the contemporaneous political chaos in China, he became convinced that cultural changes constituted a significant prerequisite for the success of a political revolution.

According to the Chinese literati, intellect and culture were the two primary molders of society and polity. This perception assumed that the basis of a society was found in its cultivation of arts and literature, as well as in the development of the character of the individuals. [3] Since the literati believed that culture was a determining factor of both society and polity, they made no distinction between the two. This organicistic view suggested that everything was interrelated. Like a growing organism, a society relied equally on all of its parts. The substitution of any one of them for a foreign element would render the society obsolete.

In Ch'en Tu-hsiu's opinion, the old ethos of Confucianism consisted of "poisonous germs" that were killing China. In his 1915 essay, "Call to Youth," he claimed that China was being suffocated by "the old and rotten," which, if permitted to accumulate, would kill a man and destroy a society. [4] Many critics of Confucianism identified the philosophy with the harshness of the family system, the rapacity of the clan officials, the conservative bias of the bureaucrats, and the brutality of the monarch. Ch'en was particularly censorious of the civil service examinations and their impact on the sociopolitical system of China. When in jail in the mid-1930s he recalled an incident during an examination that had involved "a fat candidate from Hsüchow." This Confucian scholar "stood absolutely naked except for a pair of broken shoes on his feet and a big pig-tail coiled on top of his head." He walked back and forth along an aisle in the examination yard, reading aloud his favorite essay "in a strange long-drawn-out voice." At times he gave his thigh a powerful slap and exclaimed, "Great! This time I will make it!" Ch'en was aghast. He recollected:

> As I stared at him, I began to think about the whole strange phenomenon of the examination system and the candidates involved, and then I continued to push my considerations to how much my

> *country and its people would suffer when these animals received*
> *positions of power. Because of these ideas, my mind wandered to*
> *question the whole phenomenon of selecting men of talent by the*
> *examination system. It was just like an animal exhibition of mon-*
> *keys and bears performing every few years; and then I pondered*
> *whether this system was not as defective as every other system in*
> *the nation.*

Thanks to these doubts, he changed "from being a devil's disciple of
the examination system to becoming an advocate of the party of
K'ang Yu-wei and Liang Ch'i-ch'ao." [5]

Ch'en took his last examination in the summer of 1897. For the
next ten years he tried to overthrow the Ch'ing dynasty by joining
anti-Manchu associations in China and Japan, teaching revolution
in Anhwei, and making explosives in Shanghai. Meanwhile, he entered a French-managed academy where he studied architecture
and European history. As he became disillusioned with the Manchu rulers and the political order of China, his comparison of the
Chinese civilization with its European counterpart further convinced him that changes in culture and art alone could not reform
the society and polity of China. He thus turned away from his earlier support of Liang Ch'i-ch'ao's advocacy of transformation within
tradition.

During his attack on the national heritage, Ch'en was in search of
a new culture. He insisted that the Chinese tradition had to be rejected if political changes stood any chance of success. In his essay
on patriotism, which appeared in 1916, he scolded his countrymen
for wishing to be traditional martyrs in their endeavor to save the
nation. According to him, what was really necessary for national
salvation was a change of mentality as well as a change of self-consciousness. The virtues of a truly patriotic person were, namely,
diligence, frugality, incorruptibility, inner and outer purity, sincerity, and faith. Though derived mainly from Confucian values, they
were, on the whole, related to western standards. As Ch'en maintained, the successful practice of these virtues would not only bring
about domestic order, but also help to preserve national sovereignty.[6]

In 1915–1922 Ch'en attempted to substitute a western-oriented
universal civilization for the traditional culture. With his editorship

of a new journal in 1915, he exerted strong influence on the intellectuals. Appropriately entitled *Youth Magazine* (later renamed *New Youth*), the publication attested to his anarchist, non-Marxist faith in the young leaders of the nation. In his opinion, only those who had not been trained in the old could adopt the new.

Ch'en promoted the vernacular literary movement as a vehicle of his campaign for iconoclasm. Indeed, he regarded the movement as a cultural and political process of social changes. Besides being a medium of communication and acculturation, the classical literature was representative of a social class that had sapped China's strength and destroyed its people's initiative. Similarly, the classical language was an expression of the aristocratic ideas and aspirations, as well as the sickness of the old superstitious society. Ch'en therefore called for the creation of a new language with the revolutionary images of man and society. In this respect, his literary movement was actually a cultural revolution that rejected any compromise with the old system of values.

In his 1917 essay, "On the Literary Revolution," Ch'en noted the failure of the political revolutions in 1898, 1911, and 1913, and concluded that the most powerful weapon in the arsenal of change was the cultural weapon. He likewise credited the Renaissance as the source of the political revolutions of western Europe. He favored a "literary revolutionary army," which would propagate three new forms of literature: a people's literature as opposed to the gentry's, a new, solid, realistic literature in contrast to the desiccated Chinese classics, and a popular literature in place of the one of the recluse. As he insisted, China could have a successful political revolution only if it embraced a new cultural spirit.

Anti-statist Policies

An outgrowth of Ch'en's call for a new culture was his advocacy of new politics. He opposed political associations in both traditional China and modern western countries, for he accused these elitist groups of using their power and influence to control the state for selfish purposes. He, too, resisted the demand for a nation-state. Instead, he urged to establish a political organization that would support mass participation in a social revolution. His position on political organizations must be viewed in the context of Chinese traditional attitudes toward political parties.

In 1045 A.D. Ou-yang Hsiu expressed the traditional view of political associations in China. They should ideally be groups of literati who formulated "public opinion" for the guidance of the state. The standard for judging these associations should be ethical. The moral purity of their members was much more important than their political viewpoints. With the assumption that there was a direct link between morality and polity, Ou-yang asserted that the good associations consisted of "gentlemen" or "superior men" who were unselfish, while the bad ones had as their members the "inferior men" who pursued personal gains. Thus, the major function of these groups should be to engage in moralistic activities, thereby spreading the proper code of behavior. Moral men legitimatized a moral association and even a moral state. The literati confronted their political and social issues by either praising or attacking the moral stature of the individuals. Any attempt to transform these groups into an organized political structure was illegitimate, since private associations would only nourish selfish objectives contrary to the interests of the state.

In the early twentieth century, most of the associations that sought either to overthrow the Ch'ing dynasty or, later, to preserve the republic were also organized around personalities rather than programs. Sun Yat-sen worked with secret societies, anarchists, students, and overseas Chinese. His political ideals were often inconsistent. When he founded the Chinese Revolutionary Party (Chung-hua ke-ming-tang) in 1914, he demanded from his comrades a blood oath pledging personal loyalty to him. In spite of their traditional character, however, the political parties of this period represented a new development and attracted the support of many students. Faith in a constitutional system based on parliamentarianism seemed to run high in China.

The superficial hold of political parties on the Chinese became evident after Yüan Shih-k'ai's successful counterrevolution in 1913, when he rejected the ideal of a constitutional government. A large majority of the members of the national assembly of 1913 retired from politics, and many withdrew to a life of study and self-cultivation. Of the 351 members about whom information is available, 275 retired, 23 went abroad, 12 were imprisoned, and only 41 became officials. The average age of those who retired was the mid-thirties. [7]

In 1914 Ch'en Tu-hsiu declared that the Chinese had to seek new "political forms to replace parliamentary parties." Early in 1917 he met with more than one hundred "prominent liberals" and former T'ung-meng-hui leaders such as Po Wen-wei, Tsou Lu, and Hu Han-min to discuss whether a republic could survive without political parties. They formed a club called "Beyond Politics" (Cheng-yü chü-lo-pu). [8]

In a 1918 essay Ch'en sided with both the liberals and the former T'ung-meng-hui leaders to denounce the warlords. But he parted company with his associates when he resisted the idea of a one-party government in China. He also advocated the creation of a new ethics through a broadly based political organization. Although he was uncertain of the nature of this organization, his distaste for western liberalism was obvious, especially after the conclusion of World War I. According to him, the development of German militarism and Chinese warlordism was an outcome of the politics of western statecraft. The nation-state became the servant of the military leaders, who oppressed the people while amassing wealth and power for themselves.

Throughout his life, Ch'en was consistently uneasy about the military organizations. While he was critical of their relations to the state, he accused both of usurping the power of the people. He attacked the modern Chinese army of 1911, the Kuomintang forces of the Northern Expedition, and the Red Army with equal vehemence. As secretary to the governor of Anhwei after the 1911 revolution, he aided his superior in demobilizing the modern bridges of the province. He opposed the Northern Expedition because it was no more than a purge of the rebellious warlords and was thus devoid of any social significance. He criticized the Red Army in 1931 for its imminent assimilation with the guerrilla bands and its loss of class consciousness. He noted, in particular, the increasing ineffectiveness of the Communist cadres to control the military. Moreover, as he argued, the peasants relied so much on the Red Army that they would soon lose faith in their own organization and social objectives.

In an essay on the Korean independence movement, Ch'en discussed the relationship between the military and the state. On March 1, 1919, the cultural and religious leaders in Korea read an eloquent "Proclamation of Independence," in which they declared their country free from Japanese rule. More than one million people participated in this non-violent demonstration. Ch'en applauded the Korean strategy of using "public opinion," instead of depending on "military strength." Owing to his own anti-statist beliefs, he further encouraged the Korean leaders to create "a new people's alliance." In this endeavor, however, they should "never recruit a single soldier, never make even one bullet." [9]

During the period of his stewardship in the Chinese Communist Party, Ch'en vaguely suggested the formation of a "people's army." Yet, owing to his strong reservations about the military, he made little attempt to put the idea into practice. Accordingly, his Communist associates attacked him for his failure to devise a plan for the development of armed forces in the party. [10]

Ch'en's attraction to Marxism in 1920 was based in part on the Marxist thesis that the state would cease to exist when all class distinctions disappeared. As he paraphrased the *Communist Manifesto* in a 1920 essay, there would then be an association in which the free development of each was the condition for the free development of all. [11] Hence, Marxism provided a rationale for the rejection of the nation-state, the condemnation of the political parties as representative of selfish class interests, and the creation of a classless society.

Like Marx, Ch'en did not have a clear concept of the state; in contrast to Lenin, he opposed rigid political parties. Ch'en differentiated politics from political parties. While politics referred to activities that aimed at laying a new social foundation for the promotion of human welfare, political parties were a form of monopolistic power with narrow class outlook. They were only concerned with political and economic gains. Guided by these beliefs, Ch'en became critical of the T'ung-meng-hui, the Kuomintang, and later the Chinese Communist Party and the Trotskyist Party.

Ch'en's leadership in the Chinese Communist Party did not reflect any contradiction with his distaste for the organized political structure. During the initial stage of the party, many of its members were his students at Peking University. Their association grew out of the close professor-student relationship that had developed during the May Fourth Movement. [12] Indeed, the party became tightly structured only after Ch'en's dismissal as secretary-general in 1927. His later support of Trotsky's demand for democracy within the party was therefore compatible with his political thought.

With his advocacy of the dictatorship of the proletariat, Ch'en attempted to promote mass participation in politics. He interpreted "dictatorship" as the rule of one class. He preferred dictatorship of the proletarians to dictatorship of the bourgeoisie, because the former would lead to a classless and stateless world order that would, in turn, provide for the rule of the "popular will." According to him, democracy was an instrument used by the bourgeoisie "to deceive the people and maintain power."[13] Thus, he favored the immediate transformation of China into a proletarian dictatorship. Like Trotsky, he preferred to leap over the transitional stage of bourgeois democracy and head directly into "socialist freedom."

The Significance of the Iconoclast and Anti-statist Movement

Ch'en's iconoclasm resulted in a period of confusion, during which all aspects of Chinese culture came under attack for their feudal and militarist leanings. Confucianism, the essence of Chinese civilization, was "rotten," while the gentry and the literati were "man-eaters." Save for the young intellectuals who cut across class lines, all social groups in China were regarded unredeemable. In the 1920s the Chinese Communists had difficulty in accepting any institution that exuded a breath of traditionalism. They were unable to organize the workers on the basis of their national identity and historical heritage. Instead, they turned to the appeal of international solidarity, anti-imperialism, and economic interests.

Most of the Marxist intelligentsia looked down upon the peasantry. Marx, Lenin, and Trotsky, for example, denounced the muzhik mentality as the product of "rural idiocy." Yet they still had great respect for the cream of western culture. On the other hand, Ch'en and his followers shared the Marxist prejudice against the peasants, but they could not find in their own cultural tradition any satisfactory model of behavior to base their reforms on. Consequently, in the 1920s, they sought to adapt the western bourgeois heritage to the needs of China. Only in the late 1930s and the early 1940s did the Chinese Communist Party begin to develop the peasant tradition of revolution.

In Ch'en's opinion, China's new culture would spring from the youthful intellectuals, who were still relatively untouched by tradition. It was to be modern, western, and bourgeois in nature, with emphasis on such ideals as individualism, cosmopolitanism, and liberty. Ch'en's iconoclasm prevented the Chinese Communist Party from establishing a national identity based on the cultural experience of China. The intellectual activities of the party in the 1920s centered on the study of western revolutionary movements as well as the translation of the works of Marx, Lenin, Trotsky, Stalin, and other writers who exalted the role of individuals.

Politically, Ch'en's anti-statist beliefs produced a strong sentiment of skepticism about both national bourgeois institutions and professional state armies. According to him, the national revolution was merely the harbinger of the social revolution. He never seriously considered the establishment of a state. Similarly, his comrades did not attempt to create an alternative institution to either the state or the traditional Marxist-Leninist party of the reorganized Kuomintang. Besides, their recognition of the need for a people's army was insufficient to eradicate their aversion to the military.

The National Revolution and Anti-imperialism, 1922–1931

The "decision" of the first congress of the Chinese Communist Party to adopt "an attitude of independence, aggression, and exclusion" toward existing political organizations generally reflected Ch'en's position on the subject. [14] Nonetheless, the Comintern soon forced an opposed program on the fledgling party. In 1922 it instructed the Chinese Communists to join the Kuomintang as individuals.

As the Comintern resolved to support anti-imperialist movements in colonies and semi-colonies, it sought an alignment with their national bourgeoisie. In doing so, it was torn between its ideological commitment to the native Communists and its strategic support of the bourgeois organizations. The tension that resulted from this conflict prefigured the dilemma of the Chinese Communist movement in the 1920s.

Comintern Strategy toward National Movements of Anti-imperialism

The Comintern was responsible for directing a worldwide socialist revolution. Its leaders were afraid that Communist Russia would become a stranded whale washed ashore on an unfriendly capitalist mainland. They could only save the whale if the mainland was transformed by a socialist revolution. With the collapse of the Spartacus movement in Germany and the Béla Kun uprising in Hungary, their dream of successful revolutions in Europe evaporated. Hence, they shifted their strategy by turning to the colonies and semi-colonies. Anti-imperialist movements would weaken the mother countries, thereby making them susceptible to revolution. As Lenin suggested, these nationalist movements would help to save socialism in Russia. [15]

As early as July 1920 the Comintern had decided to stress the importance of the anti-imperialist struggles in colonies and semi-colonies instead of the Marxist social revolutions. Ideologically, the Communist leaders called for the creation of a socialist order under proletarian leadership through the means of class struggle. Yet the international situation in 1922 required them to protect the revolution in Russia. To achieve this objective, they advocated the formation of an alliance with the bourgeois nationalist parties against western imperialism.[16] M. N. Roy, who opposed this policy of collaboration, recalled that his Polish comrades had hailed him as a "true Communist," while describing Lenin, the proponent of the alliance, as "a nationalist." [17]

Since Lenin assumed that the bourgeoisie in colonies and semi-colonies would act in accord with their national interests and oppose the imperialists, he denied the leaders of the social revolution the need to remain independent of the national movement. In fact, however, the bourgeois nationalists were products of imperialist domination. They played the "mediatory role between the modern and traditional economies." [18] Without risking an open break, their relationship with the mother country oscillated between dependence and hostility. It was in the form of an uneasy symbiosis.

Ch'en Tu-hsiu's Critique

Ch'en was reared in the realm of Second International Marxism, and he believed that the proletarian revolution and the bourgeois national movement should be two separate historical developments. In the "Manifesto of the Communist Party of China" adopted by the second congress in July 1922 the leaders insisted that their assistance to the national revolution should not be interpreted as the surrender of the proletarians to the bourgeoisie. [19] In

1922–1927 Ch'en often argued against the alliance with the Kuomintang. [20] Although he had been a member of a committee to work for the Kuomintang reorganization, his contribution was minimal.

As Ch'en claimed in his theory of dual revolution, every social class had its own historical part to play. The bourgeoisie would overthrow feudalism and establish a unified state with a guarantee of those political liberties generally associated with the ideal of democracy. In this initial era, the proletarians would only assume a "supervisory" role. [21] They would lead a socialist revolution later when conditions were ripe. Ch'en's strategy depended on the maintenance of a very delicate balance. He did not believe in leaping over the bourgeois stage. But, as he contended, the socialist movement would be stillborn if the proletariat became too involved with the bourgeoisie during the first period of the revolution.

Ch'en had agreed to support the nationalist movement with the understanding that this alliance was a temporary arrangement that would not require the proletarians to make any permanent commitment. He was determined to keep the Chinese Communist Party independent of the Kuomintang. Nevertheless, with neither military power nor a large organized mass following, he and his comrades could not control their own fate.

Ch'en's reluctance to abide by the Comintern strategy resulted partly from his experience with the bourgeois politics in 1905, 1911, 1913, and 1919. It was also the outcome of both his dislike of state nationalism and his Marxist interpretation of the political forces in a revolution. His critics variously attacked him for rightism and leftism. After the Chinese Communists broke with the Kuomintang in 1927, the Comintern charged him with being a right opportunist and an opponent of class struggle. Yet, in 1937, the Chinese Communist Party denounced him for being a left adventurist. [22]

The Comintern policy, however, had its positive impact on the growing Chinese party. In the promotion of the national revolution, the Chinese Communists adopted anti-imperialism as the rallying point for their struggle. Their new nationalism soon took root and worked to the disadvantage of their foreign mentors. In 1929 Ch'en accused Russia of "red imperialism" because of its seizure of the Chinese Eastern Railroad and its ensuing military conflict with the Kuomintang. [23] By 1931 the Comintern had lost much of its direct influence on the Chinese Communists, and its handpicked leaders in the party yielded their power in 1935 to the more nationalistic Mao Tse-tung. [24]

Furthermore, the Comintern provided the Chinese Communists with a fresh interpretation of nationalism that was competitive with the Kuomintang version. With a treaty-port orientation, Communist nationalism was primarily anti-imperialist. On the other hand, the nationalist beliefs of the Kuomintang were oriented to the hinterland, and their major concern was anti-warlordism. While both parties were interested in national sovereignty and unification, the Communists desired a political unity that would help to give birth to a self-sufficient national market. [25] They, too, demanded the abolition of the unequal treaties as an important step toward the restoration of China's sovereignty. According to them, imperialism was the cause of national disunity, whereas the Kuomintang charged that disunity opened the way to imperialist aggression.

Owing to their different interpretations of nationalism, the two parties developed different strategies for their revolutions. The Communists sought to expel all foreign political and economic influences from the treaty ports, since they regarded this as a prerequisite to national unification. Nevertheless, the Kuomintang was convinced that the imperialists would only take advantage of China during periods of chaos. Hence, it tried to win the support of the foreign powers in its attempt to suppress domestic unrest and disorder. Although they were the incarnation of national humiliation, the imperialists were a reliable source of investment. Besides, they seemed to be a much less disruptive ally than either the warlords or the social revolutionaries. As the Kuomintang rationalized, their attitude toward China after unification would at worst be benign and at best be helpful.

The Anti-imperialist Strategy of the Chinese Communist Party

At the second party congress in 1922 the Chinese Communists resolved to join the Comintern. This decision had its effect on both the platform and the slogan of the party. The first congress of 1921 had dealt primarily with the organization of unions, the promotion of the proletarian anti-capitalist revolution, and the establishment of socialism. In the second congress, however, the party emphasized Lenin's thesis on imperialism. It condemned the imperialist exploitation of China and analyzed the growth of the anti-imperialist revolutionary forces. The manifesto of the third congress called for a national revolution, and it identified the imperialists and warlords as China's oppressors. In short, during the years of their alliance with the Kuomintang, the Communist leaders did not develop any program for a social revolution.

In May 1922 the Chinese Communists adopted anti-imperialism and anti-militarism as their slogans. They did not expect the masses to have much difficulty in accepting the ideal of "Down with Militarism!" After all, the oppressive militarists had not allowed the people "to live in peace." Yet, the Communists admitted that the masses might not "understand, let alone accept," the slogan of "Down with Imperialism!" [26]

In an essay published on October 1, 1922, Hu Shih, a prominent American-educated intellectual, insisted that the major powers of the Washington Conference wanted a peaceful and united China. Instead of attacking the foreigners as "imperialists," he described them as "investors." As he asserted, international aggression would cease after the success of the democratic movement in China. In fact, he failed to realize the relevance of anti-imperialism in a national revolution. [27]

Hu's essay attracted immediate denunciations from the Chinese Communists. They charged that the Washington Conference represented an American attempt to seize China's resources through a strategy of "cooperative exploitation." Similarly, they ridiculed the new consortium as "an alliance of bloodsuckers." [28] For the Communists, the issues of militarism and imperialism were inseparable, since domestic disorder was the consequence of foreign aggression. In spite of Hu's denials, the imperialists collaborated with the militarists and the national intellectual compradors. For instance, Britain favored Wu P'ei-fu and Japan supported Chang Tso-lin. The United States likewise backed the "newly prosperous Chinese bourgeoisie and intellectuals," with Hu Shih as an obvious example. [29]

Its anti-Japanese uproars notwithstanding, the significance of the May Fourth Movement did not lie in its attack on imperialism. By accusing the Peking regime of betraying the Chinese interests at Versailles, the leaders of the movement established an important link between the problem of foreign exploitation and the issue of corrupt government at home. Yet, in 1919, this development was pure happenstance. It did not gain its ideological and strategic rationale until 1922 when the impact of Leninism was felt in China.

In 1922–1925 the Chinese Communists centered their anti-imperialist attacks on Britain and America. In their opinion, this was a period during which the western powers endeavored to curb the Japanese interests in China. The resentment against the British intensified after the May Thirtieth Incident of 1925 and the Canton-Hong Kong strike. In July 1926 the Communists reported that the British were "militarily more ambitious" than the Japanese. While the Japanese concentrated their attention on Manchuria, the British attempted "to annex all of China." [30]

As a result of their rupture with the Kuomintang in 1927, the Chinese Communists turned away from the nationalist struggle of anti-imperialism. They shifted their attention to an anti-feudal social revolution and devised a platform that called for land reform and peasant-worker insurrection. Their goal was to defeat the Kuomintang, rather than to drive out the imperialists. At times, this change of strategy placed the Chinese Communist Party in an embarrassing and even anti-nationalist position. The two notable examples of controversy involved the crisis over the Chinese Eastern Railroad and the Fukien rebellion.

In July 1929 when the Kuomintang seized the railway in Manchuria from Soviet control, Moscow appealed to all Communist parties to protect the socialist mother country. This presented the comrades in China with a dilemma. As Ch'en Tu-hsiu recognized, Chinese Communist support of Russia against the Kuomintang would destroy the nationalist, anti-imperialist image of the party. It would also put the Kuomintang in a favorable light. Therefore, instead of publicly backing Moscow, Ch'en suggested that his party should "oppose the faulty policy of the Kuomintang." Moreover, he urged the adoption of a slogan that stressed "universal revolutionary morality." [31]

The Fukien rebellion testified to the domestic predicament of the Chinese Communist Party. In late 1933 a group of warlords, radical intellectuals, and members of the Chinese Trotskyist Party revolted against the Kuomintang. They sought to ally with both the Japanese and the Chinese Communists. While the Japanese agreed to lend their support, the Communists were divided. Strategically, they needed the military assistance of the rebellion to break the Kuomintang campaign of encirclement. Nonetheless, they were reluctant to help because the rebels were not deemed adequately revolutionary.[32] The Kuomintang soon crushed the revolt, thus solving the problem for the Communists.

During the post-1927 years when the Chinese Communists began to move to the hinterland, they were away from the imperialists in the treaty ports. Consequently, their policy of anti-imperialism assumed a different character. For instance, they no longer used the term *imperialism* in referring only to the political, economic, and cultural aggression of the foreign powers. Rather, they often used it to attack the antisocial behavior of individuals, sometimes even their fellow Chinese. This exemplified the changes the party espoused when it left the cities for the rural interior.

In response to the Japanese invasion of Manchuria in 1931 Ch'en and some other Communist leaders proposed to ally with the Kuomintang to defend China against foreign aggression. Yet the Central Committee of the Chinese Communist Party insisted that the overthrow of the Nanking government was more important than resistance to Japanese imperialism. Although the Communists declared war against Japan the following year, they remained divided over the issue of collaboration with the Kuomintang. When they eventually decided in favor of an alliance, they once again had to curb their social revolution for the sake of national unity.

Under Ch'en's leadership, the Chinese Communist Party had little appeal to the masses. His call for "universal revolutionary morality" did not attract much support from the bourgeoisie and peasantry. With the addition of Lenin's theory of imperialism, Marxism offered a powerful analysis of the interrelations between foreign exploitation and domestic chaos. In other aspects, however, the Comintern was not consistently helpful. It failed to provide its Chinese comrades with either the organizational skill or the economic and military strength to become an independent revolutionary force. Besides, some of the decisions it made for China were based on the needs of Russia. Its strategy, too, was mostly urban-centered, more appropriate to the politics of the treaty ports than to the rural unrest of the hinterland. Adjustments were therefore necessary, as evidenced by the change in the policy of anti-imperialism. Indeed, it was largely Mao Tse-tung's rectification of the Comintern errors that gave the party a strong pride in China's self-sufficiency.

The Readjustment of Revolutionary Iconoclasm for Social Revolution

Ch'en's reevaluation of the Boxer uprising in 1924 demonstrated the influence of anti-imperialism on his iconoclast movement. While he condemned the historical tradition of peasant rebellions, he hailed the Boxers for their nationalist struggle against foreign aggression. This contradicted his earlier judgment of 1918, and it marked the beginning of an ideological transition that extended to the mid-thirties and early forties.

In an essay published in October 1918 Ch'en had directed a scathing attack on the Boxers. For their self-destructive behavior, he blamed Taoist superstition, Buddhist fantasies, and Confucian authoritarian servility. According to him, the slogan of the Boxers—"Support the Ch'ing and exterminate the foreigners!"—was similar to the Confucian teaching of "respecting the ruler and driving out the barbarians." As he further argued, China suffered a disastrous defeat because the Boxers rejected western ideas. Instead, they committed rapacious and irrational acts of destruction against both foreigners and Chinese. The one means to avoid another national humiliation was to tread the path of republicanism, science, and secularism. [33]

In another essay published two months later, Ch'en charged that the Boxers had been guilty of religious fanaticism. He defended the French missionaries in China against the accusation of superstition. He claimed that only a very small minority of the French people were superstitious, whereas every Chinese held such beliefs. The target of his indictment was not merely the Boxers, but all the Chinese and their cultural heritage. [34] As did Hu Shih in later years, Ch'en suggested in these 1918 essays that internal disorder was actually responsible for the imperialist invasion.

Shortly after the adoption of an anti-imperialist program by the Kuomintang-Communist alliance, however, Ch'en changed his views on the Boxers. As editor of the official Communist party organ, *The Guide Weekly,* he devoted the complete September 3 issue in 1924 to the commemoration of the twenty-third anniversary of the signing of the Boxer Protocol. In this publication, he and the other

contributors lauded the uprising as a movement of national resistance against imperialist aggression. [35]

As Ch'en asserted, there were two common "erroneous ideas"
about the Boxers. First, he insisted that it was mistaken to detest the
Boxers as "barbaric xenophobes." Rather, he censured "the oppression of foreign soldiers, diplomats, and missionaries," as well
as "the culture of militarists, bureaucrats, disloyal merchants, university professors, and journalists who fawn on the foreigners at the
present time." The second incorrect idea was to regard the uprising
as "the crime of a minority." Instead, it was an expression of "the
consciousness and the interests of the entire people." In Ch'en's
opinion, it was "fortunate" that the Boxers saved "part of the reputation of the Chinese people." If they were a minority, so were the
leaders of both the 1911 revolution and the May Fourth Movement.
Thus, the Boxers were the harbingers of a new movement of anti-
imperialism, and their rebellion was "the great and tragic prologue
to the history of the Chinese national revolution." [36]

In his defense of the Boxers, Ch'en revealed his ambivalent conception of the Chinese tradition. The Boxers were superstitious,
and they originated from a feudal environment. Yet Ch'en did not
suggest in an orthodox Marxist fashion that they were advocates of
class struggle. Nor did he attempt to extol them as representative of
the revolutionary character of the Chinese peasantry. The primary
objective of the Kuomintang-Communist alliance was anti-imperialism. The promotion of a social revolution was premature. At this
stage, as Borodin stated, the Communists were merely "the coolies
of the revolution."

In this manner, the Boxers were instrumental in unmasking a new
cultural tradition in Chinese history. While his anti-imperialist fervor prompted him to praise the Boxers, Ch'en's iconoclasm and dis-
dain for the peasants prevented him from resolving his quest for a
new culture. In fact, his legacy has left many still hard-pressed in
their search for a meaningful reinterpretation of the Chinese
tradition.

4

Training and Indoctrination at the Whampoa Academy

Richard B. Landis

In every political and social upheaval of modern China its leadership acknowledged the need to indoctrinate and organize revolutionary activists. While the deficiencies in such preparation adversely affected the fortunes of the Taiping and 1911 revolutionaries, the Kuomintang and Communist movements owed much of their success to the presence of indoctrinated and organizationally trained cadres. The Kuomintang revolution of the 1920s depended specifically upon the education provided at the Whampoa Academy, variously named Whampoa Military Academy or Whampoa Military-Political Academy.

During the past two decades the light of American scholarship on the Kuomintang has penetrated into the different facets of the Whampoa institution.[1] Among these roads of analysis, one of the most rewarding is to study the influence of the academy on the cadets through the medium of formal instruction and training. This approach strikes to the heart of the values and attitudes that the academy leadership wished to impart and nurture. Hence, the main concern of this chapter is to examine the training and indoctrination of the academy from its inception in May 1924 to the spring of 1926, the eve of the Third Northern Expedition in which the Whampoa system was put to a major test.

While China's revolutionary conditions developed in their own distinctive way, the impetus for the organization and programs of the Whampoa Academy evolved from the earlier Russian experience during the civil war of 1918–1921. Just after the proclamation of the Sun-Joffe manifesto in January 1923, Sun Yat-sen arranged for his close associate, Liao Chung-k'ai, to discuss with Adolph Joffe the details of the proposed Soviet aid to the revitalization of the Kuomintang. Most probably, one topic under consideration was the development of a Chinese revolutionary cadre training academy.[2]

Despite the apparent lack of Chinese and Russian materials on the Liao-Joffe discussions, much information is available on the general character of the Soviet military-political schools, or red command schools as they were familiarly known in Russia. These sources provide a basis for evaluating the nature of the Russian impact on the Whampoa system and for differentiating the Soviet experience from the Chinese one. Accordingly, this study emphasizes the example of the red command schools in the analysis of the Whampoa program of training and indoctrination.

The Red Command Schools as a Model for Whampoa Training

The system of command schools was founded in February 1918 by order of Leon Trotsky, commissar for war, to train a large number of loyal, indoctrinated junior officers and noncommissioned officers for the Red Army.[3] During the previous November, the post of commissar-in-chief of Military Educational Institutions had been established by the Soviet of People's Commissars to control the buildings, cadets, and instructional staffs of the Czarist military schools and colleges.

By January 1921 a total of 151 command courses—each of three or four months' duration—functioned concurrently in numerous schools. During the first three years (1918–1920), a total of 39,914 candidate commanders graduated from these courses. In 1918 about 37 percent of the students were listed as having "worker" backgrounds. In the absence of other documentation, one may assume that the majority of the students came from "peasant" families, with another smaller group from various other social origins, including the landlord class.

With no requirement for competitive entrance examinations, the schools accepted applicants who did not have any prior military experience as well as those from existing military units. Successful applicants, however, had to provide school or military records testifying to their ability to read, write, and utilize the four basic rules of arithmetic. In addition, they had to possess documents that vouched for their loyalty to the Soviet government.

The curriculum of the command schools included military drill, political indoctrination, and work in the Russian language, arithmetic and geometry, history, and hygiene. Students with previous military experience were enrolled in three-month programs, which stressed the study of tactics, fortifications, artillery, military topography, administration, and drills, besides indoctrination. In most cases, classes were taught by an ex-Czarist faculty.

At first the administrative direction of the schools lay in the hands of both the soviets of instructors and the committees of students. Beginning in November 1918 school directors (former Czarist officers, referred to as military specialists) and commissars were jointly appointed to supervise all school affairs. In the following months the question of ultimate responsiblity between directors and commissars arose. Instead of settling the matter unequivocally, Trotsky announced that either of them might eventually assume full responsibility for the administration of a particular school. By 1925 the concept of unitary command had been adopted by the Red Army. This was an outcome that Trotsky had earlier envisioned in many command positions.

During the second half of 1919 the schools shortened their training period and curtailed their program of political indoctrination in order to meet a heightened demand for graduates. Nevertheless, this change did not reduce the number of students who became Communists before their graduation. In fact, the courses of these schools "were important breeding-grounds for new Communist party membership."[4] The Communist members among command school graduates ranged from a low of 54 percent in 1919 to between 62 and 70 percent in 1918, 1920, and 1921.

Though patterned on the command schools of Russia, the Whampoa Military Academy differed from its Soviet counterparts in several significant ways. The Russian preference for training almost 40,000 red commanders in numerous schools was, for example, a sharp contrast to the Chinese decision to have only one school site. It was in December 1925, nineteen months after the enrollment of its first class, that the first branch of the Whampoa Academy came into operation. [5]   ∖

The total number of Whampoa graduates who participated in the Third Northern Expedition in 1926–1928 was 7,795. [6] Their socio-economic background was generally at variance with that of the Russians in red command schools. Although the terms *rural* and *urban, peasant, worker,* and *landlord* are subjected to much free usage, a careful distinction between rural and urban residences indicates that 91 percent of the Whampoa graduates were natives of rural *hsien* (districts). Moreover, the evidence suggests that they were not recruited on a random population basis. Thus, the exceptionally high percentage of graduates with their homes in rural places was a clear manifestation of the strong Kuomintang bias in favor of rural youths. Further, about 75 percent of them came from families in which the fathers were middle-sized landlords, middle-income peasants, or public officials. Seventy-six percent likewise claimed that their native provinces were either in the Yangtze valley or in South China. [7] These were areas already in political, economic, and social turmoil. The alienation of their inhabitants from the republican government in Peking often proved helpful to the recruitment activities of the Whampoa Academy.

In the beginning the Whampoa system had required its first class of students to take a written entrance examination before their enrollment. In its subsequent recruitment drives, however, the academy replaced the written test with an oral one. As a part of the admission procedures it also screened the academic records of the applicants. [8] In view of the virtual absence of information about the screening of students from the southern provinces, one may tentatively conclude that such material was withheld to enable an influx of poorly educated men from the southern military units, especially those from Hunan and probably associated with T'an Yen-k'ai. Aside from this exception, most applicants had completed a middle-school education. [9]

While the Soviet system merely provided a politically indoctrinated extension of formal education for its students in the four-month cycles, all Whampoa students joined the Kuomintang and received training for six months in particular branches of revolutionary military work. In addition, they participated in a preparatory recruit training prior to their formal admission, thus extending the duration of a class by one to thirteen months. Upon graduation, the Kuomintang required a three-year service commitment from each probationary officer, in contrast to the one-year Russian commitment.[10]

In comparison with its Chinese counterpart, the Russian system utilized a much larger staff and bureaucracy at the school level, as well as at the national level in the Directorate of Military Education. Although Commissar Trotsky was responsible for the general line of development, he did not personally work at the school level. Yet, in the meagerly staffed Chinese system at Whampoa, Liao Chung-k'ai assumed a variety of duties in the school before his appointment as its party representative. Indeed, during Chiang Kai-shek's self-imposed retirement from Canton between February 21 and April 21, 1924, Liao took charge of the Preparatory Committee. He managed all preparations for the first class, except the details of the admission procedure.[11]

Shortly after Chiang's designation as commandant in May 1924, Liao was named party representative. Nonetheless, their dual leadership in the Whampoa administration was only superficially similar to the director-commissar system of Soviet Russia. The two Kuomintang colleagues agreed most of the time on the materials presented to the students. Thanks to the heavy burden of Liao's many concurrent responsibilities, Chiang soon gained tremendous authority within the academy, even to the point of acting as a political instructor by the autumn of 1924.[12]

Because of its severe shortage of trained political workers, the Kuomintang had to transfer those already assigned to Whampoa to service in the Second Northern Expedition in the autumn of 1924, as well as in the two Eastern Expeditions in 1925. The absence of these workers helped to bring about the decline of the power of the political staff in the academy. Perilous military-political conditions in 1925 accelerated the process and resulted in a growing hegemony of the military specialists.[13] Hence, in spite of the influence of the Soviet example, distinctive Chinese problems propelled the Whampoa administration into a unitary command structure under Chiang Kai-shek's leadership.

Detailed analysis of the Chinese and Russian training systems further belies their superficial similarities. Serious problems of party loyalty plagued the Kuomintang between 1924 and the end of the Third Northern Expedition in 1928. In Russia the term *Communists* comprised a group of closely allied adherents, while it had a much more solitary connotation in China during the years of 1924–1926. Prior to the conclusion of the war against the warlords, the question of loyalty within the Kuomintang assumed the guise of a conflict between Communists and non-Communists. But the Bolshevik suppression of opponents in Russia did not assume widespread proportions until after the civil war. Clear evidence of this difference was the Kuomintang requirement that all Whampoa students had to join the party; graduates of the Soviet command schools were not likewise obligated.

Uniform membership in the Kuomintang, however, did not mitigate the ideological disagreements within the academy. Organized student rivalries began late in 1924. The Communist-inspired Association of Young Army Men contended with opposing organizations known successively as the Society of Chung-shanism and the Society of Sun Wen-ism. On the eve of the Third Northern Expedition, Chiang Kai-shek ordered the disbandment of all existing student organizations and created the Association of the Whampoa Schoolmates to take their place. Henceforth, all students would have to join the new association, and they, too, were expected to accept the Three Principles of the People in a doctrinaire fashion as prescribed by academy authorities.[14]

Within the larger framework of the political-economic realities in China, the Kuomintang faced and eventually mastered some extraordinary difficulties. For example, the party depended almost exclusively upon imported and seized arms to equip the military units that were partially staffed with Whampoa graduates. Moreover, the political and military strength of the Kuomintang did not penetrate the Yangtze Valley, the industrial heartland, until the autumn of 1926. Even in the province of Kwangtung, the power of the militarists threatened the existence of the Whampoa Academy in the spring of 1925.

Indoctrination at Whampoa

As indicated by the instructional materials presented by Liao Chung-k'ai and Chiang Kai-shek to the Whampoa cadets, the two leaders showed a remarkable degree of harmony. To many students, the commandant and party representative spoke as if they were one man. This unity was the product of regular exchange of correspondence between the two men during Chiang's retirement from Canton. With serious reservations, Chiang accepted the plan to establish a dual commandant-commissar leadership in the academy. A conflict was avoided because Liao Chung-k'ai did not have much time to devote to Whampoa owing to his concurrent appointment to many posts. In order to retain Chiang's loyal service, he was therefore prepared to make only symbolic appearances in the academy.[15]

Liao apparently lectured at Whampoa on only six occasions, the first three in May and June 1924 and the others extending to March 1925. During his latter three appearances, he mostly repeated either his earlier themes or those concepts that Chiang had already presented to the students. In addition, Liao prepared four lectures on imperialism. According to one account, he delivered them in late 1924.[16] But, as Chiang claimed, there was such a shortage of political lecturers around that time that he had to assume their functions in October. Thus, though reported otherwise, it seems likely that Liao never presented his materials on imperialism to the cadets.

In his first three lectures at Whampoa, Liao Chung-k'ai emphasized the need for unified spirit, purpose, and group organization. In his first appearance on May 11, 1924, he maintained that the lack of these qualities was the reason for the postwar problems in Germany. On the other hand, the Soviet leaders had accomplished many tasks of an unusually difficult nature primarily because they realized the importance of these forms of unity. With these two contrasting examples in mind, Liao insisted that the Kuomintang success in saving China would depend on its effort to inculcate these qualities upon the minds of the Chinese.

Liao's second lecture stressed the basic need for determination and perseverance in the mission of transforming China. He also noted that the Chinese were not familiar with the regulations of group meetings. As he recalled, Sun Yat-sen had instructed him some twenty years earlier to translate into Chinese an English language manual on the subject for members of the T'ung-meng-hui.

In the third lecture Liao dwelt at some length on Mikhail Borodin's analysis of twentieth-century China's lack of unity and organization. When Borodin asked Sun Yat-sen about his future plans, the *tsung-li* (director-general) replied that the two most important tasks

were the reorganization of the Kuomintang and the establishment
of a military school. Liao urged the Whampoa cadets to organize
themselves and act together on all matters.

On the whole, Chiang Kai-shek's lectures at Whampoa emphasized similar themes. From May through July 1924 he developed his
ideas on unified spirit and organization. He reiterated this subject
in the spring and autumn of 1925 during the period of the second
and third classes. Between the summer of 1924 and the early autumn of 1925 he elaborated on the second theme of China's organizational weakness, and he outlined various Chinese and Russian
experiences as guides to improvement and change. From November
1924 to the launching of the First Eastern Expedition in February
1925 he presented his third theme, which was an analysis of the
deficiencies in Whampoa's military education. He did not continue
to discuss the subject after this period, as he did with other themes,
probably because the Whampoa indoctrinating regiments, staffed
by Whampoa instructors and students, did not have front-line military service after the first expedition.

The fourth, and last, major topic of Chiang's lectures centered on
the military-political problems of China. When he first spoke on the
subject in October 1924 he analyzed the role of the Kuomintang and
its army, as well as their relations with the rest of the country. During the spring and autumn of 1925, however, he focused on the importance of maintaining party harmony in the face of rising factionalism at Whampoa.

In October 1924 when Chiang delivered his second speech on Chinese military-political problems, the political staff members of the
school had already been assigned to work in the Second Northern
Expedition. Consequently, he noted that he would lecture in their
place during their absence.[17]   Indeed, the topics covered by his
speeches in April 1925 were mostly the concerns of political instructors.[18] Thanks to the development of party affairs in Canton in the
following summer, he became increasingly attentive to political
problems. With the subsequent assignment of the political staff to
the Second Eastern Expedition in the autumn of 1925, he was a de
facto political instructor at Whampoa.[19]

Unified Spirit and Organization

In his first speeches Chiang Kai-shek developed his ideas of group
cohesion. According to him, the abject condition of the Chinese

people justified the existence of both a revolutionary party and its army. Although suffering, the people did not have the power to oppose their oppressors. They used their sweat and blood to furnish taxes and rents, which in turn supported the livelihood of the military leaders and paid for their weapons. In the economic sense, these militarists were totally unproductive. Their existence found meaning only if they protected the people and defended the country. [20]

As Chiang insisted, the Whampoa Academy was established to provide training in organization and discipline for the revolutionary profession. He hailed its cadets as the cream of the youthful members of the Kuomintang. To join the rank of the revolutionaries, they should examine their personal attitude and behavior, as well as develop a consistent and meaningful outlook on society. [21]

In his lectures Chiang urged the revolutionary cadets to imbibe the ideals of Sun Yat-sen's Three Principles of the People. He, too, stressed the importance of a unified spirit, purpose, and organization. [22] In Chiang's opinion, a group should act in a unified manner. Hence, its members must be willing to accept discipline. He brought up the subject of spirit in virtually every speech. In fact, the first part of the book *Huang-p'u ts'ung-shu*, which includes all his addresses to the Whampoa students, is entitled "Spiritual Education."

In his exaltation of the quality of unified spirit, Chiang Kai-shek called for the creation of leaders of the people, who would single-handedly do the work of a thousand. They would also be ready to battle a numerically superior enemy in the mode of the party's martyrs who had died at an earlier time. [23] Besides, Chiang stressed comradeship. He instructed his cadets to love their associates and welcome their guidance. They should, too, share the joys and sorrows of their comrades, as well as eat, fight, and die in their company. [24] Most importantly, the revolutionary officers must cherish the spirit of sacrifice. They should be prepared to forsake their own happiness, freedom, and equality in order to safeguard those of their party and country. [25]

Although Chiang mentioned the concept of unified purpose in his second speech at Whampoa, he never defined it in specific terms. As a military leader, he probably eschewed elaborate statements of political and social relevance and favored an overriding attention to discipline and obedience to command. Perhaps unified purpose was too obvious to require definition. When intraparty strife developed apace in the autumn of 1925, Chiang sought to accomplish a unity of purpose. He implored his comrades to accept what was harmonious in Communism and the Three Principles of the People and reject all that produced dissension.

While Chiang indoctrinated his cadets with the general concepts of unity, he also believed in the need for authority, intendancy, and hygiene in a military institution. The exercise of authority included organization in general terms, leading troops, and attending to such matters as orders, education, promotion and demotion, troop movements, as well as rewards and punishments.[26] To Chiang, intendancy involved the organization of finances, the maintenance of physical facilities, and the supply of weapons, munitions, clothing, and food.[27] Hygiene was concerned with medical care, the quality of food, the adequacy of sleep and rest, the order of daily activities, and the effect of climate upon the human body.[28]

Of these three necessities, Chiang considered hygiene the most important. Accordingly, he made strenuous efforts at Whampoa to assure its hygienic environment, which indeed surpassed that of most other Chinese military establishments. At the beginning of the academy, he demanded improvement in the quality of food and insisted on the cleanliness of the barracks.[29] After the month of May 1924, however, he did not refer to the subject anymore. It was not unlikely that Chiang had by this time already achieved this objective.

In addition to organizational qualities, Chiang asserted that a military institution had to value discipline. Not only would the work of the cadets be uniform and their marching be orderly, but they would share the same purpose as well. As Chiang argued, a cadet who underwent this kind of disciplinary training would become a soldier and, more significantly, "a man." He would "act like a man" in his daily life.[30] Chiang saw two different levels in the exercise of discipline. The first involved obedience to rules generally applicable to barracks and camp life. The second level was more important; it aimed at upholding law and order in an army and establishing an emotional bond among the troops. In this connection, Chiang stressed the necessity to place daily routines in "good order."[31]

In Chiang's conception of a military organization, he maintained that discipline was essential in order to bring about unity in spirit and purpose. Moreover, in his opinion, there was an obvious connection between disciplinary training and adherence to party ideology. He attempted to establish their relationship in two speeches delivered at Whampoa in June 1924 and September 1925. In his first lecture he noted that the Political and Academic Departments of the academy were both responsible for ethical and mental training. [32] He presented the second speech later when the split between Kuomintang and Communist supporters complicated the problem of loyalty among the cadets. He urged his students to continue their backing of the party policy of collaboration with the Communists, because it had been established by Sun Yat-sen. He also warned the cadets against any violation of academy discipline. [33]

Nevertheless, Chiang did not try to elaborate on the relationship between his concept of discipline and the party's ideological system. Neither he nor Liao Chung-k'ai devoted much time to the matter. Chiang himself had a military man's limitation in understanding the ramifications of ideology. Many of the other ranking officers at Whampoa were undoubtedly even less attuned to the problem of party organization and ideological system. In July 1924 Chiang described the establishment of the Whampoa district party headquarters as "a crisis of life and death in the destiny of our school." [34] Many of the formally trained military specialists on the staff and faculty had contended that the authoritarian character of the Whampoa Academy could not harmonize with a party organization dedicated to the spirit of equality among its members. To a large extent, Chiang agreed with these officers, and he was critical of the disorderly performance of the election of small group chiefs and party executive officers earlier in the same month. He attributed this to the spirit of individual equality and freedom among the cadets. [35]

At Whampoa the question of military discipline and ideology was the responsibility of its Political Department, as well as its small-group chiefs and party representatives. While both the group chiefs and the staff of the Political Department were in charge of the indoctrination of the cadets, the party representatives worked for the same purpose among the troops of the indoctrinating regiments led by Whampoa instructors and graduates.

In August 1924 when Chiang spoke to the small-group chiefs, he outlined their duty to evaluate and guide the conduct of their classmates in accordance with the needs of the Three Principles of the

People. The group chiefs were also to suggest ways of improvement to the academy party headquarters. Chiang exhorted them to assist the officers in guiding the cadets. As he pointed out, the unit commanders objected to his effort to "manage the students," for they were convinced that the students should direct their own affairs.[36] This attitude of the commanders opened the door to making group chiefs responsible for supervising the general conduct and ideological education of their classmates.

This separation of the functions of command and ideological indoctrination rendered it unlikely for the training unit commanders to develop a sophisticated understanding of their party ideology. This trend continued after the establishment of the system of party representatives within the indoctrinating regiments. At the end of 1924 Chiang told the graduates of the first class that the party representatives should concern themselves only with the problems of "management." These were problems of either daily living conditions or discipline among the troops. The representatives should also assist unit commanders in matters of intendancy and hygiene. But, according to Chiang, they should not apply their concepts of ideology in judgment of their unit commanders.[37]

As the military specialists gradually assumed control of ideological training at Whampoa and in the National Revolutionary Army, friction between party representatives and unit commanders probably became less and less important. During the First Eastern Expedition, however, Leng Hsin, a party representative, openly opposed his commander's disciplinary treatment of a sergeant. In view of the haughty contempt of many Chinese officers for their subordinates, one might ask whether the treatment of the rank and file deteriorated as the military specialists assumed control of the political machinery in the army. The answer must await future study.

In conclusion, because of the resistance of the military specialists to indoctrination, the relationship between the party's ideological system and the concepts of military organization and discipline was cursory and one-sided. This became more so as a result of the domination of the political administration at Whampoa by its military counterpart. Chiang's emphasis on unified spirit, purpose, and organization could have provided the foundation for an adequate military-political education. Nonetheless, the attention of the military specialists to the traditional values of organization and discipline combined with the brevity of time available for each class to make the Whampoa education extremely conservative.

As Chiang noted, discipline was arranged first in form and later in spirit. A cadet who observed discipline and obeyed command would be a good leader of society, a good officer, and a good party member. [38] In accord with this thinking, too, was the separation of customary military training from ideological indoctrination within the fifth and sixth units of the first class. When these cadets reached Whampoa in the autumn of 1924, they received intensive ideological training.[39] It was assumed that ideological training and previous military experience could be treated as separate entities. In a word, unified spirit and purpose applied only to the man who was already a member of a disciplined military unit.

Chinese Organizational Weakness and Ways to Combat It

The strong organizational and disciplinary interest shown in Chiang's speeches certainly formed relevant criteria against which to judge China in the early twentieth century. The lack of national organization, the absence of disciplined political parties, and the presence of territorial units controlled by warlords all attested to the decentralized and disorganized nature of Chinese society. To this nature of China, Chiang devoted himself time and again. In terms of frequency of consideration, problems of organizational weakness claimed second position to the stress on unified spirit and organization. In his effort to solve these problems, Chiang cited four sources of inspiration and guidance for the cadets: traditional Chinese educational ideals, Chiang's own experiences, the thought of Ch'i Chi-kuang (the Ming military commander), and the Russian revolution.

In Chiang's opinion, the Chinese people did not have the power to oppose their oppressors, and they were unable to manage their country properly. Since the Sung dynasty, they had been dilatory, negligent, and irresponsible.[40] According to Chiang, China in the 1920s was "wasteful, immovable, slovenly, disruptive, and corrupt." He further charged that this was the result of constant foreign invasions from which China had suffered since the tenth century. [41]

He complained about the improper behavior of both the Kuomintang members and the Chinese military leaders. Even the

Whampoa cadets of the first and second classes—the future hope of
the nation and the party—visited brothels, gambled, and smoked at
times of personal convenience. They were also jealous of the rank
and pay of others. Their officers likewise exhibited irresponsibility
by talking at their convenience, failing to salute, and paying little attention to their subordinates. [42]

Chiang, too, blamed the Whampoa cadets for founding provincial
associations and thus deviating from the national, unitary viewpoints of Sun Yat-sen's Three Principles of the People. He urged the
dissolution of these organizations. [43] Moreover, the cadets were
guilty of finding their only significance in feudalism, the worship of
idols, and clan society. The militarists and propertied classes were
major beneficiaries of this decadent society, and they must be
eliminated.[44]

Chiang maintained that the cadets must assume personal responsibility as members of an organized party and army. This was more
so for the small-group chiefs. [45] He quoted Sun Yat-sen to support
his belief. As Chiang recalled, the tsung-li had insisted that the Kuomintang members, including military officers, did not have any
claim to personal freedom and equality, which permitted people to
act selfishly. Those who sacrificed themselves preserved their virtue, while those who emphasized their success would not create a
meaningful revolution. [46]

In earlier centuries the Buddhists, Mohists, and Confucianists
had believed in the principle of self-denial and self-sacrifice.
Chiang, too, noted that teachers had used the ferule to regulate the
disposition of their students. Hence, he favored rewards and punishments as a means to establish and preserve a united organization
at Whampoa. [47]

Chiang accepted the traditional view that the most intimate associates of the students were their family and teachers, who were often the only ones to chastise and punish. More importantly, he was
convinced that this view had real meaning for the Whampoa education. The instructional staff of the academy and party comrades
were substitutes for the family and teachers as intimate associates
of the students. In this spirit of intimacy, the cadets should willingly
accept the dictates of military discipline. Further, they should regard their fellows as members of a cohesive group, with the slogan
of "comradely love and sincere devotion." If every student acted in

accord with this spirit, his fellow comrades would reciprocate, and this would contribute to the success of the revolution.[48]

To illustrate the importance of personal responsibility, Chiang cited his own experience as commandant at Whampoa. In order to end excuses, hesitancy, and slowness in the execution of his work, he had to manage the school without awaiting orders on every matter from either Sun Yat-sen or the Central Executive Committee of the Kuomintang. Despite the possibility of committing errors at times, Chiang insisted that superiors appreciated the effort of their subordinates to assume personal responsibility. Yet, any allowances the superiors made for errors should not preclude the application of punishment to officers. While enlisted men could be excused for their failures, officers must submit themselves to punishment. [49]

As party members, cadets should not believe that they had the right to belittle party election procedures established by the academy party headquarters. [50] After their graduation they should nourish the feeling of intimacy and reciprocity in their relations with the troops under their command. Mutual trust would develop as the troops were drilled, and as the officers attended to the problems of clothing, food, and daily activities, as well as toiled and suffered in close association with their subordinates. [51]

Chiang was indebted to Ch'i Chi-kuang when he stressed the concept of collective responsibility among the Whampoa students. Indeed, in a speech presented to the graduates of the first class in either December 1924 or January 1925, he discussed the idea in greater detail than Ch'i had ever done. [52] Basically, he stressed collective responsibility in support of the development of unified spirit and organization. He also aimed at promoting a military esprit de corps among party comrades, as well as between commanders and troops. In spite of the talks about unified spirit and organization, a more concrete form of direction seemed necessary for the revolutionary army. It would include the provision for the application of the death penalty to the junior officers who had deserted their commanders on the battlefield. This need reflected the extreme decentralization of China's political and military leadership in the early twentieth century. [53]

This phenomenon of decentralized leadership threatened to destroy Chiang's theory of military organization and discipline. For this reason the Russian success in this area offered a valuable example to the Kuomintang and its Whampoa Academy. This was, in fact, the only Soviet quality that Chiang lauded. He traced nothing else in the military field—philosophy, strategy, or tactics—to Russian origins.

On only one occasion, in early June 1924, did Chiang equate the personnel of the Soviet Red Army with the Whampoa cadets. He gave the misleading impression that all Red Army officers and men were party members. He then claimed that they supplied fuel to the Russian people, who thus respected and honored the party. [54] In three other speeches he praised the Soviet Communist qualities of dedication to duty and sacrifice of personal desire for the benefit of both the party and the people.

In the first of these speeches, delivered in the summer of 1924, Chiang stated that the Russian Communists planned only for the happiness of the people. They secured the trust of the proletariat and peasantry and fulfilled their duties more completely than other men. The Communist successes often evolved from the cooperation of a few earnest party members who brought a larger group under their influence. As a result, the Red Army often did not have to fight its enemy, who preferred to surrender "in all sincerity." [55]

In April 1925 Chiang mentioned action with dispatch as another Soviet quality that he considered desirable.[56] In September he continued to praise Russian organization but felt compelled to invoke Sun Yat-sen's authority to support the policy of reorganizing the Kuomintang on the Russian model. The specific reorganization necessary at Whampoa involved the small groups, which had not been adequately used for cadet orientation during the period of the second class. In the autumn of 1925 Chiang asked the academy's party executive officers for the third class to reemphasize training within the small groups. [57]

This was an impossible task. The small groups had probably never functioned as a satisfactory means of feeding acceptable political ideas from the party leadership and the school's district party headquarters. There were various reasons for this. The political staff at Whampoa was overworked, and the small groups lacked a unitary, highly indoctrinated leadership. Besides, as Chiang would have noted, the members exhibited too much personal freedom and equality on the part of the members. If he and Sun Yat-sen intended to equate the small groups with the cells in the Russian Red Army, they were dealing with two institutions of different origins. Nevertheless, the small groups and the cells shared one major common characteristic. They served as a source of frustration to their respective party leaders. Both institutions reflected too much of the untutored, unindoctrinated ideas of their members. [58]

During the period of the second class at Whampoa, a large portion of the political staff, including the student small-group chiefs, was dispatched on active service to the First Eastern Expedition. When the third class began its cadet training, the political staff apparently demanded renewed emphasis on the use of the small groups. Chiang's speech in the autumn of 1925 clearly made the same suggestion. Any effort in this direction, however, would have been short-lived, because many members of the political staff soon departed with the Second Eastern Expedition.

In December 1925 the Russian adviser Andrei Bubnov indicated that a much more rigorous system of political training would evolve at Whampoa. Instead of mentioning the role of the small-group chiefs in the new system, he referred only to the political instructors, whose quality and reliability could seemingly be better guaranteed. Owing to the hasty development of an understaffed political system, the Whampoa Academy suffered from an evident lack of continuous organization within the Political Department and small groups.

In conclusion, Chiang viewed the absence of dedicated loyalty to a group and its group action as the chief Chinese weakness. As a remedy, he advised his students to assume their responsibility as members of an organization, preferably the Kuomintang and, within it, the Whampoa cadet classes. Given this orientation, various Chinese and Russian models were worthy of imitation. As Chiang insisted, the Chinese revolution would succeed if the Kuomintang members served the people, accepted group discipline, loved their fellow comrades, and acted according to the principle of reciprocity. These were the essential ingredients of what became known as the Whampoa spirit.

The Military Knowledge Imparted at Whampoa

Besides the absence of a sufficiently trained political staff, there was also an inadequacy in the field of military science at the

Whampoa Academy. For the first time, in November 1924, Chiang told the graduated cadets of the first class that they had really learned very little.[59] He noted, too, that there were various ways by which the newly posted graduates (probationary officers) should improve their knowledge and capabilities. He urged them, for example, to study the duties of their new posts, especially the post of platoon commander, to which many of the probationers had been assigned. Moreover, they should learn and respect the work of the quartermaster sergeant in each company.[60]

The work of the quartermaster sergeant spanned part of the larger function of intendancy (logistics and administration) at the platoon level. Since the graduates had not received the equivalent of the one or two years of intendancy training given in foreign armies, they should study the subject during their spare time and learn the foreign methods and ideas. Intendancy was particularly important for those graduates assigned to the post of party representative. In the fulfillment of their duties, they should assist their unit commanders to solve problems of supply and finance.[61]

Related to intendancy was the lack of an independent supply system divorced from the control of the unit commanders. Chiang indicated that a financial supervisory committee would be established to handle all fiscal matters for the academy and its indoctrinating regiments. Under the new system, the unit commanders would only assume the duties of drill and battle command.[62]

Before the new system came into effect, the unit commanders continued the Chinese practice of controlling the finances and supplies within their units. This remained the case on the eve of the First Eastern Expedition even in the well-nurtured indoctrinating regiments. F. F. Liu, a military historian, maintains that the first three Whampoa classes received very little training in logistics and administration. As a result, they favored field commands above all other posts in their later careers.[63] Although intendancy training was given to specific groups of cadets beginning with the second class, only a small number of students had received such training, and it was, at best, of a limited nature. Thus, Liu's assertion accurately depicts the general situation at Whampoa.

As Chiang admitted to the cadets, he had himself received no formal training in the field of intendancy.[64] The resulting deficiency apparently blinded him to the realization of the importance of a well-organized, expertly staffed intendancy system to the overall functioning of a modern army. As with most other Chinese commanders of his day, his forte lay in the command of combat troops. When he commented on the necessary qualities of the Kuomintang army, he neglected completely the question of intendancy. Instead, he emphasized a sense of confidence, a united organization, esprit de corps, combat intelligence and liaison, quickness in movement of units on the battlefield, overwhelming concentration of strength at tactically important places, and, in general, careful calculation of the factors of time and place. [65]

Chiang's Military-Political Analyses

Until the launching of the First Eastern Expedition in February 1925, Chiang's concern was the Kuomintang vis-à-vis the rest of the country. But as early as April 1925, within a month after Sun Yat-sen's death, Chiang stressed the need for harmony between the Three Principles of the People and Communism. By this time, Kuomintang-Communist rivalries had already developed in the academy. [66] The problem of dissension subsequently became a major theme in his speeches.

Chiang presented his first military-political analysis in late October 1924. He lamented that the farther the revolution proceeded, the more distant its goals were. The speech largely reflected his views on continuity of both the party and the army. After an illness of two weeks he noted that he felt fatigued. He feared that he might die in battle prior to the completion of the revolution. Hence, he argued that the revolutionary success must depend upon the Whampoa youth, who would carry on the spirit of the martyrs of the party. Despite Sun Yat-sen's success in forming alliances and seizing territory, the only hope of solving the military-political problems in China lay in the organization of the Whampoa army. [67]

In another speech Chiang compared the success and failure of the revolutions in Russia and China. He contended that propaganda alone had not won the revolution and civil war in Russia. He attributed the success of the Soviet Communists to a variety of factors. For instance, he praised the strength of their party organization, the willingness of their comrades to assume responsibility, and their ability to implement their revolutionary slogans. In addition, he stressed the geographical factors. He noted that the Communists in Russia had benefited from the protection of both the long winters

and the Black and White seas. Owing to the absence of rivers, it was
difficult to penetrate into the Russian heartland. This had been an
advantage to the revolutionaries in view of the huge distance involved. Further, he considered their shift of the capital from Lenin-
grad to Moscow a wise decision.

On the other hand, Wuhan had proved to be a poor base of operation in the Chinese revolution of 1911, because it was so readily
served by modern forms of communication. Besides, military campaigns in China could proceed all year long, unhampered by the
weather. The oceans did not provide any protection, and the
Yangtze was a convenient avenue for penetration into the interior.
As for propaganda slogans, party members in 1911 had not implemented Sun Yat-sen's concept of "equalization of land rights" in
order to secure popular support. More importantly, the Manchu
forces had continued to hold Peking. Chiang therefore demanded
that the capital city must be seized in the revolution of the 1920s.
According to him, once Peking fell into the hands of the Kuomintang comrades, the revolution "will not be difficult to finish." [68]

In April 1925, when Chiang spoke to the recruits of the third class,
he alluded to the Kuomintang-Communist frictions for the first
time. [69] He had just returned to the academy after leading the
Whampoa army to victory against Ch'en Chiung-ming in the First
Eastern Expedition. In another speech to the recruits a few days
later, Chiang claimed that the Three Principles of the People embodied the teachings of national socialism, socialism, Communism,
and collectivism. All of them favored the struggle of the property-
less classes to survive, as reflected by the slogan "regulate capital,
and equalize landownership." To fulfill this objective, Chiang advised the recruits "to strike down the capitalists and oppose the
great landlords." [70]

In September 1925, when he lectured to the second class, Chiang
pointed out certain dissimilarities between the Three Principles of
the People and Communism. As he noted, Sun Yat-sen's main concern had been the people's livelihood, while Communism was basically materialistic. Yet instead of exaggerating their differences,
Chiang was interested in harmony. He insisted that both ideologies
advocated a revolution that looked into the future and sought un-
limited progress.[71]

In other speeches delivered prior to the Second Eastern Expedition, Chiang emphasized the common goals of defeating imperial-

ism, promoting the spirit of the Kuomintang, and eliminating inequalities within China and among nations.[72] On the other hand, he was mindful of the divergent views of Communism and Sun Yat-sen's revolutionary ideals. Hence, he demanded that the Communists accept the Three Principles of the People. Although, as he indicated, many comrades had warned him against the Communists, he would not take any action as long as they continued to support Sun's principles and acknowledge his leadership.[73]

Conclusion

In the years 1924–1925, the Whampoa leadership presented a wide-ranging array of materials designed to capitalize upon the discontent and idealism prevalent among the rural, middle-income youths. The moral and ideological materials delivered to this receptive audience provided a sense of direction. Together with training in organized student units, it formed the foundation for an indoctrinated, disciplined officer cadre.

As in the Russian experience during the civil war, a major development became obvious in the Chinese revolution. Thanks to the ineffectiveness of the system of open debate and the group decision-making process of the Kuomintang, a more authoritarian process under a military leadership prevailed. The situation worsened as the Whampoa Academy faced the question of ideological purity. From the end of 1924 to May 1926, the cadets openly debated the merits of nationalism and international Communism. When the party leaders—Hu Han-min, Wang Ching-wei, and Liao Chung-k'ai—failed to grasp the reins of leadership after Sun Yat-sen's death in March 1925, the intraparty struggle intensified. Precarious military conditions during the summer of 1925 further aggravated the crisis and provided the military leaders in the Kuomintang with an opportunity to increase their political power.

Within this milieu, Chiang Kai-shek held a unique position. He was both a popular lecturer and a battlefield commander, and he could thus claim intellectual and emotional ties with the vast majority of the young cadre of the Kuomintang. On the strength of this bond, he and other military specialists on the Whampoa staff successfully forged a harmony based increasingly on their interpretation of the Three Principles of the People. This and the resultant power laid the foundation for the launching of the Third Northern Expedition.

5

Nationalism and Revolution: The Nature and Causes of Student Activism in the 1920s

Ka-che Yip

The development of student activism symbolized a significant social phenomenon in twentieth-century China. To understand its dimensions and meaning, it is essential to examine the nature and causes of student unrest in the 1920s.

Historical precedents were not lacking for the nationalist and anti-imperialist agitations of the twenties. In 1903 students in Tōkyō, Shanghai, and Peking protested against the delay in the evacuation of Russian troops from Manchuria. Two years later the prospective renewal of the 1894 Exclusive Treaty, which prohibited the immigration of all Chinese laborers into the United States, led to an anti-American boycott. It was vigorously promoted by the students and merchants of Shanghai, Canton, and other cities of South China.

The celebrated May Fourth Incident of 1919, in which students, industrialists, merchants, and a nascent proletariat used their corporate strength against the arbitrary power of the Peking regime, was, of course, a turning point in the development of the modern Chinese student movement. Nevertheless, it was only in the twenties that an articulate, organized, and *sustained* student movement came into being. Students of that decade responded to an array of internal and external stimuli: the failure of the May Fourth

Movement to bring about the desired political and social changes, the escalation of internal conflict among warlords, the intransigence of the foreign powers, which seemingly made the realization of China's external aspirations impossible, the emergence of the Chinese Communist Party and the revitalization of the Kuomintang, the growth of labor and peasant movements, and the impetus of the rising interest in Marxist-Leninist revolutionary ideals and techniques. All these factors had an exacerbating effect on a new student generation increasingly critical of the educational system and its role in a modern society. Above all, the young intellectuals shared a common nationalistic concern for China's salvation, and they envisioned nothing less than a radical transformation of their society and polity. [1]

The student movement of the 1920s was of vital importance both in itself and as a prelude to social and political protests in later periods. This study analyzes the political behavior of students in the decade after 1919. The establishment of the Nanking government in 1928 and its repressive policy toward students ushered in a new phase of student activism, which thus constitutes the subject of another study. [2]

The New Student Generation and the Growth of Radicalism

To understand the student unrest of the twenties, one needs to examine the major social and intellectual changes that were affecting China, notably the cultural and psychological consequences of modernization and the "totalistic iconoclasm" of the May Fourth period. [3] It is, too, necessary to analyze a student's attitude toward his education as well as his perception of the role of the educational system in a rapidly changing society. In their explanation of the emergence of oppositional movement among youth, both Talcott Parsons and S. N. Eisenstadt stress the importance of the disjunction between the values of the family and those in the larger society. [4] Moreover, according to Richard Flacks, students living in societies that are undergoing a rapid breakdown of traditional authority are exposed to new cultural influences. They are becoming adults "in a historical period in which the new values have not been clarified, new roles have not been created, new authority has not been established or legitimated." As a result, they are likely to form autonomous oppositional movements with a commitment to rationalism, democracy, nationalism, and other "modern" values. [5]

Such an analysis provides only a partial explanation for the student unrest of the twenties. The new student generation was experiencing the transition from adolescence to adulthood in the decade. These young intellectuals shared many common social and political experiences and were struggling with the fundamental problem of national salvation in the period of upheavals. In fact, at least two generational shifts had taken place between the last decade of the nineteenth century and the 1920s: first, from the generation that reached its intellectual maturity in the 1890s and the 1900s to the intellectuals who became prominent in the 1910s, and second, from this "middle generation" to the student activists of the 1920s. [6] The last two groups often cherished similar views; after all, the vanguard intellectuals of the 1910s had a strong influence on such academic centers as the National University of Peking, which produced many of the student activists of the next decade.

Unlike most of the intellectuals of the generation of Hu Shih and Ch'en Tu-hsiu, the students of the twenties had not received any traditional education. They were products of the educational system introduced after the revolution of 1911. By the early twenties this first generation of students who had attended western-oriented schools reached their adolescence. In the turmoil and confusion of adolescence, they suffered from the conflict between the traditional orientation of the family and the forces of modernity in their school or university. Furthermore, they experienced frustration and discontent over the political and social stagnation that resulted from the failure of the May Fourth reforms. In this state of mind they frequently called for a radical reinterpretation of the sociopolitical reality; some of them even demanded commitment to drastic actions. [7]

These student leaders, too, were increasingly skeptical about the effectiveness of the prescriptions that the vanguard intellectuals of the 1910s offered for China's problems. According to the latter group, "meaningful political action would become possible only when the spiritual ailments of the Chinese people had been cured." [8] The young activists, however, were impatient, and they believed in the efficacy of personal engagement and direct political action. To them, the twenties were permeated by a sense of urgency that could not accommodate long delays. They were talking more and more of "revolution," a term endowed with an almost mystical and sacred quality in the language of these young students. The espousal of revolution became not only a heroic, simplistic act in tune with the psychological needs of the times, it was for many students also a mandate for action. As one of them frankly stated, "it is the realistic situation which has given us our historic mission—we can take only the road of revolution."[9] Indeed, many students were convinced that peaceful and evolutionary reforms were futile.

Moreover, these young activists began to lose faith in the integrity of many vanguard intellectuals who appeared to have abandoned their revolutionary task and succumbed to personal success and prosperity. One student, for example, accused such leaders as Hu Shih of enjoying life in comfort. As he insisted, the only thing that these older intellectuals did was "to publish a few articles and look down from their high pedestals." In consequence, the young students constituted the one social group that, still "pure," possessed the idealism and revolutionary fervor to save China.[10]

Available sources hardly permit an accurate evaluation of the social background of the students. Yet, by comparing the expenses of attending middle schools or colleges in the cities with the average income of various occupational groups, it is possible to reach some preliminary conclusions. In the early 1920s, the average yearly tuition fees in government or public academic institutions totaled approximately 45 yüan for college students and 25 yüan for middle-school students. Private institutions, however, usually charged substantially more. This was particularly so in missionary schools where the average fees amounted to 100 yüan for college students and 45 yüan for middle-school students. Furthermore, there were other expenses in both types of schools, including fees for lecture notes, laboratory equipment, and room and board in the dormitories.[11]

In comparison with the average income of different occupational groups, these expenses were high enough to make education—especially higher education—unavailable to most Chinese people. In the early 1920s the monthly salary for a professor of the Anhwei College of Law was 130 yüan, for an editor of the Commercial Press in Shanghai 60 to 90 yüan, for a Shanghai worker 6 to 12 yüan, and for a Foochow worker about 7 yüan.[12] There were sig-

nificant differences between urban and rural incomes, but those in
the rural areas, except for well-to-do peasants and landlords, were
in general lower than those in the cities. The income of Chinese
peasants varied from region to region, with the annual average
ranging from less than 50 yüan to 150 yüan. Yet the minimum
amount needed to support a rural family was 150 yüan per year.[13]

Hence, modern Chinese students were mostly drawn from well-
to-do families. They constituted a tiny percentage of the Chinese
population.[14] John Israel likewise observes that a "dis-
proportionate number of student radicals came from the lowest
groups that could afford a post-grammar school education—landlords and 'wealthy' peasants."[15] The rural origins of
these students accentuated their difficulties in adjusting themselves to the modern and cosmopolitan environment of the large urban centers where most of the institutions of higher learning were
located. Nevertheless, the lack of available data makes it impossible to determine the proportion of these radicals who took an active role in student unrest.

The Student Subculture

Whatever their background, it is evident from the voluminous body
of literature authored by students and published in numerous
magazines, journals, and newspapers that class consciousness had
developed among the students of the 1920s. It was a consciousness
derived from the students' perception of themselves as a distinctive
social group with peculiar problems. The abolition of the civil service examination system in 1905 and the emergence of new and
rival social groups, notably the military, suggested to these students
that their education could no longer be automatically translated
into political power. Indeed, their place in the political or even social arena was not so assured as before by virtue of their educational or occupational standing.[16] The need for student solidarity
was therefore connected with the entrance of new groups into the
political stage. To a certain extent, the growth of this collective consciousness among students overshadowed their differences in origin and ideology.

This development of class consciousness was clearly reflected in
the emergence of a student subculture, which extolled nationalism
and commitment to direct action in effecting political, social, and

educational changes. It defied adult authority. This subculture was fostered and promoted by the rapid spread of student newspapers, journals, extracurricular associations, and student unions. Students read and contributed to such publications as *New Youth (Hsin ch'ing-nien)*, *China's Youth (Chung-kuo ch'ing-nien)*, and *Student Magazine (Hsüeh-sheng tsa-chih)*. They organized athletic meets, debate and literary clubs, and other associations to propagate specific social and political ideals.[17] Their spiritual mentors included Darwin, Dewey, Kropotkin, Marx, and Lenin, and they were enthusiastic about the discussion and experimentation of western "ism." They, too, were interested in politics and, given the social and political instability of the time, considered sociopolitical activities their most relevant form of expression. In fact, the disorganization of Chinese society and politics in the twenties elevated the importance of such organized groups as the students, the military, and the political parties.

The concentration of students in a few urban centers helped to facilitate communication and spread the student subculture. In 1922, for example, there were in Shanghai alone 13 of the country's 132 colleges and almost 10 percent of the total college student population. Peking had 30 percent of the country's colleges and more than 41 percent of all the college students.[18] The total number of college, middle, and primary school students in any one of these and other urban centers was as high as 20,000. Most of them lived in crowded dormitories, and for many of these young students who had left home for the first time, the difficulties of their psychological adjustment probably combined with the unprecedented freedom they enjoyed to render them highly susceptible to collective action.

Students and the Educational System

For the students, especially those in the universities, the role of the educational system in Chinese society was a vital issue. They were disappointed by the inability of modern educational institutions to meet China's needs. Too little of the elaborate paraphernalia of academic life appeared to serve the purpose of strengthening and modernizing the country. As many students claimed, one reason for this failure was the control of the schools by warlords and politicians. Heads of schools were usually political appointees, dependent upon their political standing for whatever support the schools might obtain. This was particularly so with the appropriation of educational funds.[19] The lack of financial independence contributed to discontent and anger among faculty members whose salaries were frequently months in arrears. The students were similarly plagued by a sense of uncertainty, since many schools faced the possibility of closing for shortage of funds.

In their endeavor to correct the abuses of the educational system, students insisted that their schools maintain a certain degree of autonomy in academic governance. Moreover, they demanded the right to participate in the administration of school affairs. The idea of student government had become popular in the late 1910s, and it won the support of Chiang Meng-lin and other like-minded educators. As a prominent leader of the New Education Movement, Chiang emphasized the development of individuals as the foundation of a democratic society, and student government was thus a form of internship in responsible citizenship.

The young activists, however, viewed student government as a means to advance causes that they considered essential to an educational system in modern society. [20] In their opinion, student government implied the destruction of the *in loco parentis* system; it meant demands for more "relevant" courses, greater concern for student welfare, and a student voice in the selection and promotion of faculty and administrative personnel. Hence, the students were interested in the way school administrators dealt with student problems, the competence of the teaching staff as well as the conditions of the school. In fact, these issues were the causes of numerous "student storms" *(hsüeh-ch'ao)* in the twenties. For instance, there were at least 120 such protest episodes in 1922 alone.[21]

These concerns reflected the weakness of both the educational instruction and the organization of the schools. The teachers had little contact with and no responsibility for the students. They taught by lecture, written out and dictated; the students copied. This was all that the students received, with no explanation and no discussion. There was little supplementary reading. In consequence, many students found it difficult to apply their knowledge meaningfully to immediate social and political problems.

Furthermore, the teachers rarely expressed interest in the conditions of student life and seemed more concerned with their own factional squabble. They had little or no influence over the administrative staff, who showed a lack of sympathy for student problems. Innovations were almost nonexistent, because everyone was afraid that he would provoke the wrath of either the militarist or the politician. In addition, administrators were prone to use high-handed tactics in dealing with student discontent, and there was no proper channel through which students could voice their dissent. As a result, they were eager to assert their rights and were convinced that their participation in self-government was absolutely necessary for the proper functioning of the school. [22] Under these circumstances, any disturbing occurrence—the expulsion of a student, a raise in tuition fees, the feeling that an examination was unfair, or the general belief that there had been an infringement of student rights—would incite them to rebel.

Students and Anti-militarism

According to the students, problems existed in schools because education was controlled and exploited by warlords and politicians. The flaws of the educational system were symptoms of a larger malaise. Thus, one should not limit his interest to such issues as school finances, curricula, and the governance of academic institutions. He should address himself to the question of national and international policy: the unity and independence of China, the equality within the country and among nations, and the legitimacy of government authority.

The deterioration of the political situation in China disgusted many students. The May Fourth demonstrations had checked neither the arbitrary power of the Peking regime nor the incessant struggles among the warlords. The likelihood of unification was remote, perhaps even unattainable. Consequently, the students considered the overthrow of the warlords one of the prerequisites for the salvation of China.

Nationalistic desire to unify and strengthen China was certainly not new. Nationalism had begun to convulse China at the turn of the century. But the failure of the cultural approach of the May Fourth Movement and the pervasive sense of urgency brought on by the constant threat of foreign intervention in China's internal affairs aggravated the situation. As a result, the students veered toward a radical political solution. They insisted on the elimination of the warlords, and then through their own direct intervention, the political reconstruction of the nation.[23] In fact, they claimed to represent the only group uncorrupted by the political establishment, and therefore able to inject honesty and integrity into a new government.

The agitation for domestic political changes was intensely anti-authoritarian, egalitarian, and populist in nature. It was anti-authoritarian in its impassioned challenge to all forms of authority: political, social, and religious. It, too, denounced the domination of Chinese politics by warlords and bureaucrats and impugned the major clusters of old social, economic, and psychological commitments. It was egalitarian in its insistence on social and economic justice for all. It maintained the individual's right to "work and to enjoy material goods." It was populist in its concern for the well-being of the masses and in its involvement of the majority of the population in building a base for a unified and independent China.[24]

These ideological convictions manifested themselves in the twenties in the anti-militarist, anti-religious, and anti-familial aspects of the student movement. They also became the ideological underpinnings of the "go to the people" movement initiated in 1924 and of student participation in the organization of labor.[25] Although student leaders realized the need to mobilize the masses, their concern for their own social distinctiveness and the conservatism of the peasantry often prevented—at least in the pre-1925 years—the successful incorporation of the masses in the nationalist revolution. On the other hand, while they insisted on their leadership in the revolution, the students saw the need for allies and they were attracted by the political, social, and economic programs of both the Chinese Communist Party and the revitalized Kuomintang. They joined these two organizations and provided them with a vital youthful exuberance. Besides, many enrolled in the Whampoa Military Academy and became highly politicized and dedicated cadets, indispensable to the later success of the Northern Expedition.

Students and Anti-Imperialism

The problem of national unification was heightened by the foreign presence in China, and students were aware of the interrelation between unification and the achievement of full political independence. After all, the rise of modern Chinese nationalism had been a response to western imperialism. During the 1920s, anti-imperialism, as a systematic explanation of the ills of China and the contemporary world, began to influence the Chinese approaches to national problems. With the addition of Lenin's anti-imperialist theory, Marxism became exceedingly attractive to students confronted with the somber and threatening aspects of foreign imperialism. The Bolshevik revolution in Russia assumed a messianic character, while the Communist technique of political organization seemed to validate the leadership of the educated elite. At the same time, the anti-imperialist interpretation simplified the explanation of China's afflictions by attributing them to foreign aggression. Moreover, it linked China's struggle to a universal struggle of oppressed peoples of the world against international imperialism. This had special appeal to the students of the 1920s, who were anxious to put China in the inevitable trend of historical development.

Especially after 1924, students started to organize large-scale activities against what they considered to be the political, economic, and cultural aspects of imperialism in China.[26] They demanded the abolition of unequal treaties and denounced particularly the abuses of extraterritoriality, the use of military intervention to settle "incidents," as well as the economic exploitation of the powers, notably through control of China's tariffs. They, too, attacked the western missionary movement in China as cultural imperialism and initiated a vigorous campaign against Christian churches and missionary schools.[27] These activities received a tremendous boost from the May Thirtieth Incident of 1925. On that day, Chinese demonstrators, mostly students, protested the killing of a Chinese worker by a Japanese foreman in a Japanese-owned textile factory. When they amassed in front of a police station in the international settlement of Shanghai, the British officer in charge gave the order to open fire. People all over China reacted violently to this slaughter of unarmed students, and student strikes and demonstrations erupted throughout the country. To the students, this incident was conclusive evidence that China's salvation meant first and foremost the end of imperialist exploitation in China.[28]

The overthrow of imperialism was necessary for another reason: the alleged collusion between domestic warlords and foreign imperialists to keep China backward and divided. According to the prevalent belief, the capitalist countries were intimately involved in the internal strife of China, with the ultimate motive of acquiring economic gains. They were reportedly trying to stave off their own downfall. To accomplish this goal, the Japanese had supported successively the Anfu clique and Chang Tso-lin, while the British backed Wu P'ei-fu. Thus, the imperialist powers were apparently the major obstacle to China's political unity, autonomy, and external aspirations.

Student activism of the 1920s exhibited these two interacting themes of anti-militarism and anti-imperialism. The liberal tendencies of the May Fourth era had fallen victim to the demands of national unification, and the problem of national unification was increasingly interpreted in the framework of Marxism- Leninism. As Lucien Bianco defines, Marxism-Leninism was "a doctrine borrowed from the west and condemned the west." It "put China on the road to the modernization," which it badly needed, while sparing its people "the humiliation of aping more advanced nations and forever lagging in their wake." [29]

Students and the Parties: Kuomintang and Chinese Communist Party

One significant aspect of the student activism of the 1920s was its relationship with both the Kuomintang and the Chinese Communist Party. The student movement of this decade had its own sociological, cultural, and political roots and was therefore not the creation of either party. Nonetheless, the two parties exerted strong influence on its development and outcome. [30]

Students joined the parties not only because the latter had successfully captured their nationalistic aspirations, but also because they believed that a student-party alliance would be powerful enough to oust the warlords and challenge the foreign imperialists. The parties provided an additional nationwide organization (besides the unions of the students themselves) for anti-militarist and anti-imperialist propaganda. Moreover, they furnished the students with a source of power in the form of the party army, thus compensating for the students' lack of the ultimate power of coercion. As Frank Pinner hypothesizes in his study of the political behavior of students, the young intellectuals are marginal elites whose political effectiveness depends on the "derivative power they may have as members of the academic community, which may command public respect" and on their ability to enter into alliance with other groups. [31] With the rise of new and rival groups in the first decade of the twentieth century, the prestige and influence of Chinese students declined. This, in part, compelled them to seek allies. The emergence of the parties in the early 1920s seemed to provide the solution for the problems of the students.

This alliance had important consequences for the student movement. The two parties provided training and practice in manipulating propaganda and exploiting the tactics of direct action, and this resulted in the rapid politicization of the students in the twenties. Yet the parties, especially the Chinese Communist Party, were increasingly able to control the direction of student activism and set the agenda for student politics. In consequence, the students gradually lost control of the movement they had initiated. Many members of the Communist Youth Corps and the Chinese Communist Party became leaders in local as well as national student associations. Such veteran Kuomintang leaders as Wu Chih-hui, too, took a direct hand in the conduct of the activities of the Anti-Christian Federation, the most important nationwide organization of the anti-Christian campaign. [32] At the same time, the Kuomintang began to subsidize the National Student Association financially. [33]

Furthermore, the acceptance of party ideology and discipline had a significant effect on the nature of the student movement. There was an ever-present tension in student thought during the 1920s, a tension arising from the quest for individual liberty and the demand for a strong state. Because of their ultimate objective of political independence, the student leaders emphasized the need for national solidarity. Indeed, their rigid and all-encompassing nationalism replaced the earlier concern for individuals. With their eyes on foreign imperialism and its threat to China's survival, they were willing to compromise their fight for personal liberty. This ideological concession justified the collaboration of the students with parties that had strong totalistic orientations. To a great extent, however, this alliance weakened the anti-authoritarian, egalitarian, and populist commitments of the student movement and probably accounted for its failure to create a mass base of support. [34]

After the Kuomintang split with the Chinese Communists in 1927, it revised its program of anti-imperialism and stressed instead the importance of domestic reconstruction. As some party leaders claimed, "the imperialists are afraid not of processions, lectures, societies and assemblies of our people, but are afraid of our country having a strong and united government and of us having a strong central force to reform political life." [35] Thus, the student movement was to be a casualty in the Kuomintang reinterpretation of anti-imperialism.

Conclusion

With its own sociological, cultural, and political roots, Chinese student activism of the 1920s was far more than an attempt to advance the sectional interests of the students within an accepted status quo. The movement was primarily directed at the larger issue of national salvation, and it called into question the entire social and political structure. The student leaders employed direct action and other forms of militant protest because, in their opinion, such tactics were necessary catalysts of social and political change at a time when more moderate and conventional methods had proved inadequate. The proliferation of hsüeh-ch'ao (student storms) and the organization of "student armies" during the decade of the 1920s were two radical forms of protest. In a hsüeh-ch'ao, student activists often manhandled their teachers and principals, who were, at times, physically ejected from the campus. There was, too, widespread destruction of school properties. Moreover, "student armies" became extremely popular after the May Thirtieth Incident of 1925, and this was a clear indication of the growing militancy of the student movement.

In the political and social context of the 1920s, student leaders demanded a radical transformation of the political and socioeconomic order. They maintained that this was feasible only if they, in alliance with other progressive groups, could assume responsible roles in society and actively participate in the process of policy formation. As previously suggested, students of the 1920s emerged at a time when new values had not been sufficiently clarified to replace the old ones. Hence, they aimed at the creation of a modern order with a new set of values. There would also be a new interpretation of their role in society to meet the needs of the modern order.

Significantly, toward the end of the decade, some students began to interpret their role beyond the circle of their social grouping. They abandoned "the special position accorded to the intellectuals in society as well as the status of the scholar-gentry in history." [36] They were young intellectual workers or peasants. In this respect, they were antecedents of the products of the Maoist education: the cultured socialist-minded workers.

6

The Military and Nationalism: The Political Thinking of Wu P'ei-fu

Odoric Y. K. Wou

I

As Hans Kohn defines, nationalism is "a state of mind, in which the supreme loyalty of the individual is felt to be due the nation-state."[1] The Chinese equivalent of the term is *min-tsu chu-i*, the principle of the clanification of the people.[2] It requires the Chinese people to convert their traditional family and clan loyalty into an allegiance to the nation. This concept identifies the Chinese nation-state, instead of the clan, as a corporate body of national citizens to which the fealty of the individuals should be directed.[3]

Nationalism first became a dynamic revolutionary force in the late Ch'ing period. It contrasted with the traditional idea of universalism, which viewed China as a cultural entity rather than as a national sovereign state.[4] The leaders of the 1911 revolution had utilized the nationalist sentiment in China to bind the five ethnic groups together for the overthrow of the Manchu dynasty and the establishment of a republic. In the 1920s, however, Chinese nationalism assumed broader dimensions in its definition. It was no longer confined to the restricted meaning of anti-Manchuism, racial integration, and republicanism. These objectives had been accomplished in the political revolution of 1911. The leaders of the 1920s emphasized national preservation, as well as national regeneration and reconstruction. As a result, nationalism in China changed both its form and its content.

National Preservation

National preservation implied a concerted effort by the people to preserve China as a nation. During the 1920s, Chinese nationalists identified in spoken and written words certain values as symbols of national survival. These were elements that China must defend to sustain its nationhood. An analysis of these values and their historical significance would therefore contribute to the understanding of the nature of Chinese nationalism.

Republicanism, Popular Sovereignty, and Constitutionalism

Since the 1911 revolution, China emerged as a modern nation, and Chinese nationalism inevitably took on the nationalist outlook of the revolution. Expressed in the terms of "people" (*min*) and "constitutionalism" (*hsien-fa* or *hsien-cheng*), such revolutionary ideals as "republicanism" and "popular sovereignty" were deeply ingrained in the Chinese mind. They were, indeed, the very attributes of the Chinese nation. Thus, the republic was a "people's nation" (*min-kuo*), established by the people's party (Kuomintang or the Nationalist Party). Throughout the 1920s, the Chinese apotheosized the "people," and they spoke on "people's rights" (*min-ch'uan*), "people's sovereignty" (*min-chu*), "people's voice" (*min-sheng*), and "people's constitution" (*min-hsien*). Embedded firmly in these values was the idea that China was a republican nation-state, governed by the people and for the people. The Chinese nationalists considered the "people" as an important element of the nation. A government needed to legitimatize itself by seeking the support of the "people."

"Constitutionalism" was another element the Chinese valued as a national symbol. The anti-Manchu revolutionaries had decided that China should be a republic upheld by a constitution. After 1911 the Chinese came to believe that the survival of the nation depended on its ability to maintain a constitutional government. When President Yüan Shih-k'ai disregarded the constitution and attempted to proclaim himself emperor, Ts'ai Ao, Liang Ch'i-ch'ao, and T'ang Chi-yao protested against the "unconstitutionality" of the monarchical movement and denounced Yüan for betraying the nation. With Ts'ai and his comrades in command of the "National Protection Army," the anti-Yüan campaign assumed the form of a "National Protection Movement."

Since Yüan's death in 1916, Chinese nationalists regarded "unconstitutional" as synonymous with "anti-nationalist." Anyone who defied the principles of constitutionalism was "unpatriotic," "disloyal," and "anti-nationalist." Various Chinese leaders tried to justify their claim to rule with an appeal to constitutionality. In 1917 Sun Yat-sen launched the "constitution protection movement" and organized a separatist government in Canton. When Wu P'ei-fu came to power in the north in May 1922, he advocated the return of Li Yüan-hung as president in accordance with the provisional constitution of 1913. Ts'ao K'un, however, legitimatized his rule with a hurriedly adopted constitution in October 1923. After the fall of the Chihli clique, Tuan Ch'i-jui returned to power. He convened one conference after another to draft a constitution, which would give him public approval. Even the provincial leaders in Hunan, Chekiang, and Kwangtung, who favored a federalist government, worked hard on a constitution of their own in order to gain legitimacy for their regional regime.[5]

National Unification

As the Chinese leaders insisted, national solidarity was a necessary condition for China to survive. The existence of the nation depended on its unification under a stable government that could deal effectively with the outside world. Nonetheless, after Yüan Shih-k'ai's monarchical movement, China was beset by factionalism, disunity, and internal strife. The country was divided into "power bases" dominated by political-military cliques. The only way to preserve China as a nation was to reunify it under one government. Hence, "national unification" became one of the basic ingredients of nationhood.

Throughout the 1920s, political leaders in China endeavored to reunite the nation by removing their enemies, whom they attacked as "the obstacles of unification." Some of these leaders supported the idea of "unification by force." Others favored "peaceful unification," and they suggested that the northern and southern factions should discuss their differences in a "national unification conference." They should also draw up a constitution acceptable to all parties. A third group of leaders advocated a combination of the two methods. Sun Yat-sen, for example, called for the convention of a "national people's conference," while he concurrently launched his northern expeditions against Peking with the hope of bringing the country together by military force.

Anti-foreignism

Asian nationalism is generally distinguished by strong anti-foreign sentiments, with the result that anti-foreignism becomes almost an integral part of all Asian national revolutions. Resentment against western intrusion had stimulated national consciousness in China as early as 1841 during the anti-British incident at San-yüan-li.[6] With the outbreak of the Boxer uprising in 1900, anti-foreignism reached a height.[7] Yet, although the 1911 revolution demanded the overthrow of the "alien" Manchu government, its leaders were not basically anti-foreign. It took the Japanese aggression in World War I to transform anti-foreignism into a nationalist movement. The Chinese chose May 7—the day when Japan presented an ultimatum for the Twenty-one Demands in 1915—as National Humiliation Day. When China failed to recover its Shantung concessions at the peace conference in Paris, the Chinese revolution took on a new front of struggle against foreign encroachment.[8]

The Chinese nationalists of the 1920s launched a movement to fight for national sovereignty and self-determination. They denounced all treaties previously concluded with foreign nations as "unequal." Thanks to the influence of Marxism-Leninism, Chinese nationalism gained an overtone of anti-colonialism and anti-imperialism. To the Chinese leaders who were concerned with the dismemberment of China, "national salvation" required a campaign against foreign political intervention and economic exploitation.

In sum, the concept of national preservation emphasized the need for a united, constitutional republic, free from foreign domination. An individual who violated this principle invited attacks from the nationalists. In addition to its advocacy of internal solidarity, Chinese nationalism also opposed foreign aggressors. Thus, it had a twofold objective. It called for the elimination of "traitors" and the resistance of foreign aggression. Marxism-Leninism had its impact, too. In the mid-1920s the Chinese adopted the slogan "Down with warlordism! Down with imperialism!" They associated internal disorder and corruption with external encroachment.

National Regeneration and Reconstruction

During the last fifty years of the Ch'ing dynasty, the Confucian scholars had made various proposals for the regeneration and reconstruction of China. For example, Tseng Kuo-fan was a leader of the Self-strengthening Movement, and Chang Chih-tung cherished the formula of "Chinese learning for the fundamental principles, and western learning for practical application." K'ang Yu-wei was likewise an advocate of the syncreticism of Chinese tradition and western studies. In the 1920s the Chinese leaders who debated over the future course of China were generally divided into three major groups. They were traditionalist nationalists, liberal nationalists, and Communist nationalists.[9]

Traditionalist Nationalism

Traditionalist nationalism was an extension of the nationalist sentiments expressed by such Confucian scholars as Chang Chih-tung and K'ang Yu-wei of the late Ch'ing period. It had originated as a defensive movement against the pressure of western influence. The traditionalists stressed cultural nationality as the national symbol. They felt a moral obligation to preserve their national heritage and to protect it from exposure to alien influence.

In the 1920s there were still many traditionalists who were convinced of the need to sustain the Chinese culture as the very foundation of the nation. They were, namely, Chang Ping-lin, Yen Fu, Liang Ch'i-ch'ao, and Lin Shu. They wanted to revitalize Confucianism as "the national learning," and they extolled the classics and other features of traditionalism as either "the national essence" or "the national heritage." Many of them equated the Chinese culture with the Chinese nation. Yen Fu asserted that only a return to the ancient ethics and a rejection of western influence could save China from extinction. K'ang Yu-wei, who was still active, claimed that Confucianism was the religion of China as well as the soul of the republic. He compared it with Christianity in Europe. Similarly, Liang Ch'i-ch'ao argued that the Chinese nation would die if its "national character" was taken away. In short, these traditionalists contended that the present turmoil in China was an outcome of the decline of the traditional culture rather than a product of the failure of the Chinese past. China would be strengthened when its heritage was reinvigorated. [10]

Liberal Nationalism

Liberal nationalism called for the acceptance of western ideas and technology in the building of a new China. In the process of reconstruction, national progress should take primacy over the issue of cultural solidarity. As the liberal nationalists insisted, the Chinese mentality had to transcend its traditional cultural boundaries. If western values were helpful to nation-building, China should adopt them no matter how alien they might be. In this respect, liberal nationalism was iconoclastic.

The principal liberal nationalists in China were the May Fourth intellectuals. Hu Shih, Wu Yü, and Lu Hsün were the leading examples. To a large extent, Sun Yat-sen shared their aspirations. These nationalists believed that the Chinese tradition was in decay and could no longer serve the needs of the nation. Moreover, Confucianism was incompatible with the republican ideals. Since the traditional ideology and institutions were obstacles to national regeneration, their destruction was an important prerequisite to the "flourishing" of China. In order to strengthen their country against further humiliation and exploitation, they looked to the west for inspiration. They were attracted by the foreign values of democracy, science, cosmopolitanism, and utilitarianism. Consequently, progress on the western model became the goal of their nationalist movement. [11]

Communist Nationalism

The Communist nationalists found the answer to China's problems in socialism and, eventually, Communism. They traced the origins of the national crisis to the inequities of the economic system. Inequities existed not only between the economically privileged and the economically deprived at home, but they also existed externally between "the colonial nations" and "the imperialist powers." As the Communist nationalists perceived, national reconstruction involved a political revolution, a social revolution, and an intellectual revolution.

According to Ch'en Tu-hsiu and Li Ta-chao, the two major Communist nationalists, capitalism accounted for the suffering of the workers, while imperialism was the cause of poverty in China. Li looked upon China as a "proletarian nation" oppressed by international capitalism. The Chinese problems were similar to those of the international proletariat, and China's fight against the western capitalist nations was a part of the international struggle of the proletariat against their oppressors. Li thus identified the national movement with class struggle and placed the nationalist interest within the framework of a worldwide proletarian revolution.[12]

On the whole, the Chinese nationalists of the 1920s agreed that China should be a unified republic, upheld by a constitution, and immune from foreign intervention. These were the essential attributes of a "nation." Nevertheless, Chinese leaders differed on which philosophy their country should follow in the process of national regeneration. The traditionalists fell back on the system of Confucian morality, and while liberal nationalists turned to the west for guidance, Communist nationalists insisted that Marxism-Leninism was the key to the salvation of China.

In the 1920s nationalism had become an explosive issue in China, setting off strikes and anti-foreign demonstrations. Yet it is the general belief that this dynamic force produced no impact whatsoever on a group of militarists commonly called "warlords." These men in uniform were supposedly selfish militarists, who lacked any lofty principle to claim the loyalty of the people. They were power-mongers, and they used their authority indiscriminately to loot and to oppress the people. Their main concern was the expansion of their power base. They mobilized violence for selfish gains, meddled in civilian affairs, and interfered with due process of law. In short, they were pedantic military men, whose mentality was so narrowly confined by their own interests that it showed a complete lack of national perspective. They were "ideological vacuums" and outcasts of nationalism. [13]

It is, however, difficult to imagine that any leader could be oblivious to the national issues during a period of feverish nationalism. The Chinese militarists were frequently confronted with national problems, and many of their debates on these questions were as passionate as those of their intellectual contemporaries. Civil wars were often fought in the name of the "nation," the "people," and the "constitution." When the development of nationalism reached a climax in the mid-1920s, all militarists portrayed themselves as nationalists and named their troops as national armies. The two examples were Feng Yü-hsiang's Nationalist Army and Chang Tso-lin's National Pacification Army.

Most "warlords" professed that they were fighting for a national cause. But, did they actually embrace any form of nationalism or were they simply paying lip service to the nationalist aspirations? Could "warlords" be at all nationalistic? Would their military thinking prevent them from accepting some kind of nationalist values? This chapter attempts to answer some of these questions through an examination of the political thought of Wu P'ei-fu, a militarist who dominated the Chinese scene during a part of the 1920s. Obviously, a thorough understanding of the reaction of the militarists to the problems of nationalism requires an investigation of the ideology of more than one military leader. In this respect, this study represents only a preliminary effort.

II

Wu P'ei-fu was one of the most powerful military-political leaders in China during the early republican period. In many ways he was the archetype of the Chinese "warlords." After the death in 1916 of his mentor, Yüan Shih-k'ai, Wu gradually became the power behind the Chihli clique of militarists. From 1922 to 1924 he controlled the Peking government and tried to unite China by both peaceful negotiation and military force. He was betrayed by his subordinate, Feng Yü-hsiang, in November 1924, and his political influence henceforth declined. Nonetheless, he was still a major object of attack by Chiang Kai-shek's National Revolutionary Army when Chiang launched his Northern Expedition in the summer of 1926. In the following year, after the destruction of his military forces, he went into retirement in Szechwan. In 1932 he returned to Peking, which had then been renamed Peiping. The Japanese endeavored to persuade him to preside over a puppet government they were seeking to create. Wu negotiated briefly with their representatives, yet he ultimately refused to collaborate with them. He died in Peiping in 1939. [14]

Wu's political belief was the product of a lengthy process of socialization. He was first indoctrinated in Confucianism and obtained a *hsiu-ts'ai* degree. This classical training provided him with a conservative outlook. It taught him a sense of moderation. It also emphasized authority and hierarchical subordination. Of all the Confucian virtues, "loyalty" (chung) probably had the greatest influence on Wu. It demanded not only personal allegiance to the ruler, as suggested in the classics, but when applied to the country, it was synonymous with patriotism. It had inspired many patriots to defend their country against barbarian invasions in pre-modern China—for instance, Kuan Yü, Yüeh Fei, and Ch'i Chi-kuang, all of whom Wu very much admired. [15]

Furthermore, Wu's training at the Paoting Military Academy reinforced many of the values that he had acquired from his traditional education. Aside from the inculcation of knowledge in the military field, the academy taught Wu the essence of Confucian morality. Yüan Shih-k'ai, the founder of the Peiyang Army, exhorted all his commanding officers to practice prudence (chih), trust (hsin), benevolence (jen), courage (yung), discipline (yen), uprightness (cheng), and endurance (kang). [16] He often evoked the Confucian familial ideals to strengthen his military establishment. According to him, the soldiers were looked after by their parents and elder brothers before they joined the army. After they had enlisted, they should be similarly taken care of by their commanding officers, who assumed the parental and elder brotherly roles in the military organization. As it was the duty of a son to be filial to his parents at home, it was his obligation to obey his commanding officers in the army. [17] In this manner, Yüan transformed the Confucian familial principles of filial piety (hsiao) and brotherly respect (ching) into the cardinal virtues of the Peiyang Army.

The Paoting military education also strengthened Wu's concept of loyalty. As the regulation of the academy stipulated, one should be filial as a son and loyal as a subject. Besides, these regulations invoked the notion of "repaying a favor" (pao-en) and demanded loyalty from all the soldiers. Unlike many foreign nations, China did not have the law of universal conscription. It spent a large sum of money to support a standing army, since the soldiers were trained and fed at the expense of the nation. In the military establishment, the virtue of "righteousness" (i) required the soldiers to repay "the great national favor" with their loyalty. [18]

China's defeat in the Sino-Japanese War in 1895 had aroused the military to a new level of national consciousness. In the Paoting regulations, Yüan described the defeat as a "national humiliation." He argued that it had resulted in further foreign encroachment on China. Consequently, he asked the soldiers to "express a righteous indignation and face their enemy with a common animosity." According to Yüan, a soldier could repay the favor of his country by cherishing this enmity, as well as by avenging this "national humiliation" in the future.[19]

National Preservation

The concept of national preservation was not alien to the military mind. After all, the maintenance of the security of the state was a primary reason for the existence of the army. Wu's training in the Peiyang Army taught him to defend his nation against foreign invasion and domestic disorder. He conceived the military as either the "heart" (*fu-hsin*) or the "essence" (*pen*) of China.[20] The nation depended on the soldiers for protection and salvation. They were its "pillars" (*chu-shih*), and they had the duty to restore order within the country and to defend it against foreign aggression. Wu saw an interdependence between the military and the nation. Without the soldiers, a nation could not be founded and upheld; without the nation, the military would lose its usefulness.[21] Indeed, Wu had no difficulty in accepting such nationalist concepts as national unification and anti-foreignism, because underlying these ideas were the basic functions performed by the military for the country.

National Unification

While most of the Chinese militarists of the 1920s believed that the existence of the nation was closely linked with the ideal of national unity, they advocated different methods to achieve political unification. There was at this time a heated debate between the federalists and the centralists. Federalism was popular in Kwangtung, Chekiang, and Hunan. It supported the theory of regional autonomy, with the semi-independent provinces under the nominal supervision of the national federal government. As the federalists contended, this type of government would solve the immediate problem of factionalism and put an end to the fragmentation in Chinese politics.[22] Among others, Ch'en Chiung-ming of Kwangtung insisted that federalism should be only a temporary arrangement, since China would ultimately be centralized.[23]

Wu P'ei-fu, however, favored centralism. He condemned provincial self-government as "an obstacle to national unification." According to him, the evolution of a "great nation" was a gradual process from tribalism to centralism, and centralism represented a higher stage of national evolution than federalism. Moreover, China had historically been a unitary state. Wu regarded federalism as a form of tribal rule, with tyrant chieftains in control of various administrative units. He compared this with the Period of the Warring States in ancient China. As he remarked to a Reuter representative, China would be divided into eighteen countries if every one of its eighteen provinces should be allowed to have its own independent government. In his opinion, local autonomy was a symbol of political disunity, and it was a stage of the historical retrogression from centralism to tribal rule.[24]

In the beginning Wu had proposed that unification should be achieved by peaceful means and in accordance with the constitution. In 1919, when the northern and southern factional leaders agreed to hold a "peace conference" in Shanghai to negotiate their differences, he supported the idea of a peaceful settlement. After his victory in the Chihli-Anfu War in 1920, he put forth his own plan for national unification. He suggested the convention of a conference of "national citizens" to discuss such questions as the constitutional differences between the north and the south, the division of civil and military administrations, and the disbandment of troops. He maintained that there was no need for internal warfare after the defeat of the pro-Japanese Anfu clique. He further stressed the importance of "the will of the people" (*min-i*) in a republic government. Hence, he asked for the participation in his proposed conference of the representatives of the provincial assemblies, as well as of the educational, commercial, literary, legal, and agricultural associations. He would not permit any interference of the militarists. [25]

Nevertheless, other military leaders objected to the proposal. As a result, Wu modified his plan to include the military. In the conference to be held at Lushan, there would be two sections: one section would include the representatives of the provincial legislatures and public bodies, and the other, the delegates of both the army and the navy. These two groups would work out the details for the formation of a united central government and for the reconstruction of the nation. Any decisions reached by the military delegates would have to be approved by the representatives of "the people." [26]

Wu's revised proposal received much support from the populace. In a joint telegram, seven civil organizations extended to him their endorsement. They described his plan as "sound and excellent," and they complimented him for his lack of any desire for self-aggrandizement. [27] In addition, preparatory meetings were held by the Society for the Advancement of the Conference of National Citizens. In Peking, representatives from fifteen provinces founded the Assembly for the Unification of China as an initial step to bring the north and the south together.

In 1922 Wu made another attempt to unite the country by peaceful means. He recalled the national assembly of 1917 and invited Li Yüan-hung to resume his presidency. This endeavor failed. Although more than 150 members of the assembly supported the plan and established a "legal constitutional body" in Tientsin, the Canton government refused to cooperate. Other military leaders adopted a similar position. They proceeded to draft their own provincial constitutions and declared themselves autonomous.

Thus discouraged, Wu turned to the alternative of military unification. In 1924 he told an ex-premier, Chang Shao-tseng, that the prevailing chaotic political situation justified the use of force. As he argued, when the peaceful methods failed, the instrument of violence became necessary. [28]

Anti-foreignism

As in the case of many other Chinese nationalists of his time, anti-foreignism dominated Wu's nationalist sentiments. He was particularly resentful of the Japanese aggression in his native province of Shantung. He had personally witnessed the shelling of his hometown, Penglai, by the Japanese navy during the Sino-Japanese War of 1894–1895. Twenty-seven years afterward, he still remembered the sight of a bomb falling on the plaque that was hanging in the Penglai Pavilion. According to his Japanese adviser, Okano Masujirō, this incident had aroused such a strong anti-foreign feeling in Wu that he decided to join the army in defense of his country.[29]

Wu often invoked the humiliation of the Sino-Japanese War in his appeal to his soldiers to resist Japanese encroachment on China.

He once wrote a song, "Ascend the Penglai Pavilion" ("Teng Peng-lai ko"), that was saturated with anti-Japanese sentiments. A free translation is rendered as follows:[30]

Turning north to Manchuria
In the Gulf of Chihli, a great storm is gathering!
Recalling a couple of years before,
In Kirin, Heilungkiang, Liaoning, Shenyang, people
        were peacefully living
Bamboo fences lined the foot of the Chang Pai Mountain,
Cities stood serenely by the Heilungkiang.
Now, Japanese pirates are roaming, and
A storm is gathering.

Ever since the Sino-Japanese War,
Our territory has shrunken.
After the Russo-Japanese War,
Our national sovereignty has fallen.
The country beautiful as ever,
Yet, barbarians, scattered all over.
When can I lead my picked trained army,
Wage a battle to recover the territory?
Then, I will return, to go up the P'eng mountain
And say my prayers to the Buddha.

In one of his poems, "A Trip to the Dragon Gate" ("Yu Lung-men"), Wu envisioned a bloody sea battle with Japan in the Yellow Sea. He was hopeful that the Chinese navy would be blessed by the ancient sages and press home their attack on the Japanese islands.[31]

At times, Wu's anti-foreignism carried an anti-western tone. In the struggle against the westerners, he viewed the Asians collectively as an ethnic group. The emphasis then was the east against the west, instead of China against Japan. If the "yellow people" would stand together, they could maintain absolute sovereignty over their land and sea and drive the "western tyrants" out of their territories.[32]

Wu frequently used the examples of the patriotic heroes of the past to inspire his soldiers to fight for their country. For instance, he cited the career of Yüeh Fei, who fought bravely against barbarian invasions in the Sung dynasty. He also extolled Lin Tse-hsü, the imperial commissioner who fought against the British over the opium trade in the late 1830s. In spite of his failure, Lin's effort to defend his country was unparalleled in Chinese history. Wu asked the young men in China to join the army in order to fulfill Lin's dream of resisting foreign invasions.[33]

As a manifestation of anti-foreignism, Wu insisted that he would not set foot on alien soil. Nor would he seek refuge in foreign concessions in China. After his defeat in the Second Chihli-Fengtien War in 1924, he refused to accept the Japanese offer of sanctuary on the ground that his stay in a foreign concession would "bring disgrace to the nation." He informed the Japanese consul-general in Tientsin that he would rather die than accept foreign protection.[34] Similarly, he rejected the suggestion that he should travel abroad to avoid being captured by his victorious rival, Chang Tso-lin.[35]

Wu blamed the weakness of China on the pro-Japanese government in Peking, which he accused of being an agent of the foreigners. As he argued, the resistance of foreign aggression should be accompanied by a political housecleaning at home.[36] Twice in his career, in 1919 and 1921, he marched his troops to Peking to topple its government. He denounced the officials and accused them of "selling the nation" (mai-kuo).

During the May Fourth Movement in 1919 the nationalists attacked the Anfu government in Peking for its compromise with Japan on the Shantung question in return for a loan agreement. Among the demonstrations, strikes, and anti-Japanese boycotts, there were outcries for "the preservation of Chinese sovereignty and the abolition of the unequal treaties." Wu joined in the movement and accused Tuan Ch'i-jui, the leader in Peking, of concluding "traitorous agreements" with Japan. He called upon all militarists in China to give up their differences and unite in the fight for the protection of Chinese territories. He asserted that this was "the will of the people," and he implored the soldiers "to repay the favor of the nation."[37]

Two years later the question of the return of the German concessions in Shantung came up again for discussion in the Washington Conference. Chang Tso-lin and Liang Shih-yi were then in control of Peking. According to a rumor, the government had telegraphed to instruct the Chinese delegates in Washington to stop their negotiation so that Liang could discuss the issue directly with Japan. This allegedly would benefit the Japanese. When Wu heard of the rumor, he attacked the government violently in a telegram. As he stated, "there is no harm greater than selling the interests of the nation, and no treachery worse than currying favor with the foreigners."[38]

During both incidents, Wu brought down the Peking government with the use of military force, and the students commended him for his action. A Chinese student organization in Japan urged him to fight for China's "national interests." It lauded him as "a loyal general" who "loved his country." It also assured him that the Chinese people had strong faith in him.[39] When Wu's train reached Wuhan, the Hankow student body presented him with flowers and called him "a revolutionary general." Moreover, two hundred students journeyed to Paoting so that they could join Wu's army to "fight for the national sovereignty."[40]

Wu's condemnation of the "traitorous" activities of Liang Shih-yi brought forth an upsurge of nationalist sentiment in China. On January 17, 1922, an association was founded for the purpose of "national salvation" and the redemption of railways in Shantung. The nationalist fervor reached a high pitch when more than forty social groups joined Wu in denouncing Liang. In a telegram to Wu, for example, the Citizens' Diplomatic Conference charged that Liang and his associates were guilty of courting "favoritism from foreigners" and selling "their country and national sovereign rights for their own benefit." This would result in "ruining the democracy of our country and bringing the people to slavery." Thus, the conference entreated the people "to unite in driving the traitors and preventing them from taking any action . . . that will make the country suffer at later date."[41]

While Wu considered Japan as an aggressor, he did not direct his anti-foreign feeling against the Japanese alone. He, too, accused the Peking government of being subservient to the foreigners. In order to stop further alien encroachment, it was necessary to have a housecleaning at home. His effort in this direction was sanctioned by the populace, especially the students who looked upon him as a national hero trying to save the country.

National Regeneration and Reconstruction

The militarists valued security, hierarchy, authority, and obedience. They also emphasized loyalty, courage, discipline, and conformity. Most of them clung to their traditional heritage and resisted changes in the political, social, and cultural order. They were dedicated to the maintenance of law and order. Many of these military values were similar to the basic ideals of Confucianism. Conceived by Confucius during the Period of the Warring States, Confucianism was adverse to political chaos. It supported a stable and harmonious society, in which every man had his own proper role and duties to perform. As did militarism, it stressed hierarchy, authority, and obedience. It, too, preached self-discipline through self-analysis and self-cultivation.

Since Wu had experienced both a Confucian education and military training, he naturally contended that Confucianism should be retained as the national foundation of China. For the same reason, he repudiated liberalism and Communism, both of which attacked the Confucian tradition. He regarded the ethics of Confucianism as "the essence of the nation" (*kuo-tsui*).[42] Obviously influenced by Chang Chih-tung, he argued that the western material civilization was useful only for "practical application" (*yung*), while Confucianism remained the "fundamental principles" (*t'i*) of the Chinese culture. Hence, as he advocated, China would be strengthened if it would combine, say, western constitutionalism with the traditional Confucian ethics. In his speeches he often asked his audience to study Confucianism. According to him, foreigners were studying it, too. If they acquired "our national spirit," their nations would be much strengthened.[43]

Wu apparently did not believe that the Confucian virtues were no longer relevant to the Chinese society of the twentieth century. In his opinion the concept of loyalty was as important in the modern era as it had been in the past. Despite the abolition of the imperial institution in 1912, the relationship between the ruler and his subjects should always remain the same. Similar to the ruler of the past, the officials of the republican government in Peking should honor "the will of the people" and work for their welfare. In return, the people had the obligation to be loyal to their officials. Furthermore, with his identification of the officials as the representatives of the nation, Wu in effect tried to transmute the Confucian ideal of ruler-subject relationship to the modern concept of loyalty owed by the people to their nation.[44]

Typical of his military mentality, Wu perceived the republic as a nation of law and order. He also insisted that *kung-ho*, the Chinese equivalent for "republicanism," suggested the importance of "harmony" in Chinese society. In order to sustain the true spirit of kung-ho, he demanded the revigoration of the Confucian virtues of loyalty, filial piety, chastity, and righteousness.[45] Indeed, the survival of the Chinese nation relied on the maintenance of internal stability, and this was, in turn, dependent upon the practice of the Confucian values. According to Wu, because of their adoption of the teachings of Confucianism, the dynasties of Han, T'ang, and Sung had lasted several hundred years. On the other hand, the governments of Ch'in, Wei, Chin, and Yüan had been short and chaotic, thanks to their failure to follow the Confucian doctrines.[46]

Wu looked upon Confucianism as an integrating force that held the nation together. According to him, a nation was composed of a multiplicity of units, the smallest of which was the family. Since national solidarity resulted from the wholesomeness of these units, he stressed the importance of the proper regulation of the family. With the vast area and population of China, the only means to bring strong cohesiveness to the nation was the propagation of the familial virtues of Confucianism.[47]

While he admitted that Sun Yat-sen's Three Principles of the People were significant in the development of the Chinese nationalist movement, Wu did not believe that they included any novel ideas. They had been taught and practiced by many ancient sages as well as emperors of the premodern period. For several thousand years they had been "the essential elements of the nation." Sun's Principle of Nationalism, for instance, was the same as "anti-barbarianism" (jang-i). As Wu explained, nationalism was the motivating force behind the construction of the Great Wall by the First Emperor of the Ch'in dynasty. It, too, prompted Emperor Wu of the Han to send an expedition against the Hsiung-nu, and Emperor T'ai Tsung of the T'ang to wage a war against Korea. As for Sun's Principle of Democracy, it had been the central theme of the political ideals of Mencius, who preached that the people were "the most important element of a government." Similarly, Wu dismissed Sun's Principle of People's Livelihood by stating that this had always been the main concern of the Chinese rulers. They had instituted social reforms to take care of the widows, widowers, orphans, as well as those who were childless and disabled. In the Han dynasty, Emperor Wen had taken such precautious measures as storing up grain to insure against unforeseeable natural calamities.[48]

According to Wu, China was unique and, therefore, required a special type of government. As he often told his visitors, China was a "big country" *(ta-kuo)*, because it had a civilization of 48,000 years, a history of 5,000 years, a territory of 5 million square miles, and a population of 400 million people. These assets should earn China a high status in international politics, in spite of its existing domestic turmoil. Wu referred to the foreign nations as the "small countries" *(hsiao-kuo)* and insisted that they should not judge a "big country" with their own yardstick.[49]

Basically, Wu held that China should be a nation governed by men of morality instead of by law. A good government was invariably the outcome of the adherence of its rulers to the moral concepts of Confucianism. While emphasizing the Confucian value of humanism, Wu yearned for the institution of a "kingly rule" *(wang-cheng)*. With a motto, "to govern the country by morality" *(tao-te chih kuo)*, the rulers should observe the established customs and work for the welfare of the people.[50]

III

As demonstrated in this chapter, Wu P'ei-fu, a powerful "warlord," was not anti-nationalist. Both his Confucian educational background and his military training might have restricted his acceptance of certain nationalist values. Nevertheless, as a militarist, he had been trained to defend his country; hence it was not difficult for him to embrace such concepts as anti-foreignism and national unification. He expressed genuine nationalist sentiments when he opposed both Japan for its aggression in his home province of Shantung and the Peking government, which was allegedly pro-Japanese. At least during the initial stage, he thought he could bring the nation together by peaceful negotiation in a national conference.

Since he remained in power for only two years before he was betrayed by Feng Yü-hsiang, Wu had neither the time nor the military strength to implement whatever plan he had for the nation. Besides, his nationalist inclination did not prevent him from exploiting the issue of nationalism for his own ends. For example, he built up his power base by denouncing his enemies as "traitors." But he never regarded his desire to increase his power to be incompatible with nationalism, because, to him, the military, of which he was a part, was the "heart" and "essence" of the nation.

Wu was a militarist who cherished conservative moralism. Through the process of Confucian and military socialization, he identified himself with such values as law and order, authority, hierarchy, obedience, conformity, discipline, and loyalty. He treasured them as "the national essence" and argued that Confucianism would live and die with the nation. He became almost a prisoner of these concepts and could not bring himself to join either the liberal nationalists or the Communist nationalists to attack the traditional heritage in order to reconstruct China along western and Communist lines.

Wu's political thinking represented a form of cultural, traditionalist nationalism. He stressed the unique character of the nation and objected to any full-fledged intercourse with other cultures. His feeling for the Chinese tradition, however, was not merely an expression of old "culturalism." He equated the heritage with the nation and, in particular, with the survival of the nation.

In the early 1920s Wu was hailed by many people as a national hero. The western presses lauded him as the "hope of China" and "the patriot of the nation." [51] Even Ts'ai Ho-sen, a Communist leader, described him as a "more enlightened warlord." [52] Yet he was recorded in history as a "warlord" among many. All of them were anti-nationalist, unprincipled, and without ideological commitment. The reasons for this unfavorable image were various. First, the image was a product of a stereotype of some party historians. The militarists were rivals of both the Kuomintang and the Chinese Communist Party and were thus painted as villains by their historians. Moreover, many "warlords" were champions of the classical tradition, which had been so much discredited by the May Fourth intellectuals. To these radicals, the sole concern of the "warlords" was to preserve the weakening values and institutions; their mentality was so limited that they were incapable of supporting the modern ideas of nationalism. Lastly, unlike Sun Yat-sen and the intellectual leaders, the militarists lacked a modern, well-formulated ideology. They were marginal men who had difficulty in understanding many western concepts. In a period of vigorous nationalism, only those who were ideologically inclined were presumably nationalistic.

As shown in this study of Wu P'ei-fu's political thinking, these assumptions are, to a certain extent, incorrect and therefore need revision. By carefully examining Wu's ideas, one can find out the special type of nationalism he embraced and understand its limitations.

7

Provincialism within the Chinese National Revolution: The Case of Chekiang, 1926–1927

Donald A. Jordan

Led by the Kuomintang, China's national revolution of 1926–1928 channeled the surge of patriotism among many youthful intellectuals. As the Northern Expedition marched from Kwangtung toward Peking, its clarion slogans and rhetoric seemingly quickened the hearts of the modern elites. But this did not fully account for the Kuomintang success. The apparent weakness of loyalty to the resulting Nanking government of the 1930s suggests that the "national" movement had been psychologically incomplete even among the leading classes of the Chinese society. In the nominal reunification of China by 1928, there had likely been other issues, less publicized than nationalism, that had assisted the Kuomintang.

Harold R. Isaacs, for example, maintains that the radical propagandists of nationalism and socialism won over many of the enemy forces, and thus contributed to the eventual success of the Northern Expedition.[1] Without question, the well-timed defections of the military commanders at strategic points helped to accelerate the movement of Chiang Kai-shek's National Revolutionary Army through southern and central China. Yet, as historical evidences demonstrate, it took more than the ideology of national and social revolutions to win over these warlord officers, whose backgrounds and interests were very different from those of the student class.

Although they were at times able to identify themselves with the ideals of anti-imperialism, the local warlords and their retainers had survived the "competitive politics" of the warlord era mainly through the use of their personal armies, connections, and the astuteness to bend before superior military power at the right time. With national politics so ethereal in the early decades of the twentieth century, many ambitious militarists turned to their home provinces and promoted provincial autonomism within a loose Chinese federation. In the southern provinces, which were badly divided by topography, even provincialism was broken into local loyalties. For these leaders, nationalism was often hardly the prime factor for their political decisions. The following story of the three Chekiang commanders who, in late 1926, deserted their northern overlord, Sun Ch'uan-fang, to bring their troops into the ranks of the National Revolutionary Army provides a microcosm of the phenomenon of warlord defection during the Northern Expedition.

Provincial loyalty had been strong among the leaders of the Chekiang gentry during the late Ch'ing dynasty, when they became notoriously resistant to the dictates of the Manchu government in Peking. After the 1911 revolution, this tendency developed further. During the warlord period, the commanders of the local military forces either ignored the external enticements to join with the warlord hegemons or played one overlord against another. They collaborated with an outsider only when he was too well-armed to bluff. As the external cliques rose and fell, there remained in Chekiang considerable local autonomy.

Although movements for provincial independence erupted sporadically in 1916, 1917, 1922, 1924, and 1925, they failed to bring about unity within the Chekiang leadership. For instance, the wealthy merchants of Ningpo had stronger kinship with the expatriate magnates of Shanghai than with the provincial rural gentry. Similarly, many commanders of the Chekiang military forces were divided according to their sympathy with various national parties. Other factions were formed among classmates of local academies and outside schools.

Hsia Ch'ao was the first Chekiang militarist to defect to the National Revolutionary Army during the Northern Expedition. A native of Ch'ingt'ien in the southeastern part of the province, he had graduated from Hangchow's Chekiang Military Academy and risen

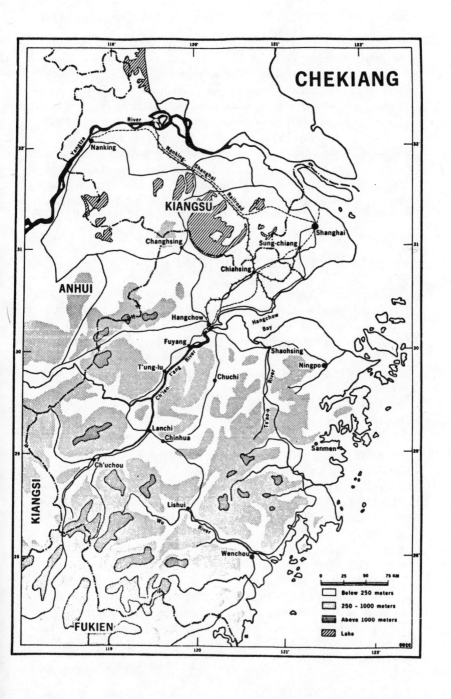

to power with the support of a clique of officers called the Kung-huo-tang. From 1916 on he held the key post of chief of the provincial police over several thousand armed policemen located throughout Chekiang. Although he often bended before outside power, he remained true to his provincial interests as he transferred his loyalty from one military governor to another with acutely pragmatic timing. In 1916 and again in 1919, instead of competing with his rivals within Chekiang, he sided with the Anfuites, a large faction with national aspirations.[2] Since the Anfu governors needed Hsia's local support as a middleman, they allowed him to retain his local power as a police chief and helped him to expand his force. By 1925 his personal army had grown to at least 5,000.[3] He was strengthened locally through his membership in the Kung-huo-tang and another provincial clique, the Shih-hsiung-ti (Ten Brothers), probably composed of classmates of the Chekiang Military Academy.[4]

Chou Feng-ch'i was another one of the Ten Brothers. From his home at Changhsing on the border with Kiangsu, he had advanced himself through his connections with the Chekiang Military Academy. In 1916 the monarchism of Yüan Shih-k'ai prompted an independence movement in Chekiang that provided both Hsia Ch'ao and Chou Feng-ch'i with new opportunities. With the aid of Hsia and the clique of the Ten Brothers, Chou continued his ascent and by 1924 commanded a brigade in one of the three provincial divisions.[5]

The last of the three leading Chekiang commanders to defect to the Kuomintang, Ch'en Yi was from the city of Shaohsing. He had also risen through his military training, which, in his case, had drawn him out of his provincial confines to Japan. A member of the fifth class of Tōkyō's Shikan Gakkō, Ch'en graduated in 1907. He thus became one of a large nationally oriented group of Chinese alumni from the Shikan Gakkō that included Sun Ch'uan-fang, many provincial warlords, and such Kuomintang officers as Chiang Kai-shek.[6]

From the time of his participation in the 1911 revolution, Ch'en joined a military unit in Chekiang and worked on the provincial military council under a succession of military governors, first Kuomintang leaders and then Anfuites. With his Japanese wife and his experience in Tōkyō, he apparently readily accepted the support the Anfu clique received from Japan. From 1919 to 1924 he served under an Anfu military governor in Chekiang, Lu Yung-hsiang.

In 1921 the Anfu overlord rewarded his collaborators in Chekiang by conceding to them a provincial constitution that provided for autonomous power in the provincial assembly.[7] Nonetheless, Hsia Ch'ao, Chou Feng-ch'i, and Ch'en Yi were dissatisfied with their medium rank in the provincial hierarchy, and they were ambitious.

In 1924 a struggle between the Anfu military governor in Chekiang and the nearby Chihli faction lord gave the aspiring provincial commanders a chance for advancement. Rather than competing with other Chekiang rivals, the three accepted offers from Sun Ch'uan-fang across the border in Fukien to oust their encircled tuchün, Lu Yung-hsiang.[8] Most likely, they saw a brighter future with a weak Chihli governor who needed them than with the status quo. With their assistance, Sun Ch'uan-fang gained access to Chekiang's western passes and emerged victorious in the Chekiang-Kiangsu War of September–October 1924. Through his connections in the Chihli-dominated government in Peking, Sun rewarded Hsia Ch'ao with the civil governorship of Chekiang, and Chou Feng-ch'i and Ch'en Yi with the command of the provincial military divisions. In light of their recent betrayal of their former superior, however, Sun retained a healthy skepticism of their loyalty to him.

Sun offered his new subordinates more than mere official titles; he helped them to consolidate a mutual hold on Chekiang. In September 1924, when a rebellion erupted in Ningpo against the new provincial leadership, Sun and his troops held Hangchow and ordered Chou Feng-ch'i to suppress his fellow provincials with his new Chekiang third division.[9] One of the leaders of this Ningpo movement was Ch'u Fu-ch'eng, vice-speaker of the national assembly and a Kuomintang partisan. He was also a nationally known promoter of provincial autonomy. His comrades in the movement included several former military governors, civil governors, Kuomintang members, and individuals linked to the Anfu clique. They formed a group of impressive diversity, but they lacked essential military support.[10] In the following year, Sun Ch'uan-fang himself was able to manipulate these strong feelings of provincial independence.

In 1925 the Anfu clique joined the forces of Manchurian Chang Tso-lin in an expedition to capture the economic center of China in the lower Yangtze Valley. Instead of facing the rapacious northern troops alone, Sun managed to gather a confederation of five southeastern provinces, including Chekiang, to block the invasion.[11] Thus, along with the other provincials, the Chekiang leaders rallied under Sun's banner and shared the fruits of his victory.

In return for their support of Sun's counterattack, which drove the northern troops out of Kiangsu, the three Chekiang commanders received new rewards. During the campaign, Sun appointed Ch'en Yi and Chou Feng-ch'i as route army commanders. He then enticed them to stay in Kiangsu (away from their home base) with a lucrative outpost for Ch'en at Hsüchow and a garrison command for Chou at the new Nanking headquarters.[12] In this way, Chou remained under Sun's close surveillance. Similarly, Sun had required Civil Governor Hsia Ch'ao to accompany him on the campaign out of Chekiang as a vice-commander. Hsia was led to believe that he would return to the province as its new military governor after Sun was entrenched in the Nanking-Shanghai area. Nevertheless, Sun intended to keep Chekiang as the keystone of his expanding empire. He left personally loyal forces in Hangchow to check Hsia and thereby guarantee his own preeminence.[13]

With the end of the threat from the north, however, a resurgence of Chekiang provincialism plagued Sun in Nanking. After pleading in vain for the return of the two Chekiang divisions stationed in Kiangsu, Hsia and the gentry declared their province autonomous from the outside regimes, and they promulgated a new constitution.[14] From Shanghai, the movement received the support of the Chekiang merchants who dominated the city's chamber of commerce.[15] Sun was not moved. On January 15, 1926, he ordered his faithful lieutenant, Lu Hsiang-t'ing, to march from Kiangsu to Hangchow. After his arrival by train, Lu accepted Sun's appointment as Chekiang's military commander-in-chief and was thus the de facto military governor of the province. Sun blocked any reinforcement from the Chekiang divisions in Kiangsu through the control of the railroad and by positioning his loyal troops across the routes to Chekiang.

With his rebellion nipped in the bud, Hsia Ch'ao readily yielded to Sun's show of force. He not only arranged a cordial welcome for Lu Hsiang-t'ing at the Hangchow railway station, but he also declared an official holiday to honor Chekiang's new chief and gave

Lu an impressive reception party, over which he himself presided. [16] Sun accepted this show of submission and graciously allowed Hsia to remain in office under Lu's supervision.

As Sun's agent in Chekiang, Lu represented the current style of political operations in China. Thanks to his origins in Shantung, he and Sun were fellow provincials. They were also "returned students" from Tōkyō's Shikan Gakkō. Lu had joined Sun in Hupeh and risen to power with him as Sun marched his forces into Fukien in 1923. He shared in Sun's victory when they later took Chekiang, and he gained promotion to the position of commander of the second division of the province in 1924. By early 1926 Lu had risen to the top military post in Chekiang mostly through his personal connection with Sun. [17]

At that time, the classmates of Shikan Gakkō held the highest government position in Chekiang, Fukien, Anhwei, and Kiangsu among Sun's five United Provinces, as well as Hunan, Yünnan, Kwangtung, and Shansi. In Chekiang, Sun seemed to be in complete control with his own man at the top of the provincial hierarchy and the backing of a submissive provincial middleman and two military commanders who owed their status and titles to him. To placate the Chekiang commanders and gentry, Sun declared in June 1926 that all his United Provinces were independent of both the Peking government and its Manchurian overlord, Chang Tso-lin. [18] In mid-1926, Ch'en Yi and Chou Feng-ch'i were thought of in Shanghai as being nearly as loyal to Sun as his longtime personal lieutenants. [19] With his frustrated ambitions, however, Hsia Ch'ao was not yet committed to Sun's confederation.

The year 1926 was not a favorable time for Sun to consolidate his hold on either Chekiang or the United Provinces. As the spirit of nationalism stirred the urban elites, he had to exert his influence through the layers of provincial vassalage that he had built upon. With their personal forces, these provincial lieutenants proved very costly to support, and Sun experienced strain in squeezing additional revenue from the provinces. In Chekiang, for example, he tried to gain crucial local support, while, at the same time, pressing the gentry and peasantry for taxes to pay his troops. Not only did he have to feed his burgeoning armed forces, but he also had to refund his debts from past wars. A poor harvest of rice in late 1925 followed shortly by grain shortage had hurt Chekiang's economy and affected the collection of taxes. The revenue of 1926 lagged behind that of the previous year. The situation worsened as the spring with its severe floods turned into an unusually dry summer. Sun's order to his tax collectors in the province to "borrow" large sums from the gentry only aggravated their alienation. By June, the hard-hit districts petitioned the provincial assembly in Hangchow to exempt them from their unpaid taxes of 1925 in order to meet the current levy. [20]

Thus, when the National Revolutionary Army launched its Northern Expedition, there existed within warlord territory divisive situations that the Kuomintang was able to exploit. Efforts to encourage defection within the ranks of militarist overlords formed an unpublicized but crucial element in the party strategy. [21] They were productive in Sun's United Provinces. The Kuomintang used members who were natives of Chekiang to negotiate with the three leading commanders in the province. Ma Hsü-lun, for example, was a provincial friend who was nationally prominent in the Ministry of Education in Peking. He and his spokesmen played on Hsia Ch'ao's dissatisfaction as a subordinate to his Shantung superiors. They also approached Hsia through their connections with the clique of the Ten Brothers. [22]

During the summer of 1926, while the Northern Expedition slogged uncertainly into Sun's eastern provinces of Kiangsi and Fukien, Hsia Ch'ao remained outwardly neutral. He claimed in an interview that he opposed any outside rule—northern or southern—over Chekiang. [23] As negotiations with Hsia continued, the Kuomintang applied pressure in Sun's provinces through the political device of organized peace movements.

Among the provincial elites, the Kuomintang promoted the formation of the All-Chekiang Society (Ch'uan-Che kung-hui). These leaders spoke out in early September 1926 against Sun's war with the revolutionaries, because the conflict threatened to ravage their province. Since Chekiang had been disrupted by several wars in the 1920s, the issue was a popular one. The society petitioned Sun at his Nanking headquarters to accept a proposed peace settlement with Chiang Kai-shek. This plea was carried to Sun by Chiang Tsung-kuei, an ex-military governor of Chekiang, and fellow classmates of both Chiang Kai-shek and Sun Ch'uan-fang at Tōkyō's Shikan Gakkō. [24] Another provincial Kuomintang member who advanced the peace movement was the ubiquitous Ch'u Fu-ch'eng, a perennial promoter of provincial autonomy and federalism and a leader of the abortive Ningpo independence movement of 1924. The All-Chekiang Society suggested that Sun and Chiang Kai-shek should combine their forces to defend southeastern China against the growing threat of a southward move by the Manchurians. [25]

Rumors abounded that Sun and Chang Tso-lin were considering an alliance against the southern revolutionaries, a possibility that both the southeastern gentry and the Kuomintang feared. Earlier in the spring of 1926 Chang had proposed the collaboration of his Manchurian army with Sun, Wu P'ei-fu, and other northern militarists, but at that time Sun had feared the Manchurians more than the unproven Kuomintang forces. In August Sun had himself favored an alliance of the classmates from Japan that could encircle Kwangtung, the base of the Kuomintang revolution. [26]

By October 1926 the spectacular progress of the National Revolutionary Army presented Hsia Ch'ao with another incentive for defection. To the winners would go the rewards. Most likely, in return for Hsia's cooperation, the Kuomintang offered him a place in the future party-appointed provincial regime. This provided Hsia with a new chance to attain the provincial status he had coveted for so long. The Kuomintang's equivalent of the military governorship was the chairmanship of the Provincial Military Committee. In October the party congress in Canton approved a division of authority between national and provincial leadership that would allow provincial leaders like Hsia Ch'ao enough autonomy to attract their support. [27] Many Kuomintang members who were natives of Chekiang relayed these enticements to Hsia. They could evoke his provincial sentiments as well as whatever budding nationalism that was present. It does not appear that Hsia was in favor of a centralized nationhood for China, unless it was necessary to hold off foreign imperialism. He could identify with Chiang Kai-shek, the commander-in-chief of the National Revolutionary Army, as a fellow provincial and as a military man who had been trained at Hsia's alma mater, the Chekiang Military Academy, before going abroad to the Shikan Gakkō. With the three Chekiang commanders, Chiang could communicate as a classmate of Hsia's and Chou Feng-ch'i's from Hangchow, and as a classmate of Ch'en Yi's from Tokyo.

The first defection of a Chekiang commander was timed to coordinate with a major offensive by the National Revolutionary Army in neighboring Kiangsi. Some of the heaviest fighting during the civil war took place in early October 1926, as the National Revolutionary Army and Sun's confederates surged back and forth across Kiangsi's fertile basin. At the Kiukiang sector of the front, the third Chekiang division under Chou Feng-ch'i had been a disappointment to Sun. Chou may have wished to disengage himself from the fighting in response to the pleas of both the All-Chekiang Society and Hsia Ch'ao, yet part of his third division was held hostage on garrison duty in Nanking. When these reserves attempted to escape on October 14, Sun's guard division surrounded and disarmed them.[28] Therefore, Chou was still in Kiangsi when Hsia rose against Sun in Chekiang. Ch'en Yi apparently refused to join the rebellion.

The National Revolutionary Army needed distractions at Sun's rear to weaken his forces at the Kiangsi front. According to his plan, Hsia's defection in Chekiang would coincide with an uprising of workers in Shanghai, an explosion of Sun's largest ammunition ship off Kiukiang, a surge in the attack of the National Revolutionary Army, and a new offer of peace from Chiang Kai-shek. With Sun's lines overextended, the Chekiang rebellion would stand a good chance of success.[29]

Although unsupported by the other provincial military forces, Hsia Ch'ao called together some Chekiang leaders on October 16. The group included a number of Kuomintang activists, and they devised plans for the expulsion of all northern officials from Chekiang and the installation of a new provincial administration.[30] Sun's northerners departed immediately for Shanghai, while Hsia formed a Committee for Political Affairs, with Ma Hsü-lun as a member. Hsia and the committee then named the provincial leaders to head eight departments, and they issued certificates of appointment for the new hsien chiefs.[31] Hsia telegraphed the Kuomintang government in Canton and accepted its designations as the provisional chairman of Chekiang and the commander of the Eighteenth Army Corps of the National Revolutionary Army.[32] In this way, the Kuomintang transformed Hsia's provincial police into an incorporated element of the National Revolutionary Army. This was an inclusive system that expanded rapidly around the inner core of the party army from the Whampoa Academy.

The purpose of the Chekiang rebels was not only to distract Sun, but also to spring a surprise attack on Shanghai. Although only a few small units from Chou Feng-ch'i's division managed to filter back into Chekiang, Hsia and the Kuomintang gambled on their ability to overcome the lightly manned defenses of Shanghai before Sun could order reinforcements from his reserve force in Nanking. With 2,500 troops under his command, Hsia might have succeeded if Sun had not been forewarned. According to one report, Hsia asked Ch'en Yi in northern Kiangsu for help and offered him the civil governorship of Chekiang in return. Ch'en did not find the proposal attractive. Besides, he lacked faith in the rebellion and its leadership. [33] A second report, however, claims that Ch'en was in communication with the Manchurian faction across the Kiangsu border in Shantung. The Manchurians knew of Hsia's plea for assistance and warned Ch'en against supporting the rebellion. [34] This latter account accords with the effort then in progress to bring Chang Tso-lin to reinforce Sun in the lower Yangtze Valley. At any rate, the defense commander of Shanghai, apparently forewarned, blocked the railway from Hangchow. This slowed Hsia's movement and required his green forces to make a long and tiring march.

Without the element of surprise on which he had counted, Hsia had to depend solely on his token force of unseasoned police. As a result, his offensive against Shanghai was doomed. After a brief skirmish on October 17 at Shanghai's western suburbs, he retreated to Chiahsing within the Chekiang border. [35] Eager to discourage defection in his provinces, Sun transferred some of his most trustworthy guard forces from his Nanking headquarters to the Shanghai area and prepared for a counterattack into Chekiang. [36]

Nonetheless, the independence movement continued with great bravado. Under Kuomintang leadership, a mass meeting at Hangchow publicized on October 18 the declaration of independence from the United Provinces and pledged its support to the southern government in Canton. [37] The situation in Hangchow further deteriorated when Chou Feng-ch'i circulated a telegram that stated his disavowal of the rebellion. [38] Faced with certain defeat, Hsia backed down. He communicated to Sun's subordinates at his border that he had acted earlier through misinformation. He also claimed to have withdrawn from Shanghai as soon as he realized his mistake. Moreover, he reported that he had dismissed his new appointees from their provincial posts. [39]

Hsia's conciliatory gesture was in vain. On October 20 Sun's troops rolled across the Chekiang border and quickly smashed the rebel defenses at the railroad town of Chiahsing. Hsia fled with his guards, while Sun's lieutenants rounded up hundreds of the poorly trained provincials and machine-gunned them in the moonlight. Hsia tried to escape to the Chekiang hills by motorcar but was overtaken, seized, and shot. His severed head was later on display at Sun's Nanking headquarters to provide a grisly example of what happened to the provincial allies who had betrayed their overlord. [40]

By late October Sun's loyal forces had suppressed the independence movement and successfully dealt with the first defection from his Chekiang ranks to the National Revolutionary Army. To serve as his new provincial middleman through which to rule the province, Sun selected his classmate from the Shikan Gakkō, Ch'en Yi, commander of the first Chekiang division. The rumor that Ch'en had betrayed Hsia Ch'ao seemed to have been borne out, when Sun transferred Ch'en back to Chekiang and by October 31 appointed him the new civil governor to replace Hsia. [41] Lu Hsiang-t'ing, Sun's personal retainer and Shikan Gakkō classmate, however, remained in the province as the all-important military governor. In the defense of neighboring Kiangsi, Chou Feng-ch'i had proved so listless that Sun, also, transferred his third division back to Chekiang.

In light of his disastrous defeat in Kiangsi, Sun hoped to bid for provincial support by conceding to the Chekiang commanders enough autonomy that they would wish to defend their home province against the National Revolutionary Army, since Chiang Kai-shek promoted a more centralized system. All else failing, Sun might still retain Chekiang as a buffer state against the Kuomintang on his southern flank. Yet his new alliance with the Anfu-Manchurian clique of North China offended the very sense of autonomy in Chekiang that he wished to stimulate.

Rumored all during the summer of 1926, the alliance was finally consummated in mid-November 1926, after Sun's ouster from Kiangsi. [42] Under the command of Chang Tso-lin, the resulting National Pacification Army included Chang's own Manchurian forces, Sun Ch'uan-fang's troops, Chang Tsung-ch'ang's Shantung units, and other northern legions. As Sun shifted Chou Feng-ch'i's Chekiang division from Kiangsu back to Chekiang, the Shantung militarist, Chang Tsung-ch'ang, moved south as the representative of the National Pacification Army. Thus reinforced from Shantung, Sun could concentrate his own forces on Chekiang.

In response to this latest show of northern military might, Chou Feng-ch'i accommodated with great flexibility. En route to Hangchow with his troops, he declared in Shanghai that the objective of his new assignment was to defend the home province against the southern offensive.[43] Then, at his reception in Hangchow on November 25, Chou countered his rumored betrayal of Sun in Kiangsi with the argument that he had never sympathized with the national revolution. Echoing Hsia Ch'ao, his executed mentor, Chou asserted that he would sacrifice anything for Chekiang. According to him, while he was friendly to neither the north nor the south, anyone who invaded the province would become his enemy.[44] Not only did this stance suit Sun, but it also allowed Chou to place himself in a favorable position to accept offers from either side.

Despite Sun's eleventh-hour scheme to retain influence in Chekiang, he failed to block the Kuomintang-promoted independence movement. In November the proponents of Chekiang autonomy negotiated with the National Revolutionary Army, while at the same time attempting to implement provincial self-rule as earlier set down in the Chekiang constitution of 1921.[45] Chiang Kai-shek agreed that his army would not enter Chekiang if its leaders would declare their independence from Sun's United Provinces.[46] In late 1926 Sun's strategy of manipulating anti-northern resentments against the Manchurians turned against him. When he vowed in November to defend his remaining territory to the last man, he weakened the credibility of the autonomy he offered the Chekiang provincials. The rumor that Chekiang would have to contribute to the maintenance of the northern reinforcements further alienated its leaders.[47] Besides, the thought of Chang Tsung-ch'ang's return appalled most of the gentry and support of the national revolution became an enticing alternative.

The Kuomintang also accelerated its peace movement, which became anti-northern in nature. It attracted many leaders in Sun's United Provinces. The Affiliated Association of Kiangsu, Chekiang, and Anhwei coordinated the protests. Its members included such Chekiang luminaries as Ts'ai Yüan-p'ei and C. T. Wang, both of whom were Kuomintang advocates of provincial autonomy. To promote a truce between the National Revolutionary Army and the northern alliance, they called for democratic self-rule in the provinces. From their sanctuary in the Shanghai settlement, they proposed the establishment of a federal government in which the provincial leaders would handle regional matters, while a national assembly in Peking would manage national and international affairs.[48]

To counter this movement, Sun made a new concession to the Chekiang provincials. He removed the pretext for a Kuomintang invasion by ordering his new civil governor, Ch'en Yi, to declare Chekiang independent.[49] The political struggle between the Kuomintang and Sun allowed the provincials to negotiate favors from both sides and play off their adversaries, although they knew that they could not ultimately stand alone against either of the two powerful regional forces.

In western Chekiang, holding a key pass into the province, Chou Feng-ch'i announced on December 11 that he and his division of troops were going over to the National Revolutionary Army. Henceforth, the provincial activists flocked to the national revolution. By early December the units of the National Revolutionary Army across the mountains in nearby Kiangsi and Fukien had consolidated a hold on the newly conquered territory and began to mobilize a vanguard for the strike into Chekiang. Astride the passes at Ch'uchou, Chou was in a position to offer the Kuomintang an uncontested entry through the mountains. To coincide with his defection was a resurgence of the Chekiang self-rule movement in Shanghai.

Claiming to represent the whole Chekiang, a group met in the international settlement on December 9–19 to elect a Provincial Government Committee. Many nominees were seasoned veterans of the self-rule movement; some had been leaders of the Ningpo movement of 1924. Highest in rank was ex-governor Chiang Tsungkuei who had led the Ningpo dissidents. For the previous several months he had been mediating between Chiang Kai-shek and Sun Ch'uan-fang as a Shikan Gakkō classmate and a Kuomintang member. Also named to the nine-man committee were the recently defected Chou Feng-ch'i, Civil Governor Ch'en Yi, and Ch'u Fuch'eng, a federalist. Meanwhile, the provincial agents of Chiang Kai-shek asked Ch'en Yi to maintain order in Chekiang until the National Revolutionary Army could advance. They also offered him the command of an army corps in the National Revolutionary Army. Chou Feng-ch'i even traveled to Hangchow on December 17 to encourage Ch'en's collaboration.[50]

With five members in a group of nine, the Kuomintang dominated the Provincial Government Committee. Yet its program was still strongly provincial. According to the six-point program, the new regime was: (1) to implement self-government through local personnel; (2) to oppose provincial militarists who might seek to carve out their own "autonomous" areas; (3) to make public Chekiang's political affairs; (4) to subordinate the Chekiang army to the provincial government; (5) to provide for freedom of assembly, press, political organization, and speech; and (6) to abolish all illegal taxes. The committee then informed both Sun Ch'uan-fang and Chiang Kai-shek of their resolutions.[51]

This latest expression of provincial autonomism lacked unity and military power. The nine members of the committee represented a loose coalition of the major political and military factions in Chekiang. All of them were natives of the province. Of the seven who had received military training, four were classmates from the Shikan Gakkō and two were graduates of the Chekiang Military Academy. Nevertheless, in the Ningpo movement of 1924, Chou Feng-ch'i had contributed to the suppression of Chiang Tsung-kuei. Chou's patron, Hsia Ch'ao, had replaced Chang Tsai-yang, and Ch'en Yi had betrayed Chou and Hsia. Now as allies, they were to work closely with each other. The two civilian leaders, Ts'ai Yüan-p'ei and Huang Fu, postponed their return to Chekiang for fear of Sun's executioners.[52]

Chou Feng-ch'i had earlier advised Ch'en Yi to join the provincial movement. But he soon returned to the mountains and left Ch'en with the only military force to defend the provincial capital. Ch'en and his agents tried in vain to negotiate with the Nanking headquarters for a political settlement that would allow Chekiang to leave Sun's United Provinces.[53] Sun believed that unless he used force, the Kuomintang would take Chekiang. On December 17 Ch'en accepted the command of the Nineteenth Army Corps offered by Chiang Kai-shek, and two days later the Provincial Government Committee declared Chekiang independent of Sun.[54]

With his usual resolution, Sun Ch'uan-fang gained the agreement of his allies to guard the western front against the National Revolutionary Army. He then staged a surprise thrust from his Shanghai arsenals. His four best divisions seized Chekiang's fertile lowlands and pushed Chou Feng-ch'i's division westward to the border passes. Sun captured Ch'en Yi and whisked him to his Nanking headquarters. With his personal retainer, Meng Chao-yüeh, as commander-in-chief of the Chekiang troops, Sun retained the offensive throughout January 1927. He seemed to have regained control of the province by the sheer use of force.

During January, however, the National Revolutionary Army had consolidated its new territory and concentrated its troops in Chekiang's western mountains for an offensive. With the defected provincial units guiding the vanguard, the Kuomintang forces began to move out of the hills later in the month. Within two weeks, they had pushed Sun's northern divisions back to Kiangsu.

Of the three Chekiang commanders who had defected to the Kuomintang, Chou Feng-ch'i was apparently the most helpful to the military progress of the Northern Expedition. With Hsia Ch'ao executed and Ch'en Yi held in Nanking, he reaped the rewards. In addition to his promotion from a Chekiang divisional chief to an army corps commander of the National Revolutionary Army, he was in charge of the provincial front when the offensive moved through.[55] Thanks to this new responsibility, he became the chairman of the Chekiang Military Committee, an equivalent to the military governorship of the past.

The compromise between the Kuomintang and the province was evident in the composition of the provisional government committee that Chiang Kai-shek appointed on March 1. All its members were Chekiang provincials. Moreover, although its chairman, Chang Jen-chieh, and its acting chairman, Ts'ai Yüan-p'ei, advocated the centralization of national political power, its other members favored provincial autonomy and federalism. Chou Feng-ch'i and Ch'u Fu-ch'eng were two obvious examples. In the summer of 1927 a multitude of Kuomintang crises kept the chairman and acting chairman in Nanking. In their absence, local decision-making power gravitated to the Chekiang autonomists. The two de facto leaders were Chou Feng-ch'i, with 12,000 soldiers stationed along the Hangchow-Shanghai railway, and Ma Hsü-lun, a civilian supported by the provincial Kuomintang organization.[56]

Chou attracted the backing of those who felt constrained by the new Kuomintang regulations in the economy, and he led them in their opposition to Ma Hsü-lun's reformist efforts. According to the

Hangchow press Ma had secreted 240,000 yüan in a bank. A rumor campaign claimed that he had, in fact, been overthrown. When Ma followed Chang Jen-chieh to Nanking, Chou's power over the province surged even higher.[57] The weakening of central authority, which had resulted from the split of the Kuomintang and Chiang Kai-shek's subsequent short-lived resignation in mid-August, also provided Chou with fresh opportunities.

On August 19, only days after Chiang's resignation, Chou was able to oust one of Chiang's associates as the defense commissioner of Shanghai and replace him with one of his own lieutenants. In collaboration with Chou was the Thirty-first Army Corps of the National Revolutionary Army, recently defected from Sun's camp. For the Kuomintang, this perilous time was the nadir of the national revolution. Rumors were rife that other former subordinates of Sun were ready to return to him should he succeed in crossing the Yangtze again.[58] In Chekiang, the bankers and Ningpo merchants with Shanghai connections were disgruntled with Kuomintang taxes and reformism, and they encouraged Chou to disregard party directions. According to allegations, Chou and this Ningpo group went so far as to conspire with outsiders to return Sun Ch'uan-fang to his recently lost United Provinces.[59] Hence, Chou's defection was not the outcome of his conversion to the cause of nationalism. Rather, he had grasped an opportunity for political advancement through his exploitation of the issue of provincialism.

By the time of Sun's amphibious crossing of the Yangtze River, the loyal Kuomintang commanders had concluded that Chou's independent stance was intransigent. On August 20, as a spokesman for Nanking's Military Council, General Pai Ch'ung-hsi ordered an end to Chou's rule in Shanghai by martial law. Ho Ying-ch'in of the First Army Corps of the National Revolutionary Army mobilized his troops to threaten Chou's communication lines between Shanghai and Hangchow.[60] Although Chou would likely have been forced to retire to Chekiang, the countermeasure halted as the National Pacification Army began its bombardment near Nanking.

When the loyal commanders of the Kuomintang forces moved their units to resist the massive counteroffensive of the northern militarists in August, Chou Feng-ch'i enjoyed practically unrivaled control in Shanghai as well as his home province. He became the de facto warlord of Shanghai, as Pai Ch'ung-hsi and Ho Ying-ch'in evacuated the city in order to concentrate their troops in the region between Nanking and Chenchiang. The previous military governors of Chekiang had yearned to dominate the nearby metropolis with its vast legal and illegal sources of revenue. In an effort to keep Chou from overtly aiding Sun Ch'uan-fang or breaking away from Nanking, the Kuomintang gave him the title of Shanghai area coastal defense commander.[61] For Chou, a victory by the National Pacification Army might have allowed him time to consolidate his hold in Chekiang, but the northerners would never have conceded Shanghai to his rule.

The Kuomintang survived its intraparty crisis with a reconciliation of the major factions, and it went on to repel the northern offensive in late August. After its forces had driven the National Pacification Army out of Kiangsu, Nanking turned to the problem of Chou Feng-ch'i's insubordination. Within Chekiang, Chou had gathered the dissidents around him by abolishing certain Kuomintang taxes and extending political freedom to particular merchants and gentry. This group opposed the outside authority of the Kuomintang, as represented by Ma Hsü-lun and his civilian officials in the provincial government and party headquarters.[62] When Nanking seemed to be secure, however, the support for Chou melted away in Chekiang.

Confident from their victories against the National Pacification Army, Ho Ying-ch'in and Pai Ch'ung-hsi moved against Chou by isolating the Thirty-first Army Corps from his influence on September 21. The disarmed troops were shipped off to Canton, and this considerably reduced Chou's military strength. He withdrew to Chekiang from the Shanghai area, thus allowing Nanking to appoint one of Chiang Kai-shek's Whampoa officers as the mayor of the city. Furthermore, the appearance of Ho's powerful forces at the Chekiang border near Hangchow compelled Chou to concede defeat in late September. The Chekiang commander quickly resigned his posts in the provincial government, boarded a train for Shanghai, and retired from politics to live in the international settlement. The troops he left behind were placed under the command of a Whampoa loyalist, Ch'en Chuo, and were led out of Chekiang to join the Northern Expedition as it moved into Shantung in the spring of 1928.[63]

Of the three Chekiang defectors, only Ch'en Yi was able to shift his attention successfully from provincial politics to national issues. Perhaps his removal from Chekiang by Sun Ch'uan-fang spared him the fate of Hsia and Chou. As a classmate of both Sun and Chiang Kai-shek from the Shikan Gakkō, Ch'en was less rigidly provincial in his outlook than Hsia, who reputedly had ventured outside of Chekiang only twice to visit Sun in Nanking.[64] Though inactive during the remainder of the Northern Expedition, Ch'en used his school ties to gain entrance into Chiang's inner circle.[65] From 1929 to 1947 he acted in the name of the National Government to administer provinces outside Chekiang. Since he had lost his personal army in late 1926, he had no alternative except to move away from the dreams of Hsia and Chou for provincial autonomy.

During the Northern Expedition, the Kuomintang military leaders saw the provincial militarists and allied autonomists as the key points in the defense of their regional overlords. Located at strategic mountain passes in their home terrain, these local commanders could have impeded the National Revolutionary Army, and the Kuomintang could not afford a long-drawn-out war. Instead of alienating these lower-level provincials, ambiguous promises of self-rule were therefore offered in place of demand for immediate political centralization. In the short run, the defection of the provincial leaders in Chekiang, as in many other provinces, speeded the forward progress of the Northern Expedition through the warlord territory. As a result, the Kuomintang was able to reunite China nominally in a military campaign that lasted only two years from mid-1926 to mid-1928.

In October 1926 Hsia's rebellion in Chekiang coordinated with other harassments in Sun Ch'uan-fang's base area. It weakened Sun's Kiangsi front. In December, the surrender by Chou Feng-ch'i of the key Chekiang passes along the Kiangsi-Fukien border doomed Sun's defense of the vulnerable lower Yangtze Valley. Finally, when Civil Governor Ch'en Yi cooperated with the invading Kuomintang to promote an independence movement against Sun, the task of ousting the overlord became simplified. As they brought nearer the hour of military victory, these negotiated defections from warlord superiors were more vital to the Northern Expedition than the nationalist propaganda.

In his study of the federalist movement in China in the 1920s, Jean Chesneaux acknowledges that federalism was a strong political force in many provinces. But, as he concludes, "by 1923 the hour of federalism had passed." [66] While nationalism and socialism may have eclipsed provincialism in the rhetoric of the modern Chinese intellectuals, there were surges of provincial autonomism in Chekiang even after 1923. Provincial merchants, gentry, and militarists participated in self-rule movements in 1924. They were followed in 1925 by Ch'u Fu-ch'eng's federalist campaign in Peking's national assembly. An autonomist movement broke out in Chekiang later in the same year and again in late 1926 prior to the incorporation of the province into the Kuomintang revolution.

Among the three commanders, both Hsia Ch'ao and Chou Feng-ch'i publicly proclaimed that their loyalty to Chekiang was more important than their fealty to either their northern overlord or the Kuomintang nationalists. After the integration of Chou's Chekiang troops into the National Revolutionary Army, the personnel of the Kuomintang Political Bureau worked to educate his soldiers toward a national orientation. [67] Nevertheless, by mid-1927, when it appeared that the party wanted to centralize political power and the northern militarists might regain the lower Yangtze Valley, Chou deserted the national revolution. Similarly, such defected warlords as T'ang Sheng-chih, Feng Yü-hsiang, and Yen Hsi-shan rose up against Nanking's central authority after 1927 and distracted the task of national reconstruction. This failure of the Kuomintang to subordinate provincial autonomists was a lesson learned by the Chinese Communist Party. Owing to their weakness of commitment to a national government, the defected militarists who had seemingly contributed to China's reunification in 1926–1927 actually kept the nation in a state of disintegration. The need remained for new ideological forces and organizational strength to pull the diverse Chinese people together.

8

Chiang Kai-shek's April 12th Coup of 1927

Tien-wei Wu

The coup of April 12, 1927, was among the most crucial events that shaped the course of modern Chinese history. It established Chiang Kai-shek's hegemony in China for the next two decades and inflicted a ten-year defeat upon the Chinese Communists, from which they did not recover until after the resumption of their relations with the Kuomintang in a united front against Japan in 1937. Yet much of the coup has remained enigmatic. There has not been adequate treatment of the subject partly because of the lack of source materials. The conflicting interpretations of both the Kuomintang and Communist historians have further clouded its development. This chapter attempts to delineate the political forces that precipitated the crisis and to examine the event and its leading participants in the context of the Chinese revolution.

Rift within the Revolution

By the fall of 1926, when the national revolution spread to the Yangtze Valley, the Kuomintang leftists and their Communist allies in Wuhan had challenged Chiang's supremacy. As a result, Chiang had to consolidate his power in Kiangsi, with Nanchang as his base. The first open contest between the two factions was over the location of the new site of the National Government. According to the resolution of the joint conference of the Central Executive Committee and the provincial party headquarters of the Kuomintang held in Canton in October 1926, the selection of the site should be guided by the necessity of work. For the time being, however, the conference decided against moving the location of the government to the battlefront. [1]

In early December 1926 the majority of the Kuomintang leaders, accompanied by Mikhail Borodin, reached Wuhan after a brief sojourn in Nanchang. A few days later they established a joint council of the members of both the National Government and the Central Executive Committee of the Kuomintang. [2] This council became the supreme authority in Wuhan in the absence of the government and the Central Executive Committee. Still in Nanchang, Chiang resented this maneuver. In late December a group of Kuomintang leaders came from Canton to join him, and they included T'an Yen-k'ai, chairman of the National Government, and Chang Jen-chieh, acting chairman of the Central Executive Committee. Chiang proposed to them that the location of the government should be in Nanchang. [3] This did not work out, although the transfer to Wuhan did not take place until early March 1927. [4]

In this struggle Chiang had initially been conciliatory, but his attitude apparently hardened after his visit to Wuhan on January 11–12, during which he was poorly received, in particular, by Borodin. [5] The relationship between the two factions further deteriorated in the following month, when 15,000 Kuomintang members from Wuhan met in Wuchang to celebrate the impending transfer of the National Government and the second uprising of the Shanghai workers. During the meeting, the participants attacked Chang Jen-chieh and "the military dictatorship." They also adopted six resolutions, one of which demanded the elimination of "all the old, rotten, unenlightened, and incompetent elements within the party." [6] The aging Chang, who had been Chiang's mentor, was the main target of this rhetoric. There were, too, in Chiang's entourage such leaders as Huang Fu and Chang Ch'ün, who indeed lacked genuine interest in the national revolution.

In early March Chiang revealed his anti-Communist sentiments by suppressing the labor unions in Kiangsi. Moreover, in a speech on March 7, he accused the Soviet representatives of employing oppressive tactics against the Kuomintang leaders, thereby impeding party activities. In his reinterpretation of Sun Yat-sen's pro-Russian policy, he insisted that the Soviet Communists had to treat China "on equal terms." [7] Nevertheless, in spite of the ill feeling, reconciliation between Nanchang and Wuhan might still have been possible, since Chiang remained seemingly reluctant to sever his relations with the leftist comrades.

The turning point came with the convocation of the third plenum of the Central Executive Committee of the Kuomintang. T'an Yen-k'ai, Li Lieh-chün, and Ch'en Kuo-fu traveled from Nanchang to Wuhan for the meeting. According to Ch'en, Chiang agreed to come to Wuhan only if the plenum would be convened on March 12 as previously scheduled. T'an's objection notwithstanding, the meeting began on March 10 without Chiang, who was officially the chairman of the Central Executive Committee. [8] Without his presence, the plenum stripped Chiang of much of his authority and increased the power of the Chinese Communists in both the Kuomintang and the Wuhan government. [9] As a result, the rift between the two groups was complete.

March to Shanghai

Chiang had started his counterattack when the plenum was still in session. He closed the Communist-dominated Kuomintang headquarters in Nanchang, and as soon as he reached Kiukiang, he shut down its municipal party organization as well. Meanwhile, he dissolved the labor unions and peasant associations in the two cities. During his campaign from Anking to Wuhu, he likewise suppressed the mass organizations that were led by the Communists. [10]

Thanks to his split with Wuhan, Chiang ran the risk of being labeled a counterrevolutionary, and he consequently alienated many of his friends and subordinates. They were, for example, Chiang Hsien-yün, Yeh Chien-ying, and Kuo Mo-jo. At the same time, he allied himself with whoever was willing to oppose his rivals. Similarly, many militarists and Kuomintang leaders supported him mainly because of his anti-Communist activities.

With the Wuhan government determined to bring about Chiang's downfall, two hostile camps developed. As each faction built up its backing, reconciliation seemed more and more unlikely. Both sides realized that their struggle would reach a climax with the capture of

Shanghai. The city was a great prize. It would give its master not only international recognition but also the lion's share of China's revenue. Thus, irrespective of the opposition from Wuhan, Chiang decided on an eastern campaign that would hopefully reward him with the control of Shanghai. [11]

In early March a series of shifts of allegiance from the warlords to the national revolution had facilitated the rapid advance of the Kuomintang forces toward the east. [12] Nanking lay open to invasion. After some hard fighting with Chang Tsung-ch'ang's northern troops, Ch'eng Ch'ien captured Nanking on the evening of March 23. The day before, the Communist-led workers in Shanghai had seized the city.

As early as mid-March, Shanghai had been surrounded by Pai Ch'ung-hsi's revolutionary army. Since he was fearful that fighting might provoke foreign intervention, he hoped to take over the city through peaceful negotiation with the northern commander, Pi Shu-ch'eng. [13] On March 21 the General Labor Union declared the third general strike, and at least 500,000 workers, including coolies and apprentices, responded to the call. In seven city zones, the strikers assaulted police stations and seized arms. They encountered little serious resistance, except at the northern train station where the fighting resulted in heavy casualties. At nightfall on March 22 they ushered in the revolutionary army. [14]

The successful seizure of Shanghai by the workers strengthened the position of the Chinese Communists, who subsequently dominated the newly organized provisional government of the city. [15] They soon proclaimed a platform for the government, which demanded the withdrawal of the military and naval forces of the powers. It, too, called for the restitution of the concessions. [16] The foreigners were in a state of hysteria, in view of the recent incidents in Hankow, Kiukiang, and Nanking. As tension mounted, the treaty powers, excluding Japan, rushed warships and troops to Shanghai, and the British Foreign Office even considered the possibility of occupying the city. [17] For some time, it appeared as if foreign intervention was imminent.

Conspiracy of Silence

In the midst of confusion, Chiang Kai-shek arrived in Shanghai from Wuhu on March 26. In an interview with foreign reporters the following day, he categorically dismissed the account of a split in the Kuomintang. According to him, the prevailing "panic" among the aliens was unwarranted. He denied that the Chinese mobs would overrun the concessions and maintained that the measures taken by the foreign authorities to defend themselves were unnecessary. [18]

Chiang was startled by the strength of the Communists, who virtually controlled both the provisional government and the Kuomintang headquarters in Shanghai. They had built an army of 2,700 workers under the command of Ku Shun-chang and Chou En-lai. [19] Chiang was reportedly discouraged by this almost hopeless situation and thought of retiring to Fenghwa, his native district. [20] Yet, before long, he received strong support from the veteran leaders of the Kuomintang, the compradors and underground societies of Shanghai, the militarists of Kwangsi, the turncoat warlords, and even the imperialists. Though of varying social origins, all of them were determined to check the spread of Communism in China.

To strengthen his political position, Chiang allied with Ts'ai Yüan-p'ei, Li Shih-tseng, Wu Chih-hui, Chang Jen-chieh, and Ku Ying-fen. As members of the Central Supervisory Committee of the Kuomintang, these five respected leaders firmly believed that the survival of their party, let alone their own power and prestige, was at stake in this struggle with the Communists. In fact, only two days after Chiang's arrival in Shanghai, Wu Chih-hui had submitted a petition to his colleagues in the Central Supervisory Committee in which he proposed to abrogate the Kuomintang alliance with the Communists. On April 2 the committee formally endorsed his proposal. It requested the Central Executive Committee to take the "dangerous Communist leaders" into the custody of the police and the army. It also insisted on the rescission of the resolutions previously passed by the joint council of December 1926 and the March plenum of 1927. [21] With the Nanchang faction thus committed, the break with Wuhan was inevitable.

For military support, Chiang relied heavily on the Kwangsi generals, particularly Pai Ch'ung-hsi. Furthermore, he commanded the loyalty of Chou Feng-ch'i, an erstwhile warlord of Chekiang. His plans for the purge of the Shanghai Communists and workers grew in scale as he met secretly in Lunghua with Li Chi-shen of Kwangtung, Huang Shao-hsiung of Kwangsi, and Ch'eng Ch'ien of Nan-

king.[22] Their decision to take action received enthusiastic backing
from the bankers in Shanghai, who advanced 3 million yüan to
cover Chiang's military expenses. On April 13, the day after the
coup, T. V. Soong likewise arranged a loan of the same amount.[23]

In his struggle with the Communists Chiang enlisted the valuable
assistance of the Green Gang, the most powerful underworld group
in Shanghai. His trusted general, Wang Po-ling, was among the honored guests of Tu Yüeh-sheng, Huang Chin-yung, and Chang Hsiao-
lin, the three prominent leaders of the gang. With the backing of his
China Mutual Advancement Society (Chung-kuo kung-chin hui), Tu
was an extremely helpful ally.[24] Partly because of his influence in
Shanghai, he won the aid of Stirling Fessenden, the American
chairman of the international settlement, and the authorities of the
French concession.[25] Indeed, with the exception of the United
States, the major powers were prepared to favor Chiang in his rivalries with Wuhan.[26] Their goodwill was desirous, since their
forces controlled the waterways and guarded the strategic localities
of the foreign concessions.

When Chiang was consolidating his position in Shanghai, Wang
Ching-wei returned from Europe on April 1. He had stopped in Moscow to consult with the Russian leaders, including, probably, Stalin.
According to some sources, the Kremlin had promised him full support.[27] After reaching Shanghai, he held several private meetings
with Chiang and Wu Chih-hui, in addition to two conferences with
other Kuomintang comrades. Many of these leaders believed that
Wang was the only man capable of reunifying the shattered party.

As an expression of conciliation and harmony, Chiang accepted
Wu Chih-hui's advice and dispatched a circular telegram on April 3
to welcome Wang's return to China. He signified his willingness to
support Wang's leadership in the political affairs of the party, while
he would concentrate on the military.[28] In exchange for Chiang's
concessions, Wang responded favorably to Wu's mediation. He
agreed to back Chiang if Wuhan should demand his dismissal as
commander-in-chief of the Kuomintang forces. In the event of an
outbreak of hostilities between the two factions, Wang would remain strictly neutral. He further promised to try to prevent a Communist uprising in Shanghai.[29]

On April 5 Wang issued a joint manifesto with Ch'en Tu-hsiu to
dispel the rumor that the workers would overrun the international

settlement in an uprising. They emphasized the importance of unity at this stage of the national revolution. In his pledge to support Sun Yat-sen's Three Principles of the People, Ch'en conceded that the dictatorship of the proletariat might never be instituted in China. [30]

On the same day Chiang met with a group of Kuomintang leaders to discuss the Wang-Ch'en manifesto. Although the majority of the gathering still advocated a separation with the Communists, they consented to solve the intraparty controversies in the fourth plenum of the Central Executive Committee, to be held in Nanking on April 15. Nonetheless, they insisted that Wang should instruct Ch'en to halt all Communist activities prior to the convocation of the plenum. In addition, the army of workers had to obey Chiang's order as commander-in-chief of the National Revolutionary Army. [31]

Frustrated by the results of the meeting, Wang was likely convinced that he would have a bright political future with the Communists. Hence, he left for Wuhan on April 6 in spite of Chiang's suggestion that he should go to Nanking instead. In a letter to Chiang, he reminded the general that Sun Yat-sen had initiated the policy of Kuomintang-Communist collaboration after much painful soul-searching. He urged Chiang to defer any action against Wuhan until after the Nanking plenum. [32] Chiang obviously did not intend to change his plans. In fact, he had already deployed his troops to gain control of Nanking from the neutral and Communist-influenced military forces. In consequence, Wang's endeavor to maintain unity within the revolutionary camp did not truly stand a chance of success.

Chinese Communist Strategy

Wang's return from Europe and his joint manifesto with Ch'en Tu-hsiu had furnished the Chinese Communists with false confidence in the goodwill of the Kuomintang leaders. Few of them apparently expected Chiang to take drastic action against them. [33] Without much success, they had earlier tried to wrestle with him for the domination of Kiangsi and Anhwei and hoped to deny him control of Nanking and Shanghai.

To win their support, the Wuhan regime had offered the governorship of Anhwei and Kiangsi to Li Tsung-jen and Chu P'ei-te respectively toward the end of March. Yet the telegraphic dispatch to Li was intercepted by Chiang's men. [34] Thus, while Chu had accepted his new appointment, Li wavered between Wuhan and Chiang for some time and eventually joined Chiang and Pai Ch'ung-hsi in Shanghai to make plans for the purge of the Communists.

Wuhan had relied principally on Ch'eng Ch'ien for its offensive against Nanking. After his departure from Hankow for the battle-front, the general allegedly received instructions, probably given at Borodin's direction, to take Chiang Kai-shek into custody.[35] Although Ch'eng captured Nanking on March 23, he hurried back to Wuhan shortly afterward when he learned of Chiang's decision to move against the Communists.[36] The effort in Shanghai ended similarly in failure. Wuhan had sent T. V. Soong and Kan Nai-kuang to the city to establish control over its revenue. After a brief period of indecision, however, they sided with Chiang instead.

As early as April 2 the Wuhan leaders had ordered Chiang, in the name of the Kuomintang, to leave Shanghai for Nanking. Henceforth, he should only take charge of the military operations. Moreover, to forestall his drive to Nanking, Wuhan declared five days later that the National Government would be transferred to the city.[37] But Ch'eng Ch'ien had already departed for Wuhan, and these measures, taken too late, proved inadequate to prevent Nanking from falling into Chiang's hands.

Under Ch'en Tu-hsiu, the central organ of the Chinese Communist Party in Shanghai lacked coordination with its comrades in Wuhan. This was partly because the rapidly changing political and military situation had rendered communication very difficult along the Yangtze Valley. Besides, most of the Communist leaders in Wuhan were too preoccupied with their own work to appreciate the critical condition of Shanghai.

At a time when strong leadership was imperative to save the party, Ch'en and his associates appeared impotent and were utterly unprepared to meet the challenges that were confronting them. After the sudden growth of mass following, they were unable either to consolidate their gains or to engage their supporters in further struggle with the enemy. Their anti-Chiang campaign depended excessively on the revolutionary potential of the workers. According to the strategy outlined by the regional committee in Shanghai, the Communists called for a military offensive by the people's forces. To emphasize the importance of mass psychology, they insisted on proclaiming Chiang's guilt.[38] Nevertheless, obsessed by its policy of a united front, Moscow ordered the Shanghai workers to avoid any confrontation with the military and the foreigners in the concessions.[39]

On April 9 Chiang made a triumphant entry into Nanking, and he immediately suppressed its mass organizations.[40] Prior to this, his backers had begun to arrest the Communists in the major cities under his control. The purges occurred in Hangchow and Ningpo on April 2 and in Foochow two days afterward.[41] The coup in Shanghai on April 12 marked the climax of the movement.

An Eventful Day

To coordinate with Chiang's anti-Communist activities in Nanking, Pai Ch'ung-hsi intensified his preparations for similar purges in Shanghai. One of the steps taken in this direction was the replacement of the army of Hsüeh Yüeh, who was friendly to the Communists and had only been stationed in Shanghai since the previous month, with the troops of Liu Ch'ih and Chou Feng-ch'i.[42] On April 6 Pai closed the pro-Wuhan political organizations in the city and imposed censorship on all telegrams and letters from Hankow.[43]

Two days later Wu Chih-hui became the chief of the newly established Provisional Political Committee of Shanghai, which was a substitute for the Communist-dominated provisional government. To influence the opinion of the Kuomintang members, the Central Supervisory Committee dispatched a circular telegram on April 9 that accused the party leftists and their Communist allies of misconduct and conspiracy.[44] Since the Communists had scheduled a mass meeting on April 12 to welcome Wang Ching-wei's return to China, Pai decided to strike without delay.

On the evening of April 11 Chou Feng-ch'i's troops began to patrol and post sentries in the Chinese sectors of Shanghai, particularly Chapei. When night fell, Wang Shou-hua, chairman of the General Labor Union, was invited to Tu Yüeh-sheng's house, where he was seized and subsequently killed.[45] The leaders of the China Mutual Advancement Society commanded more than a thousand men, who were divided into three groups under the overall charge of Chang Po-ch'i. They wore blue denim uniforms with white armbands and were sufficiently supplied with ammunitions.[46] Some of them traveled in trucks furnished by the French authorities, while others went on foot. Their main function was to precipitate clashes with the pickets of the workers, thereby providing the troops with a pretext to intervene.

Heavy fighting began at dawn in Nantao and Chapei, two important sections of Shanghai, with the attacks centering on the quarters of the worker pickets. Together with some regular soldiers in plain dress, the members of the China Mutual Advancement Society raided the Chinese Tramcar Company and the Shanghai General Labor Union. Around 5:20 A.M. they attacked the headquarters of the pickets of the workers, which was located inside the club of the Commercial Press. The fighting continued until 10:00 A.M., when the pickets, numbering 350, were finally disarmed.[47] In other areas, especially the suburb, the raids were carried out by the regular army. The pickets offered strong resistance at the third police station of Putung, with several workers killed and many wounded.[48]

On the same day, Pai Ch'ung-hsi and Chou Feng-ch'i dispatched circular telegrams in which they justified the suppression of the workers in terms of "martial laws."[49] In his later reminiscences, however, Pai admitted that he had requested the foreign representatives to permit the soldiers in plain dress to pass through the concessions. According to him, the pro-Chiang forces arrested 300 Communists, destroyed more than 70 of their organizations, and seized more than two thousand rifles.[50]

A Reign of Terror

On the afternoon of April 12 the mass meeting originally scheduled to honor Wang Ching-wei was held in the Municipal Athletic Field. It turned out to be a protest against the raids on the workers. Afterward, the participants marched to Lunghua to present a petition to Pai Ch'ung-hsi.[51] Similar meetings took place in Putung, Chapei, and other sectors of Shanghai. The Seamen's Labor Union declared a strike, which affected about forty ships then anchored in the Whampoa River.[52]

The Communist protests against Chiang Kai-shek and Pai Ch'ung-hsi were relatively mild in tone. In contrast, sixty-three commercial organizations sent a telegram to congratulate the two leaders on their success in the purges. They, too, hailed Tu Yüeh-sheng, Huang Chin-yung, and Chang Hsiao-lin as "the saviors of the country," who "led the dare-to-die comrades to destroy the General Labor Union and the worker pickets." They expressed their hope that "the whole country would imitate the example of Shanghai and slaughter all the Communists." [53]

On April 13 the Shanghai General Labor Union organized a strike that was only partially effective. It also called a mass gathering in Chapei. After the meeting the mob marched toward the headquarters of the pro-Chiang troops. In the conflict that followed, 66 of the demonstrators were killed and 316 were wounded. [54] Seven distinguished inhabitants of Chapei wrote to Ts'ai Yüan-p'ei, Wu Chih-hui, and Li Shih-tseng of the Provisional Political Committee of Shanghai to condemn this massacre of innocent, unarmed people. [55] Yet their appeal for justice and humanity failed to change Pai Ch'ung-hsi's heart, and further violence ensued. The Communist leaders in the city realized that it was futile to fight a well-equipped army. The General Labor Union called off the strike on April 15. On the same day it submitted an account of Chiang's "counterrevolutionary activities" to the Central Executive Committee of the Kuomintang and the National Government in Wuhan. [56]

In a reign of terror the pro-Chiang forces virtually rooted out all the Communist organs and cells in Shanghai during the next two months. The Communists had to conduct their activities underground in the sanctuary of the foreign concessions. The terror was not "a symbolic act," for it clearly aimed at the total elimination of Communism in China, instead of the murder of a few leaders. Edgar Snow, then on the staff of the *China Weekly Review*, estimated that more than 5,000 leftists were killed. [57]

The purge of Communism soon spread to Kiangsu, Chekiang, Anhwei, Fukien, Szechwan, Kwangsi, and Kwangtung. Governor Li Chi-shen of Kwangtung surpassed Pai Ch'ung-hsi in his violent persecution of the Communists. Two thousand suspects were arrested and many were shot. [58] The trend of reaction set in throughout China, except in Hupeh, Hunan, and Kiangsu. Under the Wuhan regime, these three provinces became, for the time being, the only havens for the Chinese Communists.

Dilemma of Revolution

The denouement of the April coup was marked not only by the defeat of the Communists in Shanghai and other areas, but also by Chiang's hegemony in the National Government, inaugurated in Nanking on April 18. More significantly, the coup disrupted the revolution at the most crucial moment and shifted it to a new direction unknown at that time even to the Kuomintang and the Chinese Communist Party. It was shortly followed by similar anti-Communist purges in Wuhan. Within half a year, the entire Communist movement in China was shattered.

In his struggle with the Communists, Chiang had compromised himself with the comprador bourgeoisie, the militarists, and the foreign imperialists in Shanghai. In the opinion of some leftist scholars, this was an anti-revolutionary triad of reactionaries, conservatives, and counterrevolutionaries.[59] Nevertheless, Chiang and his collaborators insisted that they were, in fact, the defenders of the Three Principles of the People as well as the advocates of the national revolution as bequeathed by Sun Yat-sen. They were probably right.

As Sun had done prior to his death in March 1925, Chiang contended that the "united front" between the Kuomintang and the Chinese Communist Party was never intended to be a two-party alliance. It was rather a policy by which the Communists could be admitted to the Kuomintang as individuals in order to participate in the national revolution. According to this arrangement, the anti-warlord, anti-imperialist movement was to be led by the Kuomintang and guided by the Three Principles of the People. At no time during the period of the alliance did Stalin and the Chinese Communists renounce either the Kuomintang leadership in the revolution or its ideology.

In April 1927 Stalin accused Chiang of joining with the imperialists and the national bourgeoisie against both the workers and the peasants.[60] As Mao Tse-tung likewise claimed in December 1936, the revolutionary war of 1924–1927 had failed because "the big bourgeoisie" turned traitors.[61] But in 1927 Chiang did not surrender to the imperialists and the bourgeoisie; he engineered the April coup for the purpose of suppressing the Communists, not the workers and the peasants. In general, he and his opponents had mostly come from the same social background, and they fought against each other primarily for their own interests. To the public and, more so, to the warlords, they were all dangerous revolutionaries to be ferreted out and executed.

Besides, Chiang did not befriend the bourgeoisie as Stalin alleged. In his later career, he tried to dissociate himself from Tu Yüeh-sheng, who had been indispensable to his ascendancy.[62] Although the bourgeoisie in Shanghai had rallied to Chiang's banner of anti-Communism, they suffered under his iron rule. On May 19, 1927, a senior British naval officer reported that many merchants in Shanghai were "in danger of arrest" for their refusal to pay Chiang large contributions, which, in some cases, amounted to "half a million dollars." Consequently, "feeling is said to be strongly against him." [63]

Unlike Stalin, Wang Ching-wei denounced Chiang for his alliance with the Kuomintang rightists, the Western Hills group. [64] Yet, in the April 18 manifesto, which proclaimed the establishment of the National Government in Nanking, Chiang actually condemned the Western Hills faction as counterrevolutionary, while expressing goodwill toward Soviet Russia. He further named Wang as one of the five standing members of the government council. This would leave the door open for future compromise between Nanking and Wuhan. [65]

With his authority threatened by the Communists, Chiang was convinced that his personal defeat would result in the erosion of the Kuomintang leadership in the national revolution. The purge of the Communists was thus necessary. To accomplish this, he did not believe that this modus vivendi with the bourgeoisie and the imperialists was too dear a price to pay. He had been conscious of the distinction between revolution and counterrevolution since his Whampoa days. The Chinese revolution of the 1920s was, in the main, a nationalist movement. It transcended class differences, and the Kuomintang and Communist leaders were equally dedicated to the cause of national salvation. His anti-Communist commitment notwithstanding, Chiang remained a nationalist throughout his life. At least in 1927, when the outcome of the Northern Expedition was by no means certain, he was evidently a revolutionary.

Although the coup of April 12 was not a betrayal of the Chinese revolution, it turned the "united front" into a civil war that was only suspended in 1937 in face of Japanese aggression. Chiang continued the Northern Expedition and brought about the nominal reunification of China. But he lost both the zeal for revolution and the trust of the masses that characterized his early success in Canton. In retrospect, despite the effectiveness of his coup against the Communists, it may have doomed his career as a great national leader of modern China.

9

Japanese Response to Chinese Nationalism: Naitō (Ko'nan) Torajirō's Image of China in the 1920s

Shumpei Okamoto

The history of Sino-Japanese relations from the end of the nine-teenth century to the first half of the twentieth was one of Japan's invasion of the Chinese mainland and China's resistance to Japa-nese aggression. To find out why Japan persisted for so long in an aggressive policy that resulted in its own national disaster, histo-rians must explore in various directions. One direction is to record, and examine the reasons for, the Japanese failure to grasp the changing realities of an emerging China—the basic failure to which Japan's mistaken policy can ultimately be ascribed. The principal task is to reconstruct different Japanese images of China, analyze their limitations and distortions, and discover why they so devel-oped.

As a small step in this direction, this chapter looks into the image of China held by a prominent individual when Japan was respond-ing to the rising tide of nationalism in China. Studies of Sino-Japa-nese relations in the 1920s from the Japanese viewpoint have tended to focus overwhelmingly on the so-called Tanaka and Shide-hara diplomacies.[1] Without retracing Japan's diplomatic negotia-tions with, and military interventions in, China, which have been described in detail elsewhere, this chapter concentrates on the question of Japanese perceptions of China in an effort to offer a different approach to the study of the Japanese response to Chinese nationalism.

Naitō Torajirō (1866–1934) was an eminent Sinologist. From 1907 to 1927, he held the first chair of Chinese history at Kyōtō Imperial University. Through his lectures and innumerable scholarly and journalistic writings, he greatly influenced Chinese studies in Japan. [2]

Naitō was, however, no mere dweller in an ivory tower. Prior to his appointment at the university, he had been intensely engaged in Chinese affairs for almost twenty years. In editorials, he wrote on China for such important journals as the *Nihonjin*, the *Yorozu chōhō*, and the *Ōsaka asahi shimbun*. From April 1897, he worked in Taiwan for a year as the editor of a local newspaper and commented repeatedly on Japan's colonial policy. Between 1899 and 1906 he made four extensive trips to China and interviewed such famous people as Yen Fu, Wen T'ing-shih, and Chang Yüan-chi. When the Russo-Japanese conflict over Manchuria intensified, Naitō wrote numerous editorials for the *Ōsaka asahi shimbun* strongly advocating war. In the summer of 1905 the Foreign Ministry sent him on an inspection tour to the Japanese-occupied areas in Manchuria. When he was still there, Foreign Minister Komura Jutarō summoned him to Peking to serve as his adviser in the Sino-Japanese treaty negotiations on Manchuria. In 1906 the Foreign Ministry dispatched Naitō to both Korea and Manchuria to conduct classified research on the Chientao question.

During his tenure at Kyōtō Imperial University, Naitō made as many as five trips to China, the last one in 1918. He also played an active part in the Advisory Council on Foreign Relations under the Terauchi cabinet (1916–1918). In 1933, after his retirement from the university, he made another trip to Manchuria as a member of the Japan-Manchukuo Culture Association.

In summary, Japan of his time found in Naitō Torajirō a distinguished professor, a public-opinion leader, a government adviser, and an influential and vastly learned—to borrow a current parlance—"China-watcher." It is for this reason that his image of China merits special attention.

In 1924 historian Naitō found contemporary research on China seriously deficient. He quoted three reasons for his belief that schol-

arship was retrogressing. First, on the world scene, the writings of
the British scholars were being slighted, although they had contributed much to the study of China. Yet, on the other hand, the views
of Americans, who were "most uninitiated" in Chinese affairs,
were enjoying increasing respect. Second, Chinese students who
had returned from the United States and other western countries
knew little about their own history. Nevertheless, they occupied important teaching positions at such places as the National University of Peking, from which all the "traditional profound scholars"
were excluded. The young Chinese seemed to have already forgot-
ten that their country had barely managed to "wake up," thanks to
several decades of continuous pressure from foreign powers. Indeed, they took pride in their "untested, empty" doctrines and insisted that they could make China a great nation if only they could
get rid of alien pressures. Third, the Japanese people were paying
more and more attention to the opinions of "ignorant" Americans
and to the utterances of young Chinese, who were unaware of the
actual state of affairs in their own country. Worst of all, the Japanese did not pay sufficient heed to those among them who had devoted themselves to the serious study of China. [3]

Unhappy with these developments and prompted by recent anti-
Japanese movements in China, Naitō published *Shin Shina ron* in
1924, expounding his "overall view into the distant future" of
China. [4] As he maintained in the preface, the book was to contain
only an outline of his ideas, which he would amplify in a later work.
At times, the discourse is ambiguous and even contradictory. Nonetheless, he depicted most boldly in this book his image of China of
the 1920s. This chapter examines certain basic features of Naitō's
image of China, as expressed in *Shin Shina ron* and some of his
other writings.

The "Peculiarity" of Chinese Society

At the base of Naitō's perception of China lay a persistent emphasis
on the peculiarity of Chinese society. According to him, Chinese
government after the Han dynasty ceased to have any bearing upon
the daily lives of the people. [5] Villages and clans—the "only active
and organized institutions"—filled the long-existing gap between
government and society in China and were vitally related to the interests of the people. Hence, it would be a mistake to judge China

by standards applicable to a country in which the government had more direct import upon its people.

As Naitō claimed, the Chinese were determined to seek "peace at any cost," but the maintenance of a lasting, peace-providing government depended totally upon its success in winning the allegiance of the village and clan elders (fu-lao). This was the secret of successful government in China. Revolutionaries who did not grasp this secret failed. On the other hand, Yüan Shih-k'ai prevailed largely because he understood this principle. Yet, a government based on this understanding alone could not save the nation as a whole from sinking into oblivion, for the elders were only concerned with keeping peace and security in their own village and clan. They cared little about such larger matters as patriotism and the spirit of independence from foreign powers. As long as they were guaranteed a peaceful daily life, they would willingly live under the rule of alien conquerors. [6]

Firm in his conviction that village and clan autonomy constituted the foundation of Chinese society, Naitō contrasted the Chinese national character with that of Japan, which he believed would respond as one united nation to even the most trifling challenge from abroad. China was, he asserted, like "a primitive creature such as an earthworm. If a part of it is cut off, the rest will still live with no sense of loss." [7] This lack of national consciousness affected adversely China's capacity for independence and self-government.

China's Political Capabilities

In Naitō's opinion, China's political capabilities were irreversibly declining. As a young editorial writer, he castigated his government for crediting Li Hung-chang with the ability to stabilize China during the 1898 reform, without realizing that Li had mostly been responsible for the military defeat of 1895. To Naitō, the official Japanese attitude of indifference to the people's sympathy for K'ang Yu-wei and Liang Ch'i-ch'ao was a crime against humanity, since it prolonged the struggle of Japan's 400 million neighbors to achieve the realms of civilization.[8] In 1911, as revolutionary turmoil spread in China, historian Naitō insisted that the emergence of a republican China was the inevitable result of the development of "historical trends of the last several hundred years," which could not be altered by Japan's interventionary effort. [9]

By the beginning of 1914, however, Naitō had become exceedingly pessimistic about China. To outline his views, he wrote *Shin Shina ron*, in which he claimed to "play the role of a Chinese totally for the sake of the Chinese." [10] He predicted that China would soon be subjected to military rule by foreign powers. If its people would not concern themselves with such matters as "honor" and national independence, foreign domination could lead them to a happier life. [11] Naitō's lack of confidence in China's political capabilities increased when Yüan Shih-k'ai's monarchical dream threw the nation into chaos. To Naitō, the Chinese aspiration to build a powerful, centralized government was the cause of both internal troubles and external dangers. A nominally united China might react chauvinistically to foreign aggression and thus invite overwhelming retaliation. [12]

From 1916 to early 1919, Naitō repeatedly suggested that a politically impotent China should entrust to foreigners its entire government functions—not only the maritime customs, but also the courts, police, and other activities—for "ten to fifteen years to come." [13] For instance, he argued in March 1919 that as the Chinese society was so senile, it "would be wise to invite foreigners to participate in the government." With the benefit of the alien example of public morality, the Chinese people could hopefully reform their corrupt tradition. [14]

Naitō's opinion met with criticisms in both China and Japan. But he dismissed his critics and was certain that his belief "will remain correct for the next thirty, fifty, or even one hundred years." [15] As a historian, he was inclined to present his thought in long-term perspective. In July 1918, when he was discussing the need to instill national consciousness in the mind of the entire Chinese population, he admitted that this would take at least "several decades, one hundred years, or even one hundred and fifty years" to accomplish. [16]

The May Fourth Movement brought Naitō to the nadir of his despair. He declared in July 1919:

> In a word, we no longer need to ask when China will collapse. It is already dead, only its corpse is wriggling. [17]

In 1921 he proclaimed that to carry out true reform, international control of China would be unavoidable. This represented "the natural course of events," whether the Chinese and foreigners liked it or not. [18] He further concluded in his *Shin Shina ron* that the Chinese effort to transform their society into "a normal nation" during the last days of the Ch'ing dynasty had been completely nullified by the revolution. [19]

In the course of his increasingly gloomy assessments of China's political capabilities, Naitō, too, gradually changed his views on the contemporary Chinese political leaders. The particular targets of his continuing barrage were the so-called "new people." In his eyes, these foreign-educated students who had become professional politicians were utterly ignorant of their own country's history and national character. They were lost in wild fancies when they claimed that national independence could be achieved simply by expelling foreigners from China and that success in diplomacy could be accomplished through trickery. In contrast, as far as Naitō's evaluation was concerned, the "old people"—Li Hung-chang, Tseng Kuo-fan, and Yüan Shih-k'ai—grew in stature. They had at least been serious about political reforms, however short-sighted they may have been. They had succeeded precisely because they knew their nation's history and therefore could properly appreciate the strengths of the foreigners. [20] By a knowledge of history, Naitō seemingly meant an awareness of China's inherent weaknesses and defects.

Hence, Naitō concluded that China had no indigenous political capability. This fact alone, however, did not signify a tragedy for the Chinese people. He firmly believed that international control—or whatever other means was adopted to govern the country—would not affect the life of the masses so long as it did not disrupt local village autonomy. As he insisted, the political survival of China had "no relation to the welfare of the people." [21] Once he had reached this harsh conclusion, his image of China became diffracted in two directions.

First, Naitō declared that China should free itself from the "delusion" of national defense requirements. "For the next thirty to fifty years" China would not need to defend itself. [22] National defense would merely create financial difficulties and invite troubles with the aggressive powers. The prestige and honor of the country had, in the past, been maintained not by its own military strength, but by the "interest and goodwill" of the foreign nations. According to Naitō, when China had a superior naval strength, it fought with Japan and lost both its navy and territory. Since then, although China had neither a strong army nor navy, it had lost no territory, except being forced to lease land "as tiny as a cat's forehead" to foreign powers.[23]

Second, Naitō advocated that China, with insignificant political capability and military strength, should devote itself to the life of culture, eschewing "those mundane elements among human undertakings such as politics and military affairs." [24] He urged in July 1919 that one should not be overcome with sorrow by the political demise of China. He argued:

> When a nation is endowed with such splendid cultural achievements that enjoy the respect of the entire mankind, its death in the political and economic spheres is inconsequential. Its culture will shine to the corners of the world, and the race of culture will be honored as long as heaven and earth exist. [25]

From Naitō's culturalist point of view, Japan's current prosperity in the political and military spheres was an indication that the nation was still in its infancy. He expected that a country like China, which had had a long and glorious cultural life, would simply lose interest in military and political affairs and lean more and more to the development of its culture. Japan and the western powers would be gravely mistaken, should they, as a result, consider their national character more advanced than that of the Chinese. [26]

Thus, as Naitō proclaimed, China—a culturally advanced nation—should not demean itself by competing with the backward countries in the political arena. What had drawn China into foreign entanglements was the aspiration to recover its national sovereignty and rights. Instead of struggling with the alien powers over matters of national "honor," China should adopt a policy of "moderation and patience." In this way, the nation could pursue its cultural life in peace.[27]

"What Is China?"

Naitō's perception of the relationship between China and Japan was based on his dismissal of the former's political capabilities as well as its need for national defense. It, too, was grounded on his recommendation of a policy of national devotion to culturalism. At the heart of his attitude toward Sino-Japanese relations of past and present was the conviction that Japan had only been good to China. On the day the war with China broke out in 1894, when he was twenty-nine years old, Naitō wrote an essay entitled "Japan's Mission." He justified his government's policy of continental expansion in the following terms:

> *Japan's mission is . . . to spread Japanese civilization and ways to every corner of the world. Japan is located in the Orient. Of the nations in this region, the largest is China, which therefore should become the primary target of Japan's mission.* [28]

In *Shin Shina ron*, Naitō explained that the outbreak of the Sino-Japanese War was the outcome of the mistaken policy of the Chinese, who were frustrated by their failure to modernize their country. Furthermore, they had been flattered by the irresponsible Americans and Europeans who sought to exploit a defeated China. [29]

Naitō fully endorsed the Japanese advance into South Manchuria, and he had personally played a role as an adviser to Komura in the Peking negotiations after the conclusion of the Russo-Japanese War. He insisted that Japan had been single-handedly responsible for the economic prosperity of the region. He did not deny that Japan had resorted to military means to acquire its rights and interests in China, but he was irritated by those who, out of an exclusive preoccupation with the question of "the temporary use of military force," failed to appreciate long-term economic objectives. He reasoned:

> *Suppose, with the intention to open up a huge rice field, you start digging irrigation canals. Eventually, you hit a big rock which must be cracked with a hammer or even blasted by dynamite. What would you say if someone should disregard your ultimate objective, and criticize you for destroying the land?*

He therefore concluded that "those who equate the temporary, emergency use of arms with aggression are insulting the real objective." [30]

Naitō, thus, steadfastly opposed that very small minority of Japanese of the time, such as Suehiro Shigeo, professor of law at Kyōtō

Imperial University, and Ishibashi Tanzan, editor of the *Tōyō keizai shimpō,* who proposed that Japan should give up Manchuria. Such an act on the part of Japan, Naitō maintained, would not necessarily please the Chinese. Just as someone mortally ill did not enjoy talking about life, the Chinese would not like their pride injured over a region they knew they had no ability to control.[31] The homeland of the Manchu dynasty, he noted, had been increasingly populated by Chinese from Shantung and Chihli, and they "sentimentally" longed to be reunited with the "China proper." The older inhabitants of Manchuria, however, knew the history of Japan's wars against China and Russia as well as the Japanese strength and "open-heartedness." They harbored no ill feeling toward Japanese domination. Troubles in Manchuria started after 1905, when Japan "carelessly" allowed southern Chinese to become officials there. They knew nothing of the two wars and were newly indoctrinated in the "reform and self-strengthening" propaganda. Hence, Naitō was hopeful that after those "ignorant of history" were expelled, Manchuria would return to its previously peaceful condition. Moreover, as he argued, it would be wiser for China to abandon its political control over areas it could not maintain for military and financial reasons. Manchuria was such an area.[32]

Nonetheless, Naitō disapproved of the Twenty-one Demands and the Japanese encroachment in Shantung. According to him, the demands were formulated so exclusively for the benefit of Japan that they did not contain even an ounce of consideration for China. And further, he condemned his government for its scandalous manner of negotiations. He was certain that the demands could only damage trade and have ill effect on both the welfare of Japanese residents in China and Chinese feeling toward Japan.[33] But a careful study of his writings on the issue reveals that he was displeased with the actions of his government primarily for two reasons.

First, he believed that Japan had missed the most opportune moment for presenting the demands. Second, and more importantly, he argued that it had foolishly included among the demands items that should have been excluded. He quoted the example of the extension of the Liaotung leasehold. In his opinion, Liaotung should not be returned, unless China was prepared to compensate Japan fully for the human and economic sacrifices it had made for the land. Japan should have waited until after the expiration of the lease to negotiate—"leisurely"—with China on the compensation issue; any negotiation prior to that time would amount to an admission of Japan's obligation to return the territory when the lease expired. Naitō objected on similar grounds to the inclusion of Tsingtao and the Shantung railways in the demands; after all, they were already in Japanese hands. It would be in order for China to inquire if Japan would return them. As Naitō explained, no diplomacy could be more idiotic than for the victor to discuss voluntarily with the loser about the relinquishment of the privileges. [34]

In this connection, Naitō quoted the negotiations after the Russo-Japanese War to illustrate his point. He insisted that Japan had settled matters concerning Manchuria with Russia at Portsmouth without asking whether China would accept the terms of the agreement. According to him, the subsequent Sino-Japanese negotiations were conducted merely to enable Japan to obtain further rights and interests in that region. [35] This probably revealed the true intention of some of the participants, including Naitō himself, in the Peking negotiations. Yet, despite Naitō's own emphasis on history in his arguments, he seemed to have failed to realize that one of the stipulations of the Treaty of Portsmouth was to obtain the Chinese consent before the transfer of the Russian rights in Manchuria to Japan.

In 1919, when the United States appeared sympathetic with the Chinese protest against the Japenese holding of Shantung, Naitō declared that "the power balance among nations . . . is destined to collapse sooner or later." In international politics "the final outcome depends on the strength of each nation." He, too, invoked the driving force of history to support his argument, and he proclaimed that "the rise and fall of every nation is dictated by history." Thus, he concluded that "China can blame no one but itself for its plight today." He warned:

> Through clever international maneuvers, China may temporarily succeed in elevating its position in the world. Nevertheless, it will never be able to reverse the gradual but steady downward course the country has been treading.

At the same time, he insisted that Japan, "a nation with full expansionist vitality," could not be prevented from advancing by the intervention of the powers. "Nothing is more urgent today than for everyone to recognize this truth." [36]

Naitō himself was clearly full of "expansionist vitality," and he supported Japan's "realistic" advance toward China. But he disagreed with the Japanese extremists and militarists who advocated outright subjugation of China. He objected to such irrationality primarily because history had taught him how difficult it was to control the vast and densely populated land of China for any length of time.[37] This largely explained his opposition to the Twenty-one Demands and the Japanese acquisition of Shantung.

Buoyed by his approval of Japan's past record of expansionism in China, Naitō entertained a grandiose dream about present and future Japanese activities on the mainland. In *Shin Shina ron*, he presented his enthusiastic endorsement of the role that Japanese enterprisers, particularly small capital merchants, were to play in China. As he predicted, "Japanese economic activities in China" would ultimately provide "the motive power that will destroy the traditional Chinese political structure and bring about a new, mass-based government." These activities, especially those of the small merchants who penetrated into the interior of China "with no personal regard for their lives and properties," were guided by a sense of "mission" that both Chinese and Japanese had yet to appreciate fully. These Japanese were—"without knowing it"—laboring to establish a new Oriental culture.[38]

In Naitō's opinion, Japanese enterprisers in China differed from their British and American competitors. The westerners were either content with comprador trade confined to the concession areas or motivated purely by profit-making and had no life-and-death commitment. On the other hand, Naitō likened his countrymen's economic role in China to that of the barbaric northern tribes who had in the past repeatedly revived a dying China. Thus, Japan's economic penetration was vital and indispensable for the prolongation of the very life of China, and the Chinese who attempted to stop it were "suicidal." In view of this "great mission," Naitō was convinced that "the talk of Japanese aggression or militarism in China is totally out of place."[39]

To reinforce his argument for Japan's special mission in China, Naitō proposed a thesis that emphasized "the shift of the center of Oriental culture." Nevertheless, in spite of his profound historical knowledge, the basic logic and intent of the thesis seem surprisingly simplistic.

According to Naitō, each of the nation-states in East Asia—China, Japan, and Korea—had been established with its own basis for separate existence. From a broad viewpoint of the development of Oriental culture, however, distinctions among these nation-states were inconsequential, since culture developed along a certain course that transcended national distinctions and boundaries. Moreover, the Chinese of the present day were not originally of one race; they consisted of at least two or three different ethnic groups. Racial distinctions disappeared as Chinese culture developed. Besides, the center of culture shifted as time passed. Until the Han dynasty, it was located in the Yellow River basin. Thereafter, it moved southward as well as eastward, and it was about to reach the Canton region. As culture developed with little regard for national distinctions, it would hardly be surprising if Japan, which had previously come under the influence of Chinese culture, should become the new cultural center of the Orient. If Japan and China, too, should "for some reason" develop into a single political entity, the Japanese could easily come to China and engage themselves in political and social activities. Hence, Naitō stressed that such matters as national differences were minor details in the total development of Oriental culture. [40]

As Naitō noted, some Chinese extremists demanded that China and Japan should cooperate only if the latter would relinquish the emperor system and adopt republicanism and democracy. They were "very narrow-minded," and their proposal was "impracticable." After all, Naitō argued, Japan's aim went beyond politics: it was to cooperate with China for the promotion of a grand cultural movement in the Orient. [41]

Thanks to his firm belief in Japan's mission in China as well as in the thesis of the shift of the cultural center in the Orient, Naitō was not at all impressed by the anti-Japanese movements in China. He examined these unfriendly activities in the light of his doctrine of the peculiarity of Chinese society. He charged in 1924, for example, that the age-long gap between government and society had rendered it "absolutely impossible" for the Chinese to participate in any genuine mass movement and express nationalistic indignation. He further dismissed a campaign launched under the banner of nationalism as a product of "bogus instigation," [42] which "does not deserve any serious attention." [43] Indeed, according to him, "the people ignorant of Chinese affairs" were wrong to be fearful that anti-Japanese movements would become uncontrollable if they should spread to rural areas. The principal leaders of these activities were "the delinquent students," who knew very little of their own country's history. They "extorted" funds from the rich merchants in urban centers. Yet, the "provincial peasants" would never tolerate their interference and refrain from buying Japanese goods, which were "daily necessities." As Naitō maintained:

> *In China, when certain vice spreads to the countryside, it is made immune and harmless.*

Thus, he insisted that Japan must advance its economic and cultural "mission" in defiance of the anti-Japanese movements, which were not rooted in China's social basis. [44]

In *Shin Shina ron*, Naitō cited Japan's right to survival as another reason for its need for continental expansion. [45] Earlier, in 1922, when the question "What is China?" caused some debate at the Washington Conference, he had asked the same question himself. He was convinced that resources in the world should be entrusted to those who could actually exploit them and make them available for the benefit of mankind. It did not serve the interest of humanity to permit a nation incapable of exploitation to keep its resources to itself and prevent them from being used by other nations simply on the ground of national sovereignty and territorial rights. In fact, Naitō predicted that China would soon be compelled to allow the full exploitation of its resources by the industrial nations of the world. Japan should be ready to seize the opportunity. Once again, he turned to history for inspiration and concluded that all nations which developed colonies and, in so doing, contributed to the progress of the world had "braved grave dangers and made great sacrifices." He was confident that heaven would not fail to bestow upon them "their due rewards." [46] Hence, his answer to the question "What is China?" was ominously clear. In the name of a nation's right to survival, he defended Japan's dissemination overseas of its excess population, as well as its acquisition of raw materials from other countries. As for China, he was certain that it could not become an industrial nation. It should therefore be happy with being only a supplier of raw materials. [47] As a result, when he witnessed the spread of nationalism in China in 1924, he prophesized that Japan and its neighbor would once more be on a collision course. [48]

Developments in China after 1924—the reorganization of the Kuomintang, its collaboration with the Communists, the Northern Expedition, and the ultimate reunification of the nation under the Nationalists—must have upset Naitō's historicist tranquility. With the establishment of Manchukuo in 1932, his confusion at the rapidly changing situation on the continent reached its climax.

Thanks to his emphasis on "the natural course of events" and the futility of "artificial contrivance," historian Naitō objected in principle to outright military conquest. Yet the puppet state of Manchukuo was created in utter disregard of "the natural course of events" and by the most "artificial contrivances" imaginable. Moreover, he had flatly denied any inherent Chinese capability to govern themselves, but the new state was in theory an independent nation of the Chinese in Manchuria. In July 1933, before he departed on his last trip to the region, Naitō could not help worrying about the future of the puppet state. He wrote:

> We must establish for them [the Chinese] a guideline by which a new nation can be born without having to rely upon their own national endeavor and tenacity. I know this is going to be difficult. [49]

In his perplexity, Naitō was an appropriate spokesman for Japan, as it slipped into a quagmire of fifteen years of war.

In Place of Conclusion

Naitō's perception of China in the mid-1920s was thoroughly negative. He saw its political chaos, yet was totally blind to the signs of a new era—the emergence of a nationalistic China—in the midst of the turmoil. In short, his image of China was closed, distorted, and ethnocentric.

Naitō's misconception was a typical reaction of a conservative classicist to the realities of post-1911 China, where the political scene was characterized most notably by government instability and dogfights among warlords. It, too, was a result of his excessively rigid view of the peculiarity of Chinese society. [50] His image of China represented the negative position in the controversy that arose in the mid-1920s over the achievements and potentialities of a republican China.

Nonetheless, one is disturbed by Naitō's perception of China, an undeniably distorted view that defended and promoted Japanese interests and was justified by his appeal to historicism and culturalism. Historicism convinced Naitō of the peculiarity of Chinese society and allowed him to judge China by standards different from those by which he judged other nations, above all, his own. In the name of the driving forces of history, he insisted that the Chinese had no political capability, and he thus calmly recommended—"for the sake of China"—that they abandon their aspirations for national independence as well. He almost invariably blamed the Chinese, who "knew little of their own country's history," for the conflicts between Japan and China. His knowledge of history, however, failed to enable him to recognize the movement of the "southern Chinese" to Manchuria and the emergence of the "new people" as clear manifestations of China's nationalism and resistance to Japan.[51]

In the name of culturalism, Naitō approved completely and advocated vigorously Japanese expansionism in China in the past, present, and future. He saw it as Japan's "mission" to engage in extensive economic activities and thus restore China to a new life. Furthermore, in the name of humanity, China was to become a dumping ground for Japan's excess population and was destined to remain for a long time the supplier of the raw materials that Japan needed. Naitō's views were nothing less than a reasoned justification of Japanese aggression in China in the name of history, culture, and humanity—a doctrine of Japanese imperialism with embellishments.

To dismiss Naitō as a historian who "twisted his learning around in order to flatter the age" is perhaps unfair. Nevertheless, his opinion on contemporary China surely placed him perilously close to the pitfall of "learning without thinking." As both a historian and a culturalist, he obviously abused his knowledge, and he did so in an absurdly calm manner.

His problem seemingly lies in his contemptuous attitude toward the Chinese people as well as in his total lack of any suspicion that Japan might be guilty of wrongdoings in China. Had he been aware of any misdeeds on Japan's part, he would perhaps have been less ready to see only the opportunity for Japan that China's chaos offered; he would have been able to perceive the rise of a new China.

Such an awareness should have led a person in Naitō's position to a more balanced and realistic appraisal of the changing China and its relations with Japan.

Lacking such an outlook and putting his historicism and culturalism to distorted use, however, Naitō was swept along by thought currents of the day and served uncritically to justify Japan's "manifest destiny" in China. Admittedly, he was no different from the overwhelming majority of his countrymen at the time; they, too, had little consciousness of guilt over Japan's actions in China. Not until 1945 at least was such consciousness to arise. Nevertheless, Naitō's failings represented more than his personal tragedy, for he was one of the greatest historians of China modern Japan has produced, and he profoundly influenced the Japanese image of China in the prewar years.

10

In Search of Sovereignty: The Unequal Treaties in Sino-American Relations, 1925–1930

Thomas H. Etzold

The sudden reversal of policy and relations between China and the United States during the first Nixon administration has cast the entire history of Sino-American relations into sharp relief. In "normalizing" relations, the previous relations of the two states have become essential ingredients of, and influences upon, the terms of a new formal relationship. The past promises to lay a heavy hand on the future as the consequences and implications of those relations are assessed.

Few elements of that diplomatic past have assumed more importance than the legacy of the unequal treaty system, the series of treaty agreements in the nineteenth century under which a variety of privileges inured to the imperial powers at the expense of Chinese sovereignty and self-respect. The injustice with which the powers treated China, as evidenced in the unequal treaty system among other things, often figures prominently in explanations of the motives and particular aims of the succeeding waves of revolution in China from the Taiping rebellion onward. As most commentators recognize, the inability of the Manchus to maintain formal and practical equality with foreign powers proved to be one of the most potent sources of nationalist, that is anti-Manchu, anti-foreign, and pro-modernizing, revolution at the turn of the century. As Mao was later to write in another context, there were two contradictions, two fronts on which the war for modern nationhood had to be conducted. The one front was internal to China, where various and successive revolutionary forces first contended among themselves in factions and then, with what unity they could muster, fought the reactionaries first of the dynasty and then of the warlord camp. The other front was external, and here the Chinese, nationalist and warlord alike, confronted foreign powers opposed to an integral part of the program each of the civil war antagonists had espoused. [1]

At no time in China's decades-long period of revolution did the unequal treaty system occasion more acute controversy than during the years 1925 to 1930. In those years the Kuomintang, the party of Sun Yat-sen and ultimately of Chiang Kai-shek, contended within itself and with the remnants of China's feudal government for legitimate leadership and firm control of a revived China, a control undiminished and undivided by the rights of foreign powers to exercise national jurisdiction within Chinese territory. Contrary to earlier patterns of Sino-western relations, in this short but intense interval the United States became the main western protagonist rather than the follower-participant that it had usually been in the context of East Asian international relations.

The United States acquired the principal role in discussions of revision of the unequal treaty system in the 1920s because of its willingness to liberalize relations with China, a policy that has contained paradoxical elements. Although the American government was comparatively forthcoming in response to Chinese demands for treaty revision and conducted an essentially benevolent policy toward the Chinese in this period, Americans did not actually meet Chinese demands. Despite professions of goodwill and modest efforts to bring the other powers to favorable action, the United States did not in the 1920s relinquish special privileges, and the extraterritorial systems of Britain and the United States did not end until January 11, 1943.

Scholars have asked, as did the Chinese themselves in those fateful years, why, if the Americans really were so well disposed toward Chinese aspirations to sovereign equality, they did not surrender special privileges? Why did they hesitate, delay, make excuses,

and finally refuse to concede the end of the treaty system? Because
the search for answers to these questions has primarily been confined to the context of American foreign policies and relations in
East Asia, the answers have been unsatisfactory and not compelling
enough to protect the United States from charges that liberal rhetoric and friendly oratory masked substantial remnants of unregener-
ate imperialist attitudes among American policy makers. But in addition to the circumstances of power relations in East Asia, there
were a number of elements external to East Asia that determined
American reluctance to surrender extraterritoriality. Some were
factors of international law as Americans understood it, while some
were factors of American diplomatic traditions and practices in
which were manifest an American nationalism as strong as Chinese
nationalism, though its expression was perhaps more moderate.
When these larger dimensions of the American diplomatic frame
are taken into account, American policy on extraterritoriality in
China becomes much easier to understand.

I

By the time rising Chinese nationalism seriously jeopardized the
unequal treaty system, the system was more than eighty years old.[2]
Following precedents set in British treaties with China at the end of
the war of 1839–1842, American diplomats negotiated the Treaty of
Wanghsia in 1844, in which the Chinese granted most-favored-
nation treatment and in which certain clauses laid the foundation
for later development of the unequal relationship. In the main,
these articles provided for consular jurisdiction over criminal and
civil cases involving Americans in China and foreclosed Chinese involvement in legal disputes or criminal activities that involved only
foreigners, even though incidents might take place on Chinese soil.
The British and American treaties of the early 1840s became models
for treaties between China and many other western powers in ensuing years, and one should add that the Chinese were not by any
means adamantly opposed to extending the privileges granted in
the original documents to still more powers. Americans had not
found it necessary to wrest consular jurisdiction from a reluctant
Chinese government but had found the imperial representatives
more than ready to bestow that grant of power.[3] It seemed wise to
the Chinese, at this early point, to let the barbarians take care of

their own criminals and to grant similar privileges to a number of the western nations as a way to encourage debilitating competition among them. [4]

Had foreign exercise of jurisdiction in China remained confined to the modest formulations of the Treaty of Wanghsia, much controversy would have been unnecessary. But in ways that no one could have foreseen, those modest powers so readily extended to many foreign states after the British had forced Chinese concessions grew out of all proportion to the original intentions and expectations either of the western powers or of the Chinese. In subsequent treaties, western powers demanded expansions of the earlier grants of power and more importantly, in decades of diplomatic concourse and in the exercise of the jurisdictional powers and immunities, extended their practical application into a system so comprehensive that even western diplomats conceded that it amounted to *imperium in imperio*, a logical and legal absurdity. [5]

From modest beginnings as limited grants of consular jurisdiction, the unequal treaty system and the allied extraterritorial powers and privileges of the western states expanded to include western control of Chinese tariff rates, foreign supervision of Chinese postal and customs services, unfettered operation of radio stations and postal agencies serving the foreign communities, rights of trade and travel in the interior in addition to the forced opening of coastal and riverine ports, toleration of Christianity and, later, rights of missionaries to travel and proselytize throughout China. In the archetype of nineteenth-century imperialism, some of the powers, not including the United States, carved "leaseholds" out of Chinese territory, which they treated like ordinary pieces of property, as they transferred the holdings back and forth among themselves according to the vicissitudes of international politics and the fortunes of war. Foreigners lived in concessions or settlements where Chinese officials could exercise no authority, and they lived under the protection of warships stationed in or near virtually all of the cities and ports that had been forced open to trade and foreign residence. Finally, in one of the worst abuses of the special privileges, some of the foreign powers permitted their consuls to extend protection to so-called protégés, Chinese nationals who had become friendly with or useful to the foreign community, and who were in effect given immunity from the laws of their own country by virtue of the

powerful foreign friends who would actually intervene diplomat-
ically in their behalf just as if they had been foreigners. [6]

II

The persistence of the unequal treaty system in the age of burgeoning Chinese nationalism could not have been more than a temporary phenomenon. How could a modern nation-state tolerate conditions in which foreigners were immune to its laws, immune even
from deportation, in which foreign corporations paid no taxes and
carried on business under preferential arrangements whose continuation was assured by the presence in Chinese waters of foreign
warships? How could the Chinese build a unified nation or with-
stand the social and cultural shocks and dislocations resulting from
aggressive missionary endeavors, likewise protected by agreement
and implicit force? [7] The answer, of course, was that the Chinese
could not, and in the years following the first republican successes
in China, after 1911, there were increasingly frequent instances of
anti-foreign violence and a rising level of governmental activity directed toward winning western agreement to revision, really abrogation, of the old privileges.

   In the context of a national and nationalist revolution, extraterritoriality had been certain to become an issue. The most fundamental source of Chinese revisionism was long-standing, with beginnings that considerably antedated the particular revolutionary
era of the middle twenties. At the earliest, anti-foreignism and the
alloyed resentment of the privileges foreigners enjoyed and exer-
cised in China had been one of the primary causes of Chinese dissatisfaction with the Manchus. As John K. Fairbank demonstrates,
in the late nineteenth century, Chinese acceptance, even approval,
of the treaties negotiated from 1842 to 1880 disintegrated into bitter
conviction that China had been the victim of concerted western discrimination and exploitation, a conviction heightened by obvious
and even flagrant abuses of treaty rights, which were becoming
more frequent as time passed. [8] The complicity of the dynasty in this
long serial humiliation and the inability of the dynasty to bring the
foreign powers to surrender special privileges convicted the Manchus, in the minds of many Chinese, of ineffectuality at the least
and of inexcusable failure to recognize and vindicate China's na-

tional interests at worst.[9] Thus, anti-foreignism and the determination to alter the status quo characterized the entire revolutionary
era and were prominent in each succeeding phase.

Japanese incursions and Chinese participation in World War I
heightened both the need for and the expectation of improved treatment by the powers. But Chinese hopes were dashed at the Paris
Peace Conference. The disappointment of Chinese diplomats found
quick reflection in the riots of May 4, 1919, as young nationalists
vented their frustration over continued foreign pretensions of supe-
riority and the incapacity of Chinese government officials to alter
the humiliating formal inequality. Rather vague western promises
of treaty revision came at the Washington Conference in 1921–1922,
partly because the nationalist violence of 1919 and thereafter had
impressed the powers, as it had Chinese officials, with the potential
for disorder if there was no accommodation to nationalist ambitions. But the promises remained unfulfilled as the powers vacil-
lated and the Chinese floundered through a period of increasing
governmental weakness into the early phases of renewed civil war
and then revolution.

The Chinese search for equality in foreign relations took on a
newly militant dimension in 1923 when Sun Yat-sen redefined one
of the Three Principles of the People, the Principle of Nationalism,
to mean anti-imperialism. Sun explicitly called for revision of the
treaty system and made it a part of the Kuomintang program.[10] As
the Kuomintang consolidated following Sun's acceptance of Soviet
aid and guidance, his proclamations on this issue took on vital significance for the western powers. A vague, occasionally manifested
anti-foreignism and a series of polite pleadings from various weak
governments of China had been disturbing to those powers and had
augured future difficulties. But the organization of a revolutionary
party with mass support, foreign aid, military capability, and an
anti-imperialist program presented a much more serious threat to
the structure of Sino-western relations.[11]

Of course, the Kuomintang most directly threatened not western
privileges, but the power of the warlord government in Peking. That
increasingly ominous threat doubtless played a part in the considerations that led to Peking's attempt in 1925 and 1926 to abrogate or
revise some of the unequal treaties. Thus, well before the opening

of the Northern Expedition, the anti-foreign pronouncements of the Kuomintang had presented a twofold challenge to the stability of the status quo in Sino-western treaty relations.

Still another challenge to the old system of relations arose directly out of the prosecution of revolutionary war. In competition for popular support and in the conduct of military operations, both the leaders of the Kuomintang and the various warlords of the Peking government violated the rights of foreigners in China time and time again. Foreigners were killed, their property destroyed, their rights of travel and residence interrupted or refused. Western remonstrances called forth ambivalent and contradictory reactions, but few apologies and little satisfaction, from the contenders for predominance in the Chinese revolution. Sovereign equality had become so popular a principle that neither warring party could do anything but defend it aggressively, even if one faction would have wished not to do so. [12] In any case, both warlords and Kuomintang leaders wished to destroy as much of the old system as possible. On this one topic, as on no other, the enemies were in almost complete accord. [13] Beyond the necessity of maintaining a firm public stand on the question, the opponents in war faced the manifold difficulties of controlling large armies in combat, of managing the violence of a mammoth civil war so as to avoid incidental offenses against foreigners. That, as it proved, was a nearly impossible task. In a sobering demonstration of that fact, anti-foreign violence reached a peak in the Nanking Incident of 1927 when a Nationalist Chinese army apparently went berserk and killed foreigners and seized foreign-owned property and buildings throughout the city, though there were countless hundreds of minor instances in which foreigners were mistreated, killed, or despoiled, casual victims of hostility whose misfortunes were submerged in the untranquil milieu of revolutionary struggle. [14]

Thus, the unequal treaty system came to the front of Sino-western relations in the middle twenties as a result of a new and intense phase of China's modernizing revolutions. Sun Yat-sen's creation of a strong revolutionary party with an anti-imperialist platform in 1923–1925 set the stage for revisionism. By acquiring substantial military power, Sun established a first condition in China that held certain novelties for the western powers seeking to maintain special privileges. Sun's military support and friendship with the Soviet Union made him more immune to western displeasure than earlier nationalists and anti-foreign leaders had been. And, most important, that military power gave him the opportunity to contest the legitimacy of the central government, a contest in which success would bring decisive opportunity to force the alterations in foreign relations so long desired.

III

American responses to Chinese initiatives on the subject of extra-territoriality and the general system of special privileges, to this "ebullition of national self-consciousness," were crucial to Chinese aspirations in the mid-twenties for several reasons. [15] Of all the great powers, the United States was probably the most favorably disposed toward Chinese hopes for a thorough revision of the treaty system, a friendly attitude that American officials demonstrated many times in those difficult years. [16] Additionally, there was some hope in the American government and populace for the potential of a China becoming republican, democratic, and outward looking. To the extent that Americans believed the Kuomintang to embody this prospect, they favored Kuomintang success and were willing to make promises as evidence of good intentions toward a Kuomintang-governed China. [17] The trouble, of course, was that the Kuomintang did not yet govern China and that it needed more than promises to win the revolutionary war. Finally, because of its liberal orientation on the issues, Americans seemed the most likely of all the western powers to "break the ranks" of great power cooperation in relations with China, a step that was essential to the substantial alteration of treaty terms. [18]

Like the war of revolution, American responses to these Chinese initiatives were divided into two main fronts or categories, with aspects internal to the terms of Sino-American relations in Asia and aspects external to that relationship but integral to broader American diplomatic traditions and practices. The most important element of American response within the Asian context was the tradition of cooperation among western powers. From early in the nineteenth century onward, British, French, and American policies and activities had been coordinated, sometimes explicitly, sometimes tacitly, but always practically. As more great powers actively entered the Asian sphere late in the century, this triad of powers

admitted others into a cooperation marred by friction and competition but sustained by the fact that the competing western powers and Japan had more interests in common than any of them had
with China. Pondersome as the traditional cooperation could be,
Americans in the mid-twenties had no intention of giving up the
comfortable security of that habit. President Calvin Coolidge pointedly reminded the Department of State of the dangers that could attend inadequate attention to concert among the powers. [19]

In this context, some of the reasons why Americans, liberal and
friendly as their inclinations were, did not fulfill Chinese hopes
that they would make precedential concessions become under-
standable. American leaders in the 1920s had not departed from the
essential aspiration embodied in the Open Door policy of the turn
of the century, in which Americans indicated that they did not particularly wish to exploit China in new and more extensive ways
than those already established, but that on no account would the
United States settle for less than other powers obtained in relations
with China. Americans were willing in the 1920s to encourage other
powers to grant some Chinese wishes, but they were not willing to
give up extraterritorial privileges before the other powers did so.
The attitudes fundamental to the Open Door remained strong, and
for much the same reasons they had at the turn of the century.
Americans had no wish to conduct business in China on a basis inferior to that of other foreign powers, both because of the commercial disadvantage and because of the loss of prestige that would
result. [20]

The second factor internal to the Chinese situation that had notable significance for American policy related to the timing of the
revision initiatives and the outbreak of active military campaiging.
In a way, revolution was ironically counterproductive, for the tremendous internal disorder of the revolution provided both an ex-
cuse and a real reason for American refusal to grant concessions in
treaty revision. [21] Americans had spent a lot of diplomatic time and
energy from 1922 to 1926 urging the other powers to fulfill promises
made to the Chinese at the Washington Conference and hearing in
reply that conditions in China were too unstable and the future too
uncertain for the powers even to consider surrendering the privileges that made them at least partially immune to the vicissitudes of
China's internal affairs. After Kuomintang military campaigns began, the United States found itself in company with the other for-

eign powers in refusing to grant official recognition to any of the contenders in the internal power struggle. Revolutionary disturbances, violence, and overwhelming governmental instability more than proved the contention that termination of special privileges would be premature. Americans could only agree that treaty revision would have to await restoration of order and the emergence of a victor who could govern China. [22]

This latter factor, the disintegration of central authority and the failure of any Chinese faction to win western recognition between 1926 and 1928, in part bridged the division between the internal and external factors in American responses to the Chinese search for equality in sovereign relations. One of the most critical ingredients of Chinese revisionism had been the conviction that the unequal treaty systems, however willingly accepted earlier, had after all constituted an illegal and immoral violation of China's sovereignty. That conviction still finds potent expression today in the writings of scholars, both Chinese and western, who have criticized the imperialism and amorality of western powers in Asia. Questions of the nature, location, and exercise of sovereignty lay at the center of Sino-western disagreements on the effect of the treaty system and on their more pointed disagreements over the procedures by which that system might be altered. It was unfortunate for Chinese aspirations in the mid-twenties that there was no central government, for in the context of arguments over sovereignty, such a lack severely handicapped the Chinese.

Because it lay at the heart of Chinese arguments for treaty revision, because western powers disagreed with those arguments, and because it has survived to color most secondary treatments of Sino-western relations, the question of China's sovereignty requires close investigation. [23] Apparently, as Chinese officials prepared to seek entry into the international community of the turn of the century, dominated as it was by the European great powers and by their principles of law and traditions of diplomatic concourse, they attempted to absorb the ideas, principles, and rules of international law and diplomacy procedure, a system of law that was alien to Chinese traditions and difficult to assimilate. In the 1920s, additionally, several Chinese with western legal training, some in the United States, became influential officials in the Chinese government. Thus, in the mid-twenties, Chinese approaches to treaty revision and the abolition of extraterritoriality took on new aspects.

Previously, the issue of treaty revision had been treated by Chinese and western powers alike as a question subject to the same diplomatic processes in which the original treaty arrangement had been realized. Western special privileges were legal, defined in treaties negotiated between legitimate Chinese government and the western powers. The arrangements could be revised, modified, or abolished, but only in the same process as they had first been established, that is in bilateral or multilateral negotiation, not by unilateral revision or abrogation by fiat. In the heyday of imperialism, with the great powers ever ready to back up diplomatic positions with gunboats, the Chinese of necessity had to recognize the futility of attempting to deal summarily with the treaty system and associated western rights.

In the 1920s, however, some of the realities of the earlier situation seemed to be changing; and as a result, in part, of changing power factors and, in part, of the introduction of western legal theory into Chinese representations, Chinese positions assumed more and more dependence on legal theories and political fictions, which, as it proved, were inadequate counters to the practical components of western and American postures. In the legal category, the Chinese argued that sovereignty was absolute and indivisible. Since western powers were in fact exercising jurisdiction in China, the treaty system constituted illegal and intolerable infringements of China's sovereignty and had to be eradicated promptly.[24]

But the diplomacy of the United States and other western powers had always been tempered with an element of practicality in which the theoretical principles of law underwent modification before becoming diplomatic precept or practice. There was a place in law textbooks for absolute sovereignty, in which all sovereigns were equal, but not in the world of diplomacy. In that latter realm, sovereigns were equal *before* the law but not *in* the law and certainly not in fact. According to the American consensus, the rights of sovereigns were inseparable from the duties. To possess sole and undivided jurisdiction by right, a sovereign had the duty to exercise complete control of government, population, and territory and had to meet certain standards of modernity in judicial administration and procedure.

Further, western international law recognized that the absolutes of theory could legally be modified in practice, that sovereignty could be limited, the rights foregone or foreclosed by contractual, that is treaty, agreement. As one jurist aptly summarized it, sovereignty amounted to those rights left to an individual sovereign by the community of nations. Lester Pearson put it even more pointedly some years later when he said of his own day that no nation was truly sovereign that did not possess the hydrogen bomb.

As far as the United States was concerned in the mid-twenties, China could demonstrate little ability to fulfill the duties of a sovereign, for the courts were in disarray, the laws antiquated, and after 1926, the government beleaguered. [25] Of course, Americans admitted that the Chinese had the right to attempt to alter circumstances unilaterally, in the same way that every sovereign determines its own interests and can resort to force to vindicate its point of view. But in that near approach to a "might makes right" philosophy, the Chinese would have to bear whatever consequences and risks attended on unilateral alterations of treaty obligations.[26]

From the American point of view, Chinese representations in the mid-twenties rested on still another fantasy. Chinese pretensions, as Americans saw them, to the establishment of an internal administration and ordered government had few elements of reality. In common with the other western powers, the United States recognized no government of all China during the years of active revolutionary conflict. That fact made it impossible for the United States even to carry on substantive discussions on topics as broad or as high level as treaty relations between the Chinese and the Americans.

Thus, as it developed, Americans and Chinese were almost completely divided on the questions arising out of the interplay between legal and political theories and realities. Americans insisted that the Chinese establish a government of all China, demonstrate its control and good intentions, reform the judiciary and laws, and demonstrate a real likelihood that foreigners would be able to trade, live, and travel and teach in China free from discrimination and safe from violence. When these changes had occurred, when such conditions could be guaranteed, Americans would gladly, in company with the other powers, surrender the special privileges of extraterritoriality. [27] At the same time, Chinese officials wondered how they could conclude a national revolution and construct a strong central government, one with popular support and sufficient influence, before the powers had ceased violating China's sovereignty. It seemed to the Chinese that the western powers were asking for an impossibly paradoxical achievement. [28] Somehow, Chinese officials were supposed to erect a fully sovereign and functioning government while the imperial powers continued to limit and share that sovereignty.

IV

The philosophical differences that divided Chinese and Americans in the mid-twenties were significant, but not as important as the actual problems that arose out of concrete cases in which American citizens needed protection in China. In protection of citizens, Americans had long-established policies that were integrally bound up with the accession of the United States to modern world power at the turn of the century. Protection policies thus rested on a body of practice and precedent much greater than the admittedly large body of cases and offenses at issue within China. In the protection issue there was head-on conflict between nationalist pride and the needs of an emerging China and similarly nationalistic emotions in the United States, which was still self-conscious about its new role and capabilities in foreign relations.

It had seemed to Americans at the turn of the century, when the United States first began to act like a world power, that one of the most basic functions of a state in international relations was to protect the lives, property, and interests of citizens abroad. Theodore Roosevelt, who in large part presided over the construction and early use of new national power, showed acute perception of this point. A constituent state's first task in foreign affairs was to protect citizens, and protection began not with the grand designs of national defense in the self-limiting and isolationistic sense of the nineteenth century, but with the individual who traveled, conducted business, or carried Christian enlightenment abroad. Indeed, the protection obligation was the ultimate rationale behind the more generalized diplomatic and security policies through which constituent states regulated their foreign affairs. Treaties of amity, commerce, and consular rights were not abstract elements of interstate relations, but fundamental building blocks on which not only large questions of national trade and economy depended, but on which the legal rights of each individual American rested and through which American diplomats could vindicate citizens' rights and win reparations for injuries to person, property, or business interest.

As records of protection work show, Americans were zealous in defense of citizens not just in countries of lesser power, but in the great and powerful states of the twentieth century. Following Theodore Roosevelt's vigorous lead, Americans courted a break in relations with Britain in the midst of World War I, primarily over British violations of the rights of American citizens and merchants as neutrals, and then went to war with Germany on much the same grounds. Americans maintained capitulatory arrangements, the Mediterranean counterpart to extraterritoriality, in Turkey, Persia, and Morocco as long as possible. And protection disputes figured prominently in the deterioration of German-American relations in the 1930s as the two countries drifted toward war.

In short, when Americans insisted on the importance of protection work in China, when they expressed fears about probable violations of American rights or enumerated violations, demanded reparations, and called for the creation of order and competent administration, they were not making excuses for the continuation of an imperialist position simply because they were in a position to stave off Chinese initiatives. American diplomats considered it their first and most serious duty to provide protection for Americans in China. [29]

The importance with which Americans approached the protection obligation is to some extent demonstrated in the work of the Commission on Extraterritoriality in China, which met from January to June 1926. In this international investigating commission, the signatories of the Washington Conference redeemed their pledge to consider Chinese requests for treaty revision, though not to the satisfaction of the Chinese since the commission recommended at best gradual abolition of extraterritoriality, beginning at some future time when conditions in China were not so unstable. But it was especially notable that American representatives provided by far the largest portion of cases and records for the commission to consider in reaching its recommendations. American representatives supplied to the commission records of 482 cases involving American rights in China, while Japan offered none in evidence and the British only a few of minor nature. [30]

In actual attempts to protect citizens, Americans found their most convincing evidence that China was not yet ready for unrestricted sovereignty. The hundreds of cases Americans submitted to the Commission on Extraterritoriality in China dated, of course, from years before the opening of active civil war.[31] When the Kuomintang began its northward drive late in 1926, the number of offenses against foreigners, including a substantial number of Americans, increased dramatically. As the violence of the civil war grew and spread, so the difficulty of winning satisfaction in protection cases increased. To work effectively for American interests, American diplomats were forced to the utmost practicality, to dealings in which the niceties of formal diplomacy became the least of considerations. The confusion of the revolutionary struggle produced an almost inconceivable complication for diplomatic and consular officers. The government that had been recognized previously by the United States had lost control of parts of China in which Americans were being mistreated. The Peking government had lost effective control of many of its own vassals and their troops, so that the central government could neither restrain nor punish its own people for offenses against foreigners. Where nationalist troops were stronger or in control, Peking authorities were powerless, of course. To provide help that was timely and effective, American diplomats had to ignore the complicated and important formal questions of recognition, risk the possibility that they might be charged with incorrect behavior amid competing factions in a fluid revolutionary struggle, and concentrate single-mindedly on the citizens in distress, as well as conduct other essential business of state.

The importance to Americans of protection work and its imminence—the fact that disposition of or reaction to cases often could not be deferred—continued to extend the effects of protection far beyond the issue of extraterritoriality. The beginnings of recognition for the Kuomintang, and the beginning of the end of recognition for the Peking warlord government, came out of the circumstances of protection work. Within a few months of the opening campaigns of the Northern Expedition, American diplomats realized the futility of protesting to Peking the excesses of nationalist troops or treaty violations that took place in areas not controlled by the Peking government.[32] Thereafter, American diplomats protested directly to nationalist leaders and military commanders the offenses of southern troops and those that occurred in the regions occupied by Kuomintang forces. Both to Peking and to the various nationalist leaders and headquarters, Americans repeated stern warnings reminiscent of Woodrow Wilson's 1915 reaction to the sinking of the *Lusitania*, when he said that Germany would be held "strictly accountable" for violations of American rights. Americans cautioned both sides in the war that full reparation would be expected and that the United States was keeping track of offenses and would remember them all.[33]

Pragmatically, although the United States no longer recognized the Peking regime as the sole and de facto government of China, it did not break relations. The State Department in Washington continued to receive the minister of the Peking government and to respect his accreditation, even though it likewise was regularly conversing with representatives of the Kuomintang. Rather than imply recognition by receiving an official representative from the KMT, the department was content to talk informally, but as all parties knew, quite seriously, with Frank Lee, whose letter of introduction or credence the secretary of state cautiously refused to give to the president.[34]

Most prudently of all, the American government coupled its protection representations with efforts to move American citizens out of China and away from the disturbances of an uncontrolled, and perhaps uncontrollable, situation. Americans in the interior were urged and ordered by consuls to seek the relative safety of coastal and riverine ports. Thousands of Americans were carried out of China by private and naval vessels, sometimes under the very flashes of gunfire and exploding bombs and shells. Determined as they were, American diplomats were hard-pressed to match the stubbornness of some Americans, especially missionaries, who repeatedly declined to evacuate their missions or residences, who wandered about China, sometimes into the midst of military engagements or into the paths of enraged, exhausted, or embittered soldiers who cared little about the treaty rights of foreigners. Even when injury or death resulted from the foolhardiness of the victim, the American government reminded appropriate Chinese authorities of Chinese treaty obligations.

As Americans and Chinese had finally divided on the questions of sovereignty involved in the issue of extraterritoriality, so they found themselves with paradoxically opposite attitudes within the context of protection problems. Americans judged the legitimacy of the pretensions of civil war contenders in part on the basis of their ability and willingness to fulfill treaty obligations. But Chinese competitors for national power were struggling to see which of them could wrest the greater concessions in treaty revision from the western powers, and failing that, to see who could violate western rights with the most impunity. That latter aspect of the Chinese attitudes showed most notably in the increasingly confident Kuomintang reactions to American protests. By 1928, and especially as success came nearer for the expeditionary forces, Nationalist leaders grew noticeably less penitent and more argumentative about the violations with which American officials reproached them, a development that the practical excuses afforded by the war's circumstances doubtless eased considerably.[35]

V

The declining penitence of Nationalists in 1927–1928 was just one more indication that the end of an era in Sino-western relations was at hand. The conviction of Chinese leaders in both Peking and Nationalist factions in the mid-twenties at last had approached that long dominant among younger, sometimes radical Chinese.[36] Times had changed and with them the circumstances in which the treaty system had been wise or tolerable. Until the leaders had validated their conviction in practical contests with the powers, however, there could be no benefit in that perception for China or its governors. Chinese leaders were cautiously assessing the consequences of unilateral action, assaying modest risks in an endeavor to measure Chinese strength and determination against western power and resolve.

Thus, it was no accident that the Chinese warlords already in 1925 introduced another western legal doctrine into discussions of treaty revision.[37] The principle *rebus sic stantibus*, according to which treaties remained effectual and binding only as long as the conditions envisioned in the treaty or at its signing persisted, captured the very essence of Chinese contentions. It mattered little to the Chinese that *rebus sic stantibus* had fallen into disrepute among western diplomats and jurists, though it was unfortunate that Americans found it an especially reprehensible principle associated with the "old diplomacy" of a corrupt, cynical, and Machiavellian era in European international politics. The construction of Chinese argu-

ments on that principle's basis simply became another point of le-
gal-philosophical divergence to impede Sino-American agreement
on the future of extraterritoriality. As a doctrine, *rebus sic stantibus*
was not likely to impress the United States and the other powers.
Not until a new, powerful, competent, and modern China faced the
powers would it matter, and then not as legal doctrine but as demon-
strable political and diplomatic reality. The beginnings of that reality had been established in 1926, for even before the Northern Expedition had begun, the Peking government had denounced the
treaty that embodied Belgian special privileges.[38] In the summer
and fall of 1926, Peking had gone on to abrogate a similar treaty with
Spain and to call into question the rights of France and Japan.

Where the Peking government necessarily left off its exploration
of the range in which its unilateralism would be tolerated, the Nationalists resumed, and after 1928 moved rapidly toward a point at
which the imperial powers would either concede the end of extraterritoriality or face Chinese abrogation of treaties. Chinese leaders
of both sides in the revolution found, as they surely had hoped, that
the imperial powers, especially the United States but including Japan, were much less willing to resist Chinese appeals than they
once had been. Perhaps most important for the success of the Chinese in ending extraterritoriality, there was a notable disinclination
to coerce the Chinese with military force as the imperial nations
had so often done in the past.[39] Ultimately, the maintenance of
treaty rights after the Chinese began to resent them had depended
on the willingness of the treaty powers to use gunboats and marines
to protect citizens, leaseholds, concessions, and to punish Chinese
cities and citizens for infractions of foreign rights. Undeniably, in
the 1920s, that resolute willingness to coerce the Chinese had diminished, with the result that Chinese initiatives could proceed much
further without engendering decisive opposition.[40]

Once again, the reasons for the diminishing American interest in
forcible maintenance of rights had as much to do with factors outside the Asian situation as with factors integral to it. Of course,
there were important components of changing American policy to
be found in the terms of Sino-American relations. Americans had
been friendly to Chinese aspirations for a long time, and the secre-
taries of state of the 1920s were among the foremost Americans of
the day in their liberal attitudes toward the Chinese revolution, in-

cluding the determination to end foreign privileges. Their liberal
attitude derived from several perceptions and assumptions. American leaders had been convinced in the aftermath of World War I
that China had a great future, that it would become a powerful and
important nation, and that it stood on the threshold of transition
into that future. Americans wanted to be on good terms with China
when that happened. [41]

But, beyond American concerns for the future tenor of relations
with China, there were serious doubts in the United States about
the effectiveness of coercion in international relations. Indeed, the
1920s were a time in which Americans massively rejected intervention, at which they had no little experience, as immoral and out-
dated, and worst of all, ineffective. [42] Americans had just completed two decades of intervention in various countries of the
Western Hemisphere, where American interests were clearly significant and relatively easy to define. Americans had sought peace,
stability, and friendship in relations with Latin America and had intervened from time to time to control or alter conditions that imper-
iled these goals. To cap it all, Americans had at last intervened in
the Great War for much the same reasons. All those interventions,
from Cuba to Santo Domingo to Haiti to the World War, had, as it
seemed to Americans in the late 1920s, been futile. None of the
goals for which Americans had striven had been achieved through
intervention. There was no reason to think that intervention would
be any more useful in American relations with China. [43]

Because there was no other means appropriate to influence the
course of affairs in China, Americans trusted to time to bring about
conditions in which a more definite and satisfactory resolution of
the tension between Chinese aspirations and American interests
could come about. [44] Time would tell which faction would rule in
China. Time would moderate, Americans hoped and thought, the
impetuousness of revolutionary rhetoric, and the end of war, when
it came, likewise would introduce restraint in language, behavior,
and expectations. When the revolution had ended, when China had
returned to a more normal and ordered life, the validity of Chinese
views on how times had changed would be easier to assay.

As it happened, the end of civil war brought something less than
validation of Chinese convictions, something more than mere rever-

sion to earlier terms of relations. In the months following the end of civil war, Kuomintang leaders grew increasingly frustrated at their failure to move the United States and the other powers to treaty revision and to surrender extraterritoriality. [45] When Americans proved unwilling to negotiate independently of the powers and unable to force the pace of British and Japanese deliberations, Chinese leaders reproached them and tried almost to shame American diplomats into making concessions. [46]

Finally Chinese leaders, angry, frustrated, and determined, progressed beyond recriminations to threats.[47] Perhaps emboldened by success in the war, they prepared to treat the great powers as summarily as they had the weaker European powers in 1926.[48] From the middle of 1929 onward there were rumors in China—undoubtedly of official origin—that further stalling by the powers would force the Chinese to decree an end to extraterritoriality, and late in December, the Central Committee of the Kuomintang did in fact determine to abrogate the unequal treaties as of January 1, 1930.

With that official pronouncement, the aspirations of Chinese nationalists to full sovereignty were put to their most severe test. Unhappily for the Kuomintang government, conditions had not changed as far as it had judged. With the declaration of January 1, 1930, both Chinese and Americans reached the virtual end of diplomatic repertoires, a highly uncomfortable circumstance since they were no closer to agreement or to the end of extraterritoriality than they had been at the middle of the preceding decade. Sino-American relations entered a period of ambiguity and fantasy in which Americans pretended to misunderstand the Chinese declaration, although they realized that the ground was slowly slipping from underfoot (an apt metaphor for the erosion of extraterritoriality). [49] Americans accepted the declaration as a statement of policy intent rather than of immediate implementation, continued to speak optimistically of a gradual, negotiated end to the treaty system, and worried about the paucity of tools and weapons in their diplomatic inventory should the Chinese proceed to actual rather than verbal abolition of extraterritoriality. [50] It was an uneasy decade for Chinese and Americans alike, one in which relations avoided crisis perhaps only because there were so many and serious distractions as Chinese pretensions to sovereign equality received shattering blows at the hands first of the Japanese army and then at the hands of resurgent Communist rebels.

Ironically, in one important sense, Americans had been more right than the Chinese when they said that an end to extrality would be premature, for the revolution was far from over. The completion of revolutionary change, the maturation and modernization of China's institutions, and the ardors of modern nation-building remained ahead. It was only a final irony that American and British governments surrendered extraterritoriality in 1943 more to forestall the completion of processes they had earlier favored than to facilitate or recognize them.

Notes

Preface

1. Mary C. Wright, "From Revolution to Restoration: The Transformation of Kuomintang Ideology," in *Far Eastern Quarterly*, Vol. XIV, No. 4 (August 1955), pp. 515–32.
2. Brandt, *Stalin's Failure in China, 1924–1927* (Cambridge, 1958); and Isaacs, *The Tragedy of the Chinese Revolution* (Stanford, 1962).

Introduction / A Decade of Challenge

1. *The May Fourth Movement: Intellectual Revolution in Modern China* (Cambridge, 1960), p. 182.
2. Paul S. Dull, "The Assassination of Chang Tso-lin," *Far Eastern Quarterly*, Vol. XI, No. 4 (August 1952), pp. 453–63; Morishima Morito, *Inbō, Ansaku, Guntō* (Tōkyō, 1950), pp. 21–24; and Sadako N. Ogata, *Defiance in Manchuria: The Making of Japanese Foreign Policy, 1931–1932* (Berkeley, 1964), p. 13.
3. H. G. W. Woodhead (ed.), *The China Year Book, 1924–5* (Tientsin, n.d.), p. 863.
4. Chang Kuo-t'ao, *The Rise of the Chinese Communist Party, 1921–1927: Volume One of the Autobiography of Chang Kuo-t'ao* (Lawrence, Kansas, 1972), p. 277.
5. A good French source, now available in English translation, is Jean Chesneaux, *The Chinese Labor Movement, 1919–1927* (Stanford, 1968), pp. 42, 262–71, 361–63 and *passim*; and Teng Chung-hsia, *Chung-kuo chih-kung yün-tung chien-shih* (Tientsin, 1949), pp. 5–26 and *passim*.

6. For details, see Arnold J. Toynbee, *Survey of International Affairs, 1927* (London, 1929), pp. 334–38.

7. For a classical study of the Peking raid and the salvaged materials, see C. Martin Wilbur and Julie Lien-ying How (ed.), *Documents on Communism, Nationalism, and Soviet Advisers in China, 1918–1927* (New York, 1956), pp. 8–9; and Toynbee, *Survey of International Affairs*, pp. 335–585.

8. Boyd C. Shafer, *Nationalism: Myth and Reality* (New York, 1955), pp. 7–8; and Louis L. Snyder, *The New Nationalism* (New York, 1968), pp. 2–6.

9. According to Teng Wen-i, Sun Yat-sen had made six northern campaigns before 1926: in 1913 (the so-called "Second Revolution"), 1914, 1915, 1917, 1920, and 1923. See his "Huang-p'u ching-shen," in *Lu-chün chün-kuan hsüeh-hsiao chih shih-chou-nien hsiao-ch'ing chuan-chi* (Feng-shan, Taiwan, 1964), p. 74.

Chapter 1: Sun Yat-sen and the Origins of the Kuomintang Reorganization

1. Quoted from Wang Ching-wei's telegram to Liang Shih-yi, in Ts'en Hsüeh-lu, *San-shui Liang Yen-sun hsien-sheng nien-p'u* (Taipei, 1962), Vol. I, pp. 428–29. Cf. Sun's letter to Ts'ai Ping-jo on June 18, 1919, in *Kuo-fu ch'uan-chi*, ed. by Kuomintang Archives (Taipei, 1965), hereafter cited as KFCC, Vol. II, p. 70. Lyon Sharman describes the years 1918–1925 as "the most active literary period" of Sun's life. See Sharman, *Sun Yat-sen, His Life and Its Meaning: A Critical Biography* (Hamden, 1965), p. 227.

2. KFCC, Vol. IX, p. 403.

3. Hu, *The Chinese Renaissance* (New York, 1964). The best books on the revolution—commonly known as the May Fourth Movement—are Chow Tse-tsung, *The May Fourth Movement: Intellectual Revolution in Modern China* (Cambridge, 1960); and its companion volume, Chow, *Research Guide to the May Fourth Movement: Intellectual Revolution in Modern China* (Cambridge, 1963). See also Joseph T. Ch'en, *The May Fourth Movement in Shanghai: The Making of a Social Movement in Modern China* (Leiden, 1971); and Benjamin I. Schwartz (ed.), *Reflections on the May Fourth Movement: A Symposium* (Cambridge, 1972).

4. In his report to the Secretary of State on September 10, 1919, Paul S. Reinsch analyzed the causes of the May Fourth Incident. He stressed the disappointment of the Chinese with the decision of the powers on the "Shantung Question." According to him, "the belief had become general throughout the country that the conference was disposed to regard China's representations favorably. . . . This belief in many circles amounted to conviction." In consequence, "the first report to reach China of the decision of the conference to embody Japanese pretensions in regard to Shantung in the peace treaty therefore were received with incredulity." See United States Department of State, *Records Relating to Internal Affairs of China, 1910–29* (hereafter cited as USDS), 893.00/3235. The details of the May Fourth Incident and its aftermath are recounted in Chow, *The May Fourth Movement*, pp. 84–116. In his September 10 report, Reinsch maintained that Ts'ao Ju-lin, one of the three ministers, "resigned," partly because of the "loss of face" occasioned by the attack on his residence by the students. See USDS, 893.00/3235. Ts'ao defends his own position in his memoirs, *I-sheng chih hui-i* (Hong Kong, 1966), pp. 195–204.

5. Huang Chi-lu, "Ts'ai Yüan-p'ei hsien-sheng yü kuo-fu ti kuan-hsi," in *Chuan-chi wen-hsüeh*, Vol. V, No. 3 (September 1964), p. 21.

6. As Yü-ju Chih notes, Ch'en did not join the Revolutionary Alliance "allegedly because of his disapproval of its narrow nationalistic strain." See Chih, "Ch'en Tu-hsiu: His Career and Political Ideas," in Chün-tu Hsüeh (ed.), *Revolutionary Leaders in Modern China* (New York, 1971), p. 340.

7. Hu enrolled at Cornell in September 1910. He remained there until he moved to Columbia University in the autumn of 1915. See Jerome B. Grieder, *Hu Shih and the Chinese Renaissance: Liberalism in the Chinese Revolution, 1917–1937* (Cambridge, 1970), pp. 41–42.

8. KFCC, Vol. IX, p. 453.

9. Chang, *Suan-t'ien-ku-la ti hui-wei* (Taipei, 1968), pp. 15–19.

10. Chiang, "Chui-i Chung-shan hsien-sheng," in Yü Yu-jen et al., *Kuo-fu chiu-shih-nien tan-ch'en chi-nien lun-wen-chi* (Taipei, 1956), Vol. III, pp. 3–4; and Russell, *The Autobiography of Bertrand Russell, 1914–1944* (Boston, 1968), p. 180.

11. This short essay is reprinted in KFCC, Vol. XII, pp. 17–18.

12. Quoted from the preface of the English version of the treatise, *The International Development of China* (Taipei, 1953), p. v. The Chinese version, entitled *Shih-yeh chi-hua*, is included in KFCC, Vol. III, pp. 241–364.

13. *Tai Chi-t'ao hsien-sheng wen-ts'un*, ed. by Ch'en T'ien-hsi (Taipei, 1959), Vol. II, p. 583.

14. Josef Fass, "Sun Yat-sen and the May Fourth Movement," in *Archiv Orientalni*, Vol. XXXVI, No. 4 (1968), pp. 577–83. Cf. Sharman, *Sun Yat-sen*, p. 223; and Y. C. Wang, *Chinese Intellectuals and the West, 1872–1949* (Chapel Hill, 1966), pp. 333–35.

15. Quoted in *Tai Chi-t'ao hsien-sheng wen-ts'un tsai-hsü-pien*, ed. by Ch'en T'ien-hsi (Taipei, 1968), Vol. II, p. 657.

16. See Chu's letter to Sun (original document in Kuomintang Archives), partially quoted in *Kuo-fu nien-p'u tseng-ting-pen*, ed. by Lo Chia-lun, with additions by Huang Chi-lu (Taipei, 1969), hereafter cited as KFNP, Vol. II, p. 793. See also Teng Tse-ju, *Chung-kuo kuo-min-tang erh-shih-nien shih-chi* (Shanghai, 1948), p. 247.

17. *North China Herald* (hereafter abbreviated as NCH), January 8, 1921, p. 94; and Walter E. Gourlay, "The Kuomintang and the Rise of Chiang Kai-shek, 1920–1924" (unpublished Ph.D. dissertation, Harvard University, 1966), p. 16.

18. Hu Han-min, "Liu-yüeh shih-liu chih hui-ku," reprinted in Wu Hsiang-hsiang (ed.), *Chung-kuo hsien-tai-shih ts'ung-k'an* (Taipei, 1950–1964), Vol II, p. 411.
19. KFNP, Vol. II, pp. 808–10.
20. *Ibid.*, p. 815.
21. KFCC, Vol. VIII, p. 112.
22. Quoted from "Manifesto to the Foreign Powers Issued by Dr. Sun Yat-sen, May 5, 1921," included in USDS, 893.00/3866.
23. Vice Consul (Canton) to Secretary of State, April 20, 1921, in *ibid.*, 893.00/3868; and Vice Consul (Canton) to Secretary of State, April 6, 1921, in *ibid.*, 893.00/3869.
24. NCH, February 5, 1921, p. 31; and Bonnie Lawrence, "Sun Yat-sen, Ch'en Chiung-ming and the Coup d'Etat of June 16, 1922" (unpublished manuscript, Columbia University, 1971), pp. 10–11.
25. USDS, 893.00/3868; and Great Britain Foreign Office, *Further Correspondence Respecting China*, F 2831/1629/10, #98, China Command Intelligence Diary, April 21, 1921.
26. USDS, 893.00/3868; and *China Weekly Review* (hereafter cited as CWR), April 23, 1921, p. 395. Cf. Li Chien-nung, *The Political History of China, 1840–1928*, trans. by Ssu-yü Teng and Jeremy Ingalls (Stanford, 1967), pp. 414–15; and T'ao Chü-yin, *Pei-yang chün-fa t'ung-chih shih-ch'i shih-hua* (Peking, 1957–1959), Vol. VI, p. 15.
27. Ernest B. Price, American Vice Consul in Canton, praised Ch'en as "a practical patriot," who "will support Dr. Sun until and unless he is convinced that Dr. Sun's policy will injure Kwangtung." See USDS, 893.00/3868. Cf. KFNP, Vol. II, p. 826.
28. "Manifesto to the Foreign Powers," in USDS, 893.00/3866.
29. KFNP, Vol. II, p. 840; and United States Minister (Peking) to Secretary of State, December 3, 1921, in USDS, 893.00/4148.
30. Consul General (Canton) to Secretary of State, January 3, 1922, in USDS, 893.00/4209.
31. KFNP, Vol. II, pp. 862–65; and Lawrence, "Sun Yat-sen, Ch'en Chiung-ming and the Coup d'Etat," pp. 26–31. Cf. Walter E. Gourlay, who finds "no convincing evidence that Ch'en Chiung-ming had any hand in the assassination." See Gourlay, "The Kuomintang and the Rise of Chiang Kai-shek," p. 98. In a letter to his "party comrades," dated September 18, 1922, Sun offered his version of the events leading to the June 16 coup (KFCC, Vol. IX, pp. 544–49). He claimed to have "documentary proof" of Ch'en's conspiracy with "the authorities in Hunan" (p. 545).
32. NCH, May 27, 1922, p. 590.
33. KFNP, Vol. II, pp. 865–66; and Hu, "Liu-yüeh shih-liu chih hui-ku," pp. 413–14. See also Sun's September 18 letter, in which he argued that the retreat from Kweilin in April 1922 had resulted from Ch'en Chiung-ming's "obstruction" (KFCC. Vol. IX, p. 545).
34. Vice Consul (Canton) to Secretary of State, June 22, 1922, in USDS, 893.00/4526. Cf. Li, *The Political History of China*, which states that Sun "summoned Ch'en for an interview. Ch'en dared not go" (p. 417).

Similar views are expressed in KFNP, Vol. II, pp. 866–67; Tsou Lu, *Chung-kuo kuo-min-tang shih-kao* (Taipei, 1965), Vol. III, pp. 1037–38; and Hu, "Liu-yüeh shih-liu chih hui-ku," p. 414.

35. Kuomintang sources characterize Ch'en's June 16 coup as an act of "betrayal" and "treason." For a typical example of Kuomintang interpretation, see Li Shui-hsien, "Ch'en Chiung-ming p'an-kuo shih," reprinted in Wu (ed.), *Chung-kuo hsien-tai-shih ts'ung-k'an*, Vol. II, pp. 432–96, and Vol. III, pp. 403–38.

36. United States Consul (Canton) to Secretary of State, April 26, 1922, in USDS, 893.00/4399.

37. NCH, May 6, 1922, p. 372.

38. Hu, "Liu-yüeh shih-liu chih hui-ku," p. 415. Bonnie Lawrence describes these paper notes as "worthless." See Lawrence, "Sun Yat-sen, Ch'en Chiung-ming and the Coup d'Etat," p. 38. Sun himself expressed his opinion of the printing of paper currency in an interview with Rodney Gilbert. He claimed that "it is not essential to provide a cash reserve nor to promise to redeem paper money on demand." See NCH, May 6, 1922, p. 373.

39. Tsou, *Chung-kuo kuo-min-tang shih-kao*, Vol. III, pp. 1035–37.

40. Jacob Gould Schurman to Secretary of State, June 25, 1922, in USDS, 893.00/4493.

41. Vice Consul (Canton) to Secretary of State, June 22, 1922, in *ibid.*, 893.00/4576; Vice Consul (Canton) to Secretary of State, June 30, 1922, in *ibid.*, 893.00/4578.

42. Ho Hsiang-ning, *Hui-i Sun Chung-shan ho Liao Chung-k'ai* (Peking, 1957), pp. 26–30; and Ho Hsiang-ning, "Wo ti hui-i," in *Hsin-hai ke-ming hui-i-lu*, comp. by Chung-kuo jen-min cheng-chih hsieh-shang hui-i ch'uan-kuo wei-yüan-hui wen-shih tzu-liao yen-chiu wei-yüan-hui (Peking, 1961), Vol. I, pp. 32–41.

43. KFNP, Vol. II, pp. 877–83; and Hu, "Liu-yüeh shih-liu chih hui-i," pp. 416–20. See also Mao Ssu-ch'eng, *Min-kuo shih-wu-nien i-ch'ien chih Chiang Kai-shek hsien-sheng* (Hong Kong, 1956), Vol. VI, p. 24a; and Pichon P. Y. Loh, *The Early Chiang Kai-shek: A Study of His Personality and Politics, 1887–1924* (New York, 1971), pp. 70–73.

44. USDS, 893.00/4493.

45. KFCC, Vol. IX, pp. 544, 548–49.

46. For the text of the manifesto, see *The China Year Book, 1924–5*, ed. by H. G. W. Woodhead (Tientsin, n.d.), pp. 868–70. Allen S. Whiting analyzes this controversial document in his "The Soviet Offer to China of 1919," in *Far Eastern Quarterly*, Vol. X, No. 4 (August 1951), pp. 355–64. On the Soviet policy toward the Chinese revolution, see Whiting, *Soviet Policies in China, 1917–1924* (New York, 1954), pp. 236–47.

47. As Benjamin I. Schwartz notes, "It would be impossible to overestimate the impression produced in China by Karakhan's proposal." See Schwartz, *Chinese Communism and the Rise of Mao* (Cambridge, 1952), pp. 214–15, n. 44. Regarding the impact of Marxism on the Chinese intellectuals, see Maurice Meisner, *Li Ta-chao and the Origins of Chinese Marxism* (Cambridge, 1967), especially pp. 52–121.

48. Ts'ui Shu-ch'in, "The Influence of the Canton-Moscow Entente upon Sun Yat-sen's Political Philosophy: I. The Principle of Nationalism," in *The Chinese Social and Political Science Review*, Vol. XVIII, No. 1 (April 1934), p. 118.

49. See, for instance, his "The True Solution of the Chinese Question," which he wrote in English in 1904 with the help of Wang Ch'ung-hui. KFCC, Vol. VII, p. 141.

50. The text of Sun's letter to Harding is enclosed in Personal Representative of Dr. Sun Yat-sen to President Harding, June 16, 1921, in USDS, 893.00/3913.

51. KFNP, Vol. II, p. 771; and KFCC, Vol. IX, pp. 496–97.

52. Charles R. Crane to Secretary of State, February 28, 1921, in USDS, 893.00/3817.

53. *Ibid.*, 893.00/3889.

54. Secretary of State to Consul General in Canton, June 25, 1921, in *ibid.*, 893.00/3902.

55. See the chapter entitled "The Lost Opportunity" in Akira Iriye, *After Imperialism: The Search for a New Order in the Far East, 1921–1931* (Cambridge, 1965), pp. 26–56.

56. Ho, *Hui-i Sun Chung-shan*, p. 12.

57. "Polozhenie v vostochnoi Azii," in *Kommunisticheskii Internatsional*, Vol. XIII (September 1920), pp. 2553–62.

58. A partial translation of Voitinsky's article, "Moi vstrechi s Sun Yat-seno," is included in Xenia Joukoff Eudin and Robert C. North, *Soviet Russia and the East, 1920–1927: A Documentary Survey* (Stanford, 1957), pp. 218–19. The original essay appears in *Pravda*, No. 61 (March 15, 1925), p. 2.

59. See Dov Bing, "Revolution in China: Sneevlietian Strategy" (unpublished M.A. thesis, University of Auckland, New Zealand, 1968). For a much shorter version of the work, see his "Sneevliet and the Early Years of the CCP," in *The China Quarterly*, No. 48 (October/December 1971), pp. 667–97.

60. Bing, "Revolution in China," pp. 66–67.

61. In *The Inner History of the Chinese Revolution* (New York, 1930), T'ang Leang-li claims that Maring visited Wu prior to his meeting with Sun (p. 155). Conrad Brandt confirms this, and he further states that Wu agreed to give the Chinese Communists much freedom of activities in his sphere of influence in return for Maring's promise of support. See Brandt, *Stalin's Failure in China, 1924–1927* (Cambridge, 1958), pp. 24–25. See also Shao Chuan Leng and Norman D. Palmer, *Sun Yat-sen and Communism* (London, 1961), p. 55; and Meisner, *Li Ta-chao and the Origins of Chinese Marxism*, p. 211. Nevertheless, Dov Bing remains skeptical about this, since Maring's own writings make no reference to this alleged meeting. See Bing, "Revolution in China," p. 47. n. 10.

62. See the first document, "Notes on a Conversation with H. Sneevliet: The Chinese Question, 1920–23," included in "Documents on the Comintern and the Chinese Revolution, Introduction by Harold R. Isaacs,'' in *The China Quarterly*, No. 45 (January/March 1971), p. 104. Cf. Teng Chia-yen, "Ma-t'ing hsieh tsung-li shih-chi," in *Ke-ming wen-hsien*, comp. by Kuomintang Archives (Taipei, 1953–   ), hereafter abbreviated as KMWH, Vol. IX, p. 1409.

63. Teng, "Ma-t'ing hsieh tsung-li shih-chi," p. 1410. Bing, however, maintains that Maring stayed in Sun's headquarters "for more than a week." See his two works, "Revolution in China," p. 73; and "Sneevliet and the Early Years of the CCP," p. 682. Maring himself informed Harold R. Isaacs in an interview on August 19, 1935, that he "spent two weeks with Sun Yat-sen at his headquarters." See "Notes on a Conversation with H. Sneevliet," p. 104. Chang Chi asserts that he, a friend of Maring's, introduced the Dutch guest to Sun in Kweilin. See *Chang P'u-ch'uan hsien-sheng ch'uan-chi* (Taipei, 1951), p. 195.

64. "Notes on a Conversation with H. Sneevliet," p. 104; and Maring's reminiscences, written under the name, H. Sneevliet, "Met en bij Soen Yat-sen, enige persoonlijke herinneringen," in *Klassenstrijd* (Amsterdam), No. 3 (March 1926).

65. Quoted in Eudin and North, *Soviet Russia and the East*, p. 220.

66. Wang Ching-wei, "Tui Chung-kuo kuo-min-tang ti-erh-tz'u ch'uan-kuo tai-piao ta-hui cheng-chih pao-kao" (hereafter cited as "Political Report of 1926"), in KMWH, Vol. XX, p. 3855.

67. Sneevliet, "Met en bij Soen Yat-sen." Cf. "Notes on a Conversation with H. Sneevliet," p. 104.

68. Teng, "Ma-t'ing hsieh tsung-li shih-chi," pp. 1410–11.

69. George E. Sokolsky, "The Kuomintang," in Woodhead (ed.) *The China Year Book, 1928*, pp. 1320–21; and Josef Fass, "Sun Yat-sen and Germany in 1921–1924," in *Archiv Orientalni*, Vol. XXXVI, No. 1 (1968), p. 137.

70. Sneevliet, "Met en bij Soen Yat-sen." Significantly, this source is a commemoratory essay written after Sun's death, and it appeared in print at a time when the Comintern cooperation with the Kuomintang seemed to be going well. Maring's comments on Sun were less glowing during his interview with Harold R. Isaacs, as evidenced in "Notes on a Conversation with H. Sneevliet," pp. 103–104.

71. Wang, "Political Report of 1926," p. 3855.

72. See the minutes of the twenty-second committee meeting in *Chung-kuo kuo-min-tang lin-shih chung-yang chih-hsing wei-yüan-hui hui-i chi-lu* (original document in Kuomintang Archives).

73. Without the substantiation of the Kuomintang sources, Chang Kuo-t'ao contends that Sun Yat-sen actually "sent" Chang Ch'iu-pai to represent the party in the congress. See Chang, *The Rise of the Chinese Communist Party, 1921–1927: Volume One of the Autobiography of Chang Kuo-t'ao* (Lawrence, 1971), p. 188. Chang Ch'iu-pai later played an important role in the Kuomintang reorganization. For example, he was elected an alternate member of the Central Executive Committee on January 30, 1924. See KFNP, Vol. II, p. 1068.

74. KFCC, Vol. XI, p. 46. Josef Fass dates Sun's plan for the alliance from "the beginning of 1922." See Fass, "Sun Yat-sen and Germany," p. 139.

75. These were two of the three documents allegedly found by Ch'en Chiung-ming in Liao Chung-k'ai's safe after the June 16 coup of 1922. *Hong Kong Telegraph* printed the photocopies of the documents on September 22. See Ts'ai Ho-sen's analysis in *Hsiang-tao chou-pao*, No. 4 (October 4, 1922), pp. 25–28. Cf. NCH, October 7, 1922, pp. 3–4; and CWR, October 7, 1922, pp. 181–82.

76. Dalin, "Velikii povorot: Sun Yat-sen v 1922g," in *Sun Yat-sen, 1866– 1966, K stoletiiu so dnia rozhdeniia: Sbornik statei, vospominanii i materialov* (Moscow, 1966), p. 256. Cf. Ch'en Tu-hsiu, "Kao ch'uan-tang t'ung-chih shu," included in *Kung-fei huo-kuo shih-liao hui-pien*, comp. by Chung-hua min-kuo k'ai-kuo wu-shih-nien wen-hsien-hui (Taipei, 1963), in which the author dates Sun's meetings with Dalin in July (Vol. I, p. 427). This is likely a mistake, because Sun was then a refugee on a gunboat.

77. Dalin, "Velikii povorot," pp. 263–64.

78. *Ibid.*, p. 273.

79. *Ibid.*, p. 269.

80. *Ibid.*, p. 276.

81. *Ibid.*, pp. 283–85.

82. KFCC, Vol. XI, pp. 46–47.

83. Quoted by Chiang in a speech on April 25, 1929, in *Chiang tsung-t'ung chi* (Taipei, 1963), Vol. I, p. 540.

84. Fass, "Sun Yat-sen and Germany," pp. 140–41.

85. Sneevliet, "Met en bij Soen Yat-sen."

86. H. Sneevliet, "Het Chineesch-Russisch conflict over den Oost-Chineeschen Spoorweg," in *De neiuwe weg* (Amsterdam, 1929), p. 234.

87. Mao, *Min-kuo shih-wu-nien i-ch'ien*, Vol. IV, pp. 39a–40a.

88. KFNP, Vol. II, pp. 906, 911–12.

89. A complete list of the fifty-three participants in the September 4 meeting is given in Li Yün-han, *Ts'ung jung-Kung tao ch'ing-tang* (Taipei, 1966), Vol. I, p. 184, n. 25. See also KFNP, Vol. II, pp. 908–909; and Chang, *The Rise of the Chinese Communist Party*, p. 267.

90. Chang, *The Rise of the Chinese Communist Party*, p. 293, n. 8.

91. *Ibid.*, p. 87. The phrase "the death of a dream" *(i-ko li-hsiang huan-mieh liao)* appears only in the Chinese version of Chang's autobiography. See his "Wo ti hui-i," in *Ming-pao yüeh-k'an*, No. 5 (May 1966), p. 64.

92. Chang, *The Rise of the Chinese Communist Party*, p. 100.

93. Ch'en, *The Communist Movement in China: An Essay Written in 1924*, ed. with an introduction by C. Martin Wilbur (New York, 1966), pp. 74–78.

94. Ch'en Kung-po, a participant in the congress, reports that the Chinese Communists adopted a "non-compromise" policy in order to ensure "an attitude of independence, aggression and exclusion," thus rejecting any possibility of an alliance with "the existing parties." See *ibid.*, pp. 80–81.

95. Ch'en, "Kao ch'uan-tang t'ung-chih shu," p. 427.
96. Dalin, "Velikii povorot," p. 257.
97. Quoted from "The Decisions of the Second Conference of the Communist Party of China of 1922," one of the few valuable documents included in Ch'en, *The Communist Movement in China*, pp. 119–20.
98. Ch'en, "Kao ch'uan-tang t'ung-chih shu," pp. 428–29. Cf. Chang, *The Rise of the Chinese Communist Party*, pp. 253–57. Chang Kuo-t'ao is apparently wrong to state that the plenum met "early in August 1922" (p. 253). See also Bing, "Sneevliet and the Early Years of the CCP,'" p. 690.
99. See Ch'en, "Kao ch'uan-tang t'ung-chih shu," pp. 428–29. In his 1935 interview with Harold R. Isaacs, Maring denied that he had ever invoked the Comintern authority to overrule the opposition of the Chinese Communists. See "Notes on a Conversation with H. Sneevliet," p. 106. For an analysis of the controversy, see Bing, "Revolution in China," pp. 94–116.
100. In response to the charges of the Communist sabotage in 1923, Sun attempted to convince the Kuomintang "rightists" that Soviet Russia had imposed the idea of collaboration with the Kuomintang on the Chinese Communists. See his remarks in "T'an-ho Kung-ch'an-tang liang ta yao-an," reprinted in Teng, *Chung-kuo kuo-min-tang erh-shih-nien shih-chi*, p. 317. Ts'ui Shu-ch'in describes "the alliance with Soviet Russia" and "the toleration of Communists" as "a twin policy." See his "The Influence of the Canton-Moscow Entente upon Sun Yat-sen's Revolutionary Tactics," in *The Chinese Social and Political Science Review*, Vol. XX, No. 1 (April 1936), p. 120. Cf. Chung-gi Kwei (Ch'ung-chi Kuei), *The Kuomintang-Communist Struggle in China, 1922–1949* (The Hague, 1970), pp. 8–9.
101. Wang Ching-wei, "Wu-han fen-Kung chih ching-kuo," a speech delivered in Canton on November 5, 1927, included in KMWH, Vol. XVI, p. 2854; and Chang, *The Rise of the Chinese Communist Party*, p. 260.
102. C. Martin Wilbur, "Sun Yat-sen and Soviet Russia, 1922–1924" (preliminary report to University Seminar on Modern East Asia: China, Columbia University, March 10, 1965), p. 8; and Chang Chi's speech on September 21, 1941, included in Chang, *Chang P'u-ch'uan hsien-sheng ch'uan-chi*, p. 195.
103. Quoted in Whiting, *Soviet Policies in China*, p. 201.
104. For the text of the declaration, read Woodhead (ed.), *The China Year Book*, 1924–5, p. 863.
105. See his remarks in "T'an-ho Kung-ch'an-tang liang ta yao-an," p. 312.

Chapter 2: Soviet Russia and Chinese Nationalism in the 1920s

1. See Voitinsky's own account in *Pravda*, March 15, 1925, p. 2.
2. John Hart, "Mr. Joffe and the Failure of the Chinese-Russian Negotiations," *China Weekly Review*, hereafter cited as CWR, January 27, 1923, p. 340.

3. Allen S. Whiting, *Soviet Policies in China, 1917–1924* (New York, 1954), pp. 78–86, *passim*.

4. Archives of the Military Section, cited in R. A. Mirovitskaya, "Pervoe desyatletie," in *Leninskaya politika SSSR v otnoshenii Kitaya* (Moscow, 1968), p. 26.

5. *Ibid.*

6. Home Office (Great Britain), File on Mikhail Markovich Borodin, #436.947/11.

7. M. Borodin, "Kto byl Mikhail Borodin," *Otchizna*, No. 8 (1971), p. 9.

8. V. V. Vishnyakova-Akimova, *Dva goda v vosstavshem Kitae, 1925–1927* (Moscow, 1965), p. 178.

9. Dan N. Jacobs, "Recent Russian Material on Soviet Advisers in China: 1923–1927," *The China Quarterly*, No. 41 (January–March, 1970), pp. 108–109.

10. A. I. Cherepanov, *Zapiski voennovo sovetnika v Kitae: Iz istorii pervoi grazhdanskoi revolutsionnoi voiny, 1924–1927* (Moscow, 1964), p. 14.

11. N. Mitarevsky, *World-wide Soviet Plots, as Disclosed by Hitherto Unpublished Documents Seized at the USSR Embassy in Peking* (Tientsin, 1927), pp. 130–31.

12. CWR, September 8, 1923; and September 23, 1923.

13. Cherepanov, *Zapiski voennovo sovetnika v Kitae*, pp. 35–37.

14. *Ibid.*, pp. 37–39.

15. M. F. Yur'ev, *Revolyutsiya 1925–1927 v Kitae* (Moscow, 1968), p. 157, and Cherepanov, *Zapiski voennovo sovetnika v Kitae*, pp. 40–41.

16. Yur'ev, *Revolyutsiya 1925–1927 v Kitae*, p. 158.

17. Lyon Sharman, *Sun Yat-sen, His Life and Its Meaning: A Critical Biography* (Hamden, 1965), p. 267.

18. T'ang Leang-li, *The Inner History of the Chinese Revolution* (New York, 1930), p. 165.

19. Sharman, *Sun Yat-sen*, p. 279.

20. Cherepanov, *Zapiski voennovo sovetnika v Kitae*, pp. 66–67.

21. Yur'ev, *Revolyutsiya 1925–1927 v Kitae*, p. 92.

22. Chang Kuo-t'ao, *The Rise of the Chinese Communist Party, 1921–1927: Volume One of the Autobiography of Chang Kuo-t'ao* (Lawrence, 1971), p. 426, and Yur'ev, *Revolyutsiya 1925–1927 v Kitae*, pp. 166–67.

23. *ibid.*, p. 168.

24. Nym Wales (pseud. of Helen Foster Snow), *Red Dust: Autobiographies of Chinese Communists* (Stanford, 1952), p. 28.

25. Lewis S. Gannett, "Bolshevism in China?" *Nation*, August 25, 1926.

26. Jean Chesneaux, *The Chinese Labor Movement, 1917–1927*, trans. by H. M. Wright (Stanford, 1968), pp. 291–92.

27. A. I. Cherepanov, *Severnyi pokhod natsional'no-revolyutsionnoi armii Kitaya* (Moscow, 1968), p. 26.

28. V. K. *Blyukher v Kitae, 1924–1927 gg.* (Moscow, 1970), pp. 40–41.

29. Yur'ev, *Revolyutsiya 1925–1927 v Kitae*, p. 314.

30. Chang, *The Rise of the Chinese Communist Party*, p. 509.

31. *Ibid.*, p. 512.

32. CWR, April 17, 1926.

33. A. Bulatsel, "Revolyutsionny plakat v grazhdanskoi voine Kitaya," *Novyi Vostok*, No. 12 (1926), pp. 197—200.

34. James C. Bowden, "Soviet Military Aid to Nationalist China, 1923—41," in Raymond Garthoff (ed.), *Sino-Soviet Military Relations* (New York, 1966), pp. 48—49.

35. S. Dalin, *Ocherki revolyutsii v Kitae* (Moscow-Leningrad, 1927), p. 45.

36. *Ibid.*, p. 149.

37. A. V. Blagodatov, *Zapiski o kitaiskoi revolyutsii, 1925—1927 gg.* (Moscow, 1970), p. 168.

38. *Peking Leader*, June 3, 1926, in the Huston Collection, Hoover Institution on War, Revolution and Peace, Stanford University.

Chapter 3: From Revolutionary Iconoclasm to National Revolution: Ch'en Tu-hsiu and the Chinese Communist Movement

1. Antonio Gramsci, *Prison Notebooks: Selections*, ed. by Quintin Hoare and Geoggrey N. Smith (London, 1971), p. 151 and *passim*.

2. For the number of members in the Chinese Communist Party during the 1920s, see James Harrison, *The Long March to Power: A History of Chinese Communist Party, 1921—72* (New York, 1972), pp. 5, 39, 52, 61, 64, 70, 119, 148, and 161.

3. Lin Yu-sheng, "The Crisis of Chinese Consciousness: Iconoclasm in the May Fourth Era" (unpublished Ph.D. dissertation, University of Chicago, 1970), *passim*.

4. Ssu-yü Teng and John K. Fairbank, *China's Response to the West* (New York, 1963), p. 240.

5. Richard C. Kagan, "Ch'en Tu-hsiu's Unfinished Autobiography," *The China Quarterly*, No. 50 (April/June 1972), p. 314.

6. Ch'en Tu-hsiu, "Wo chih ai-kuo chu-i," originally published in *Hsin ch'ing-nien*, October 1916; reprinted, with the first three lines missing, in *Tu-hsiu wen-ts'un* (Shanghai, 1926), Vol. I, pp. 85—94.

7. These statistics are derived from research by Sam Kupper of the University of Michigan, Ann Arbor.

8. Edward Friedman, "The Evolution of Early Revolutionary Parties in China as an Inheritance of the Chinese Communist Party" (paper delivered at the Connecticut Symposium on the Chinese Communist Movement, 1921—1971, at Storrs, Connecticut, March 25—27, 1971), p. 47. Cf. Friedman, *Backward toward Revolution: The Chinese Revolutionary Party* (Berkeley, 1974), p. 215. "Beyond Politics" as a translation of "cheng-yü" is borrowed from Friedman. During the conference in January 1974, when all the contributors of this volume met at Miami University, Professor Ssu-yü Teng suggested that "Extracurricular" might be a more appropriate name for the club.

9. Ch'en Tu-hsiu, "Ch'ao-hsien tu-li yün-tung chih kan-hsiang," in *Tu-hsiu wen-ts'un*, Vol. II, pp. 607—608. Originally published in *Hsin ch'ing-nien*, March 22, 1919.

208   China in the 1920s

10. Ch'en Tu-hsiu, "Tsao-kuo lun," in Hsiang-tao chou-pao, No. 2 (September 20, 1922), pp. 9–10. Cf. Sze-shun and Chün-yu, "Tu Tu-hsiu chün 'Tsao-kuo lun' te i-wen," in ibid., No. 4 (October 4, 1922), pp. 34–36.

11. Ch'en Tu-hsiu, "T'an cheng-chih," in Tu-hsiu wen-ts'un, Vol. I, pp. 541–56. Originally in Hsin ch'ing-nien, September 1, 1920.

12. Maurice Meisner, Li Ta-chao and the Origins of Marxism in China (Cambridge, 1967), p. 118.

13. Ch'en Tu-hsiu, "Min-chu-tang yü Kung-ch'an tang," in Tu-hsiu wen-ts'un, Vol. II, p. 110.

14. Ch'en Kung-po, The Communist Movement in China: An Essay Written in 1924, ed. with an introduction by C. Martin Wilbur (New York, 1960), p. 105.

15. V. I. Lenin, "Better Fewer, But Better," a speech given in March 1923, cited in Robert V. Daniels (ed.), A Documentary History of Communism (New York, 1960), p. 233.

16. Warren Lerner, Karl Radek: The Last Internationalist (Stanford, 1970), pp. 96ff.

17. Cited in Branko Lazitch and Milorad Drachkovitch, Lenin and the Comintern (Stanford, 1972), p. 386.

18. Herbert P. Bix, "Japanese Imperialism and the Manchurian Economy, 1900–31," in The China Quarterly, No. 51, p. 443.

19. Ch'en, The Communist Movement in China, p. 115.

20. Julie Lien-ying How, "Ch'en Tu-hsiu's Leadership of the Chinese Communist Party: On the Kuomintang Issue, 1922–1924" (paper delivered at the Connecticut Symposium on the Chinese Communist Movement, 1921–1971, at Storrs, Connecticut, March 25–27, 1971).

21. Chih Yü-ju, "The Political Thought of Ch'en Tu-hsiu" (unpublished Ph.D. dissertation, Indiana University, 1965), p. 70.

22. Hsüeh Chün-tu, "Chang Kuo-t'ao and the Chinese Communist Movement," in Hsüeh Chün-tu (ed.), Revolutionary Leaders of Modern China (New York, 1971), p. 453.

23. See Ch'en Tu-hsiu's three letters on the Chinese Eastern Railway incident, in his Chung-kuo ke-ming yü chi-hui chu-i (Shanghai, 1929), pp. 67–70, 71–85, and 86–118. It was this controversy that precipitated his expulsion from the Chinese Communist Party and his adoption of Trotskyism. Ironically, Trotsky sided with Stalin on this issue.

24. Richard C. Kagan, "The Comintern, the 29 Bolsheviks, and the Alumni of Sun Yat-sen University," in International Review of History and Political Science, Vol. XI, No. 1 (February 1974), pp. 79–90.

25. In the August 7 conference, the Chinese Communist Party declared that two of its four goals should be the "complete liberation from 'the oppression of foreign capital'; and the creation of a national market by uniting the country and overthrowing militarism." See Harrison, The Long March to Power, p. 127.

26. C. Martin Wilbur and Julie Lien-ying How (ed.), Documents on Communism, Nationalism and Soviet Advisers in China, 1918–1927 (New York, 1956), p. 63.

27. Hu Shih, "Kuo-chi te Chung-kuo," in *Hu Shih wen-ts'un* (Shanghai, 1926), Series II, Vol. III, pp. 128a–i. Originally published in *Nu-li chou-pao*, October 1, 1922.

28. Ch'en, *The Communist Movement in China*, p. 110 Cf. articles by Ts'ai Ho-sen and Chang Kuo-t'ao in *Hsiang-tao chou-pao*, No. 6 (October 18, 1922), pp. 45–51.

29. Ch'en, *The Communist Movement in China*, p. 109.

30. "Political Report of the Central Committee," in Wilbur and How (ed.), *Documents on Communism, Nationalism and Soviet Advisers*, p. 273.

31. Ch'en Tu-hsiu, "Tu-hsiu t'ung-chih tui Chung-tung-lu wen-t'i i-chien," in *Chung-kuo ke-ming yü chi-hui chu-i*, pp. 67–70.

32. Bill Dorrill, "The Fukien Rebellion and the CCP: A Case of Maoist Revisionism," in *The China Quarterly*, No. 37 (January/March 1969), pp. 31–53; and Richard C. Kagan, "Ch'en Tu-hsiu and the Chinese Trotskyist Movement" (unpublished Ph.D. dissertation, University of Pennsylvania, 1969).

33. Helene Carrere d'Encausse and Stuart Schram (ed.), *Marxism and Asia* (London, 1969), pp. 210–11.

34. Ch'en Tu-hsiu, "I-ho-ch'uan cheng-fu le yang-jen," in *Tu-hsiu wen-ts'un*, Vol. II, pp. 1–2.

35. *Hsiang-tao chou-pao*, No. 81 (September 3, 1924), pp. 645–56.

36. D'Encausse and Schram (ed.), *Marxism and Asia*, pp. 223–24; and *Hsiang-tao chou-pao*, No. 81, pp. 645–46.

Chapter 4: Training and Indoctrination at the Whampoa Academy

1. See, for example, Richard B. Landis, "Institutional Trends at the Whampoa Military School: 1924–1926" (unpublished Ph.D. dissertation, University of Washington, Seattle, 1969); and Roderick L. MacFarquhar, "The Whampoa Military Academy," *Papers on China* (Harvard University), Vol. IX (1955), pp. 146–72.

2. Fook-lam Gilbert Chan, "Liao Chung-k'ai (1878–1925): The Career of a Chinese Revolutionary," *Essays on Chinese Studies Presented to Professor Lo Hsiang-lin on His Retirement from the Chair of Chinese, University of Hong Kong* (Hong Kong, 1970), pp. 319–48.

3. The following summary of the red command school system is derived from Dimitrii Fedotoff-White, *The Growth of the Red Army* (Princeton, 1944), pp. 56–62; and John Erickson, *The Soviet High Command: A Military-Political History, 1918–1941* (London, 1962), pp. 32–33.

4. Fedotoff-White, *The Growth of the Red Army*, p. 59.

5. Chiang Kai-shek's *San-nien-lai te kuo-min ke-ming* (Shanghai, 1929) enumerates the chronology of the main school and its branch classes (pp. 151–55). Each training cycle lasted for six months. A formal recruit, or preparatory, session preceded the opening of the third, fourth, and fifth classes. See Landis, "Institutional Trend at the Whampoa Military School," p. 37. The branch in Ch'aochou was the only one to open prior to January 12, 1926, when the name of the parent school was changed to Central Military Academy.

6. This figure is based on Chung-yang lu-chün chün-kuan hsüeh-hsiao, *Chung-yang lu-chün chün-kuan hsüeh-hsiao shih-kao* (Nanking, 1936), Vol. IV, pp. 1b–92a; and Chung-yang lu-chün chün-kuan hsüeh-hsiao, *Chung-yang lu-chün chün-kuan hsüeh-hsiao te shih-san ch'i t'ung-hsüeh lu* (T'ung-liang, 1938), pp. 37–77. Slight differences in number per class between the two sources probably reflect problems in including Communists or suspected Communists.

7. See Landis, "Institutional Trends at the Whampoa Military School," for the rural bias and social-economic class origins of the graduates (pp. 10–11); the provenance (pp. 29 and 56); and the recruitment of cadets (chapters II and III).

8. On the development of screening and testing procedures for the first four classes, see *ibid.*, pp. 27–40.

9. The question of differential standards for admission and testing at Whampoa is discussed in *ibid.*, pp. 33 and 38.

10. *Ibid.*, pp. 170–92.

11. *Ibid.*, pp. 23–26.

12. Chiang's addresses to the students are included in Kuo-min ke-ming-chün chung-yang chün-shih cheng-chih hsüeh-hsiao, *Huang-p'u ts'ung-shu* (Shanghai, 1928), hereafter cited as HPTS.

13. Landis, "Institutional Trends at the Whampoa Military School," pp. 105–14.

14. Author's interviews with General Leng Hsin (retired) in Taipei on August 5 and 12, 1966.

15. On this Chiang-Liao relationship, see Richard B. Landis, "The Development of Chiang Kai-shek's Influence on the Whampoa Cadets" (paper delivered at the Western Conference, Association for Asian Studies, San Diego, 1971). Liao's correspondence with Chiang in March 1924 is included in *Liao Chung-k'ai chi* (Peking, 1963), pp. 128 and 130.

16. For Liao's three lectures to the first class, see *ibid.*, pp. 157–64. His lectures on imperialism appear in pp. 204–23.

17. HPTS, Vol. I, p. 131.

18. *Ibid.*, Vol. II, pp. 52–54, 61–66.

19. *Ibid.*, Vol. II, pp. 118–26, 127–33, 134–40, and 141–48.

20. *Ibid.*, Vol. I, pp. 13–20, 39–43, and 46–54.

21. *Ibid.*, Vol. I, pp. 14–15, and 47; Vol. II, p. 66.

22. *Ibid.*, Vol. I, pp. 20–24, *passim*.

23. *Ibid.*, Vol. I, pp. 13, 31–35, 83–87, and 155–67; and Vol. II, pp. 63–64.

24. *Ibid.*, Vol. I, pp. 31, 43–46, 77–83, and 140–48.

25. *Ibid.*, Vol. I, pp. 68–77, 83–87, 88–94, and 94–103; Vol. II, pp. 52–54, 61–66, 127–33, and 141–48.

26. *Ibid.*, Vol. I, pp. 35–38.

27. *Ibid.*, Vol. I, pp. 182–83.

28. *Ibid.*, Vol. I, pp. 35–36.

29. *Ibid.*, Vol. I, pp. 34–36, 45–46.

30. *Ibid.*, Vol. I, pp. 20–24, *passim*, and 27–30; Vol. II, 141–42.

31. *Ibid.*, Vol. I, pp. 43–44, 54–62.

32. *Ibid.*, Vol. I, p. 76.
33. *Ibid.*, Vol. II, p. 139.
34. *Ibid.*, Vol. I, p. 95.
35. *Ibid.*, Vol. I, pp. 88–92.
36. *Ibid.*, Vol. I, p. 111.
37. *Ibid.*, Vol. I, pp. 184–85.
38. *Ibid.*, Vol. I, pp. 28–29, 57.
39. *Ibid.*, Vol. I, p. 124.
40. *Ibid.*, Vol. I, p. 108.
41. *Ibid.*, Vol. I, p. 109; and Vol. II, p. 120.
42. *Ibid.*, Vol. I, pp. 109–10, 115–16, and 183–84; Vol. II, pp. 120, and 130–31.
43. *Ibid.*, Vol. I, pp. 83–84.
44. *Ibid.*, Vol. I, p. 186.
45. *Ibid.*, Vol. I, pp. 110–14.
46. *Ibid.*, Vol. I, pp. 96–97; and Vol. II, pp. 54–55, 128.
47. *Ibid.*, Vol. I, p. 76.
48. *Ibid.*, Vol. I, pp. 63–68, 82, 126–30, 142, 159, and 167.
49. *Ibid.*, Vol. I, pp. 116–17, and 159.
50. *Ibid.*, Vol. I, pp. 88–89; and Vol. II, p. 141.
51. *Ibid.*, Vol. I, pp. 64, and 188–96.
52. *Ibid.*, Vol. I, pp. 193–94.
53. *Ibid.*; the "appendix" of the book includes the text of the "Revolutionary Army's Law of Collective Responsibility" (pp. 5–7). The concluding section is entitled, "The Text of the Regulations on Collective Responsibility." Cf. Frederick F. Liu, *A Military History of Modern China, 1924–1949* (Princeton, 1956), p. 13.
54. HPTS, Vol. I, pp. 64–65.
55. *Ibid.*, Vol. I, p. 86.
56. *Ibid.*, Vol. II, p. 63.
57. *Ibid.*, Vol. II, p. 143.
58. *Ibid.*, Vol. I, p. 110.
59. *Ibid.*, Vol. I, p. 143.
60. *Ibid.*, Vol. I, pp. 142–43.
61. *Ibid.*, Vol. I, pp. 182–83, and 185.
62. *Ibid.*, Vol. I, p. 183.
63. Liu, *A Military History of Modern China*, pp. 58–59.
64. HPTS, Vol. I, p. 183.
65. *Ibid.*, Vol. I, pp. 164–67.
66. Interviews with Leng Hsin in August 1966.
67. HPTS, Vol. I, pp. 127, and 129.
68. *Ibid.*, Vol. I, p. 138.
69. *Ibid.*, Vol. II, p. 52.
70. *Ibid.*, Vol. II, p. 65.
71. *Ibid.*, Vol. II, pp. 125–26.
72. *Ibid.*, Vol. II, pp. 139, and 144–45.
73. *Ibid.*, Vol. II, pp. 139, and 146.

Chapter 5: Nationalism and Revolution: The Nature and Causes of Student Activism in the 1920s

1. On the student movement of modern China, see Wang Tsi-chang, *The Youth Movement in China: Some Aspects of Chinese Civilization* (New York, 1927); Kiang Wen-han, *The Ideological Background of the Chinese Student Movement* (New York, 1948); and John Israel, *Student Nationalism in China, 1927–37* (Stanford, 1966). See also Chow Tse-tsung, *The May Fourth Movement: Intellectual Revolution in Modern China* (Cambridge, 1960); and Benjamin I. Schwartz (ed.), *Reflections on the May Fourth Movement: A Symposium* (Cambridge, 1972). Various aspects of student activism are also discussed in Ka-che Yip, "The Anti-Christian Movement in China, 1922–1927, With Special Reference to the Experience of the Protestant Missions" (unpublished Ph.D. dissertation, Columbia University, 1970); Doreen H. Woo, "Chinese Student Attitudes in Peking, 1925: A Case Study" (unpublished M.A. thesis, Columbia University, 1970); and Thomas A. Creamer, "Hsüeh-yün: Shanghai's Students and the May Thirtieth Movement" (unpublished M.A. thesis, University of Virginia, 1975).

2. See Israel, *Student Nationalism in China*; and my article "Education and Political Socialization in Kuomintang China: *San-min chu-i* Education," in a forthcoming book, F. Gilbert Chan (ed.), *China at the Crossroads, 1927–1949: Republicanism versus Communism*, to be published by New Viewpoints.

3. For a provocative analysis of totalistic iconoclasm in the May Fourth period, see Lin Yu-sheng, "Radical Iconoclasm in the May Fourth Period and the Future of Chinese Liberalism," in Schwartz (ed.), *Reflections on the May Fourth Movement*, pp. 23–58.

4. Talcott Parsons, "Youth in the Context of American Society," *Daedalus* (Winter 1962), pp. 97–123; and S. N. Eisenstadt, *From Generation to Generation: Age Groups and Social Structure* (Glencoe, 1956). Richard Flacks discusses the application of the Parsons-Eisenstadt hypothesis to both developing and advanced industrial societies in his article, "Social and Cultural Meanings of Student Revolt," in Edward E. Sampson and Harold A. Korn (ed.), *Student Activism and Protest* (San Francisco, 1970), pp. 118–41.

5. Korn (ed.), *Student Activism and Protest*, p. 122.

6. Schwartz (ed.), *Reflections on the May Fourth Movement*, p. 4. In his introductory essay, Schwartz stresses the shift between the first two generations. My focus in this chapter, however, is on the differences between the "middle generation" and the student activists of the 1920s. Cf. Henry Dewit Smith II, *Japan's First Student Radicals* (Cambridge, 1972), pp. viii–xiii.

7. For an important study of the process of radicalization of youth, see Kenneth Keniston, *Young Radicals: Notes on Committed Youth* (New York, 1968).

8. Schwartz (ed.), *Reflections on the May Fourth Movement*, p. 7.

9. "Hsüeh-sheng ho ke-ming," *Pei-ching hsüeh-sheng lien-ho-hui jih-k'an*, February 1923. Quoted in *Wu-ssu shih-ch'i ch'i-k'an chieh-shao* (Peking, 1958–1959), Vol. II, p. 273.

10. Lo Hsiang-lin, "Ch'ing-nien ch'iu-hsüeh yü chiu-kuo yün-tung," in *Hsüeh-sheng tsa-chih*, January 1926, p. 14. See also T'ung Chu, "Hsien-tai Chung-kuo chung-hsüeh-sheng ying yu te tse-jen," *ibid.*, December 1926, pp. 72–73.

11. See, for instance, the educational expense for various schools as listed in Chu Ching-nung (ed.), *Chiao-yü ta tz'u-shu* (Taipei, 1964), pp. 346, 664–65, 971–72, 975–77, and 1510.

12. T'ao Hsi-sheng, *Ch'ao-liu yü tien-ti* (Taipei, 1964), pp. 63–64; and Jean Chesneaux, *The Chinese Labor Movement, 1919–1927* (Stanford, 1968), pp. 97–98. Also, Y. C. Wang, *Chinese Intellectuals and the West, 1872–1949* (Chapel Hill, 1966), p. 183.

13. R. T. Tawney, *Land and Labor in China* (Boston, 1966), pp. 69–70.

14. According to Chow Tse-tsung, only about 3 percent of the Chinese population had received some form of the new education in 1919. See Chow, *The May Fourth Movement*, pp. 379–80. The exclusiveness of education in both the middle schools and colleges persisted into the 1930s. See Olga Lang, *Chinese Family and Society* (New Haven, 1950), pp. 72 and 365.

15. Israel, "Reflections on the Modern Chinese Student Movement," in *Daedalus* (Winter 1968), p. 239.

16. For a discussion of the process of social mobilization and differentiation, see S. N. Eisenstadt, *Modernization: Protest and Change* (Englewood Cliffs, N. J., 1966), pp. 2–19.

17. Students in these associations often insisted on a puritanical life-style. For example, members of one association vowed to abstain from drinking, gambling, visiting brothels, and having concubines and maids. See *Hsüeh-sheng tsa-chih*, June 1924, p. 119.

18. Wang, *Chinese Intellectuals and the West*, pp. 365–67. The number of colleges in Peking was 40. The college student population in Peking and Shanghai was 15,440 and 3,643 respectively.

19. For a detailed analysis of educational funds in modern China, see Ch'eng Ch'i-pao, "Chung-kuo chiao-yü ching-fei kang-yao," in *Hsin chiao-yü*, September 1924, pp. 1–10.

20. Ts'ao Nien-mei, "Ts'ung shih-nien lai hsüeh-sheng huo-tung li so-chien te hsüeh-hsiao tsui-kuo," *Hsüeh-sheng tsa-chih*, January 1923, pp. 5–6; and "Ts'an-yü hsiao-wu yün-tung," *Chung-kuo ch'ing-nien*, September 1925, pp. 632–37.

21. Yang Chung-ming, "Min-kuo shih-i-nien chih hsüeh-ch'ao," *Hsin chiao-yü*, February 1923, pp. 295–312.

22. Ts'ao, "Ts'ung shih-nien lai hsüeh-sheng huo-tung," pp. 1–8; and "Hsüeh-sheng yü hsüeh-ch'ao," in *Hsüeh-sheng tsa-chih*, February 1923, pp. 1–11.

23. See, for instance, Hsiung Pao-feng, "Hsüeh-sheng yü cheng-chih," *ibid.*, September 1923, pp. 1–4; and Ch'en Wei-jen, "Hsien-tsai hsüeh-sheng

so-shou yü cheng-chih ho ching-chi te ying-hsiang chi ch'i chieh-chüeh feng-fa," *ibid.*, August 1923, pp. 1–4.

24. See Ch'en, "Hsien-tsai hsüeh-sheng," pp. 1–4; Yün Tai-ying, "Hsüeh-sheng yü min-ch'uan yün-tung," *Hsüeh-sheng tsa-chih*, May 1923, pp. 2–4; and Hsiung, "Hsüeh-sheng yü cheng-chih," pp. 1–4.

25. Shih-hsün, "Wu-san hou i-nien-lai chih Chung-kuo hsüeh-sheng yün-tung," in *Chung-kuo hsüeh-sheng*, May 1926, pp. 230–38; Sung-yu, "Wu-ssu i-lai Chung-kuo hsüeh-sheng sheng-huo chih tsung-chieh," *Hsüeh-sheng tsa-chih*, January 1930, pp. 11–19; Yang Chia-ming, *Min-kuo shih-wu-nien Chung-kuo hsüeh-sheng yün-tung k'ai-k'uang* (Shanghai, 1927); Tai-ying, "Yu-pei shu-chia te hsiang-ts'un yün-tung—'tao min-chien ch'u.' " *Chung-kuo ch'ing-nien*, May 1924, p. 4; Chou Chün, "Tao min-chien ch'u te i-ko ch'iao-liang," *Hsüeh-sheng tsa-chih*, February 1925, pp. 19–21. Cf. Chesneaux, *The Chinese Labor Movement, passim.*

26. The National Student Association laid down plans for the anti-imperialist movement in both its sixth and seventh national congresses, held in August 1924 and July 1925 respectively. See *Chung-kuo ch'ing-nien*, August 1924, pp. 1–7; and *Hsüeh-sheng tsa-chih*, August 1925, pp. 102–104.

27. For a detailed account of the anti-Christian movement, see Yip, "The Anti-Christian Movement in China."

28. L. Wieger, *Chine Moderne* (Hien-hien), Vol. V (1925), pp. 37–38.

29. Bianco, *Origins of the Chinese Revolution, 1915–1949* (Stanford, 1971), pp. 50–51.

30. Ka-che Yip, "The Chinese Student Movement, 1920–1928: A Preliminary Study," in *The Montclair Journal of Social Sciences and Humanities*, Vol. III, No. 1 (spring 1974), pp. 42–54.

31. Pinner, "Students—A Marginal Elite in Politics," *The Annals of the American Academy of Political and Social Science*, May 1971, p. 133.

32. *Chine Moderne*, Vol. IV (1924), pp. 233–34.

33. *Wu-ssu shih-ch'i ch'i-k'an chieh-shao*, Vol. II, p. 263; and Tsou Lu, *Chung-kuo kuo-min-tang shih-kao* (Taipei, 1965), Vol. I, p. 458, n. 21.

34. Ling-kuang, "Wo-pei ch'ing-nien te jen-wu—ta ke-ming chi-ch'u," *Tu-li ch'ing-nien*, August 1925, pp. 10–12.

35. Quoted in P. Cavendish, "Anti-imperialism in the Kuomintang, 1923–8," in Jerome Ch'en and Nicholas Tarling (ed.), *Studies in the Social History of China and Southeast Asia* (London, 1970), p. 51.

36. Lin Chung-ta, "T'ai-p'ing-yang shih-tai chih Chung-kuo hsüeh-sheng te shih-ming," *Hsüeh-sheng tsa-chih*, March 1930, p. 12.

Chapter 6: The Military and Nationalism:
The Political Thinking of Wu P'ei-fu

1. Kohn, *Nationalism: Its Meaning and History* (New York, 1971), p. 9. See also Louis Snyder, *The New Nationalism* (New York, 1968); Karl W.

Deutsch, *Nationalism and Its Alternatives* (New York, 1969); Karl W. Deutsch, *Nationalism and Social Communication: An Inquiry into the Foundations of Nationality* (Cambridge, 1972); Elie Kedourie, *Nationalism* (London, 1971); and Yehoshua Arieli, *Individualism and Nationalism in American Ideology* (Baltimore, 1966).

2. For nationalism in China, see James P. Harrison, *Modern Chinese Nationalism* (New York, 1970); and Chalmers A. Johnson, *Peasant Nationalism and Communist Power: The Emergence of Revolutionary China* (Stanford, 1962).

3. Donald W. Treadgold, *The West in Russia and China: Volume II, China 1582–1949* (New York, 1973), p. 88.

4. Joseph R. Levenson, *Confucian China and Its Modern Fate: A Trilogy* (Berkeley, 1968), Vol. I, pp. 95–108.

5. Franklin W. Houn, *Central Government of China, 1912–1928* (Madison, 1959), pp. 147–50.

6. Frederic Wakeman, Jr., *Strangers at the Gate: Social Disorder in South China, 1839–1961* (Berkeley, 1966), pp. 11–21 and *passim*.

7. Chester C. Tan, *The Boxer Catastrophe* (New York, 1971), pp. 35–55 and *passim*.

8. Chow Tse-tsung, *The May Fourth Movement: Intellectual Revolution in Modern China* (Cambridge, 1960), pp. 84–116.

9. Louis L. Snyder classifies them as traditionalist nationalism, westernized nationalism, and Communist nationalism. It is more appropriate to use the term "liberal nationalism" than "westernized nationalism," since Communism also came from the west. See Snyder, *The New Nationalism*, pp. 161–69.

10. Chow, *The May Fourth Movement*, pp. 61–72; and Levenson, *Confucian China and Its Modern Fate*, Vol. I, pp. 95–116.

11. Chow, *The May Fourth Movement*, pp. 61–72; and Levenson, *Confucian China and Its Modern Fate*, Vol. I, pp. 125–133.

12. Chester Tan, *Chinese Political Thought in the Twentieth Century* (New York, 1971), pp. 66–110; and Maurice Meisner, *Li Ta-chao and the Origins of Chinese Communism* (Cambridge, 1967), pp. 144–46, 151–54, 188–94, 263–64, and *passim*.

13. Dun J. Li, *The Ageless Chinese: A History* (New York, 1965), pp. 442–48; and John K. Fairbank, Edwin O. Reischauer, and Albert M. Craig, *East Asia: The Modern Transformation* (Boston, 1965), pp. 649–58. It is interesting to note that the image of the military is different elsewhere. In the west and in Japan, the militarists are considered patriotic and nationalistic, since national defense is their primary duty and the security of the state is the main concern of their profession. In some areas, such as Latin America and Japan, the militarists sometimes turn into "superpatriots" and "ultranationalists," growing on the national ideology and justifying their actions in the interests of "national sovereignty and integrity." According to Bengt Abrahamson, nationalism is an axiom of military ideology. See Abrahamson, *Military Professionalization and Political Power* (Beverly Hills, 1972), pp. 80–85. Cf. Quincy Wright, *A*

Study of War (Chicago, 1965), pp. 212–25; John J. Johnson, *The Military and Society in Latin America* (Stanford, 1964), pp. 134–52; and D. M. Brown, *Nationalism in Japan: An Introductory Historical Analysis* (Berkeley, 1955).

14. For a biographical study of Wu, see Odoric Ying-kwong Wou, "Militarism in Modern China: As Exemplified in the Career of Wu P'ei-fu, 1916–1928" (unpublished Ph.D. dissertation, Columbia University, 1970).

15. Wu P'ei-fu, *Wu P'ei-fu hsien-sheng chi* (Taipei, 1960), pp. 268–69, 282.

16. Liu Feng-han, *Hsin-chien lu-chün* (Taipei, 1967), p. 184.

17. Yüan Shih-k'ai, *Hsün-lien ts'ao-fa hsiang-hsi t'u-shuo* (Taipei, 1966), Chapter I, pp. 6a–6b.

18. Liu, *Hsin-chien lu-chün*, pp. 183–84, 189–90.

19. *Ibid.*, p. 190; and Yüan, *Hsün-lien ts'ao-fa hsiang-hsi t'u-shuo*, Chapter I, p. 1.

20. Wu P'ei-fu, *Wu P'ei-fu cheng-shu* (Shanghai, 1922), pp. 1b and 10a.

21. *Ibid.*, pp. 5a, 10a–b, and 16a.

22. Li Chien-nung, *The Political History of China, 1840–1928*, trans. by Ssu-yü Teng and Jeremy Ingalls (Stanford, 1967).

23. Winston Hsieh, "The Ideas and Ideals of a Warlord: Ch'en Chiung-ming (1878–1933)," in *Papers on China* (Harvard University), Vol. XVI (1962), pp. 198–252.

24. Wu, *Wu P'ei-fu hsien-sheng chi*, p. 284; and *North China Herald*, November 12, 1921, p. 431.

25. Wu, *Wu P'ei-fu hsien-sheng chi*, p. 348.

26. *Ibid.*, pp. 351–53.

27. *North China Herald*, August 14, 1920, p. 413.

28. Wu's conversation with ex-Premier Chang Shao-tseng in mid-February 1924, in Wu, *Wu P'ei-fu hsien-sheng chi*, pp. 286–87.

29. Okano Masujirō, *Go Hai-fu* (Tokyo, 1939), p. 1269; and Wu, *Wu P'ei-fu hsien-sheng chi*, pp. 306–307.

30. T'ao Chü-yin, *Wu P'ei-fu chiang-chün chuan* (Shanghai, 1941), pp. 30–31.

31. Wu, *Wu P'ei-fu hsien-sheng chi*, p. 178.

32. Wu's poem, "Shu-kan" ("Painful Recollection after Reading"), in *ibid.*, p. 178.

33. Wu's poems, "Huai-ku" ("Memory of the Past"), in *ibid.*, p. 177. The first poem is on Yüeh Fei, and the second one on Lin Tse-hsü.

34. *Ibid.*, p. 408.

35. *Ibid.*, p. 144. Cf. *North China Herald*, February 28, 1925, p. 334; and *Papers Relating to the Foreign Relations of the United States, 1924* (Washington, 1955), Vol. I, p. 408.

36. *North China Herald*, September 4, 1920, p. 600.

37. Wu, *Wu P'ei-fu hsien-sheng chi*, pp. 343–44.

38. Li, *The Political History of China*, p. 411.

39. *Wu-ssu ai-kuo yün-tung tzu-liao*, ed. by Chung-kuo k'o-hsüeh li-shih yen-chiu-so ti-san-so chin-tai-shih tzu-liao pien-chi-tsu (Peking, 1959), Vol. II, p. 273.

40. T'ao, *Wu P'ei-fu chiang-chün chuan*, p. 31; and *Millard's Review of the Far East*, August 14, 1920, p. 572.
41. "Members of Old Parliament Join in Chorus," *China Illustrated Review*, January 14, 1922, p. 5.
42. Speech to the middle school in Kuang-an county, Szechwan, in the summer of 1931, quoted in Wu P'ei-fu, *P'eng-lai Wu-kung chiang-hua lu* (Peking, 1934), p. 10a.
43. *Ibid.*
44. *Ibid.*, pp. 10a-b.
45. *Ibid.*, p. 6a.
46. Speech given to middle school in Kuang-an county, Szechwan, in *ibid.*, pp. 8a–10a.
47. Speech to the Wu clan in Kuang-an county, Szechwan, in the summer of 1931, in *ibid.*, p. 17a.
48. Speech delivered at the graduation ceremony of the Military School for the Eighth Division at Fengchieh county, Szechwan, in the autumn of 1927, in *ibid.*, pp. 1a–3a.
49. Wu, *Wu P'ei-fu hsien-sheng chi*, pp. 275–83, 285; and Okano, *Go Hai-fu*, p. 327.
50. Wu, *Wu P'ei-fu hsien-sheng chi*, pp. 285–87.
51. "The Malady of China," in *The Round Table*, December 1922; Geo Broson Rea, "The Tail of the Dog," *Far Eastern Review*, Vol. XIX, No. 6 (June 1923), pp. 367–72.
52. See Ts'ai Ho-sen's essay on reunification, foreign loan, and the Kuomintang in *Hsiang-tao chou-pao*, No. 1 (September 1922), pp. 4–6.

Chapter 7: Provincialism within the Chinese National Revolution: The Case of Chekiang, 1926-1927

1. Harold R. Isaacs, *The Tragedy of the Chinese Revolution* (Stanford, 1961), pp. 111–29 and *passim*.
2. Edwin S. Cunningham, American Consul General (Shanghai), "A Brief Historical Sketch of the Political History of the Chekiang Province since the Year 1911" (September 30, 1925), p. 11. The document is included in State Department, Diplomatic Post Records, Group 84, Vol. 1237 (Section 2, No. 10). See also *Chung-kuo kuan-shen jen-ming lu* (Tōkyō, 1918), p. 366; and *Min-kuo chün-fa ch'ü-hsien* (n.p., n.d.), pp. 195–97.
3. In his "Quarterly Report to the Foreign Office," April 31, 1925, H. F. H. Derry, British Consul General in Ningpo, claimed that Hsia had 5,000 armed police (Great Britain, Foreign Office records, FO 371/10919). This estimate was considerably lower than the 10,000 reported earlier by *North China Herald*, September 20, 1924, p. 452. According to Ch'en Pu-lei, *Kuo-min ke-ming-chün chan-shih* (Nanking, 1936), the number rose to 15,000 in 1926 (ch. 2, p. 9).
4. Ma Hsü-lun, *Wo tsai liu-shih-sui i-ch'ien* (Shanghai, 1947), p. 96. The author was a provincial Kuomintang member, who worked to gain Hsia's defection in 1926.

5. *Ibid.*; and *Chung-kuo kuan-shen jen-ming lu*, p. 230. See also Cunningham, "A Brief Historical Sketch," p. 11.

6. *Shen-pao*, November 9, 1926; Howard L. Boorman (ed.), *Biographical Dictionary of Republican China* (New York, 1967–1971), Vol. I, pp. 251–53; and *Biographical Sketches: Members of the 6th Kuomintang Central Executive Committee* (Yenan, 1945).

7. Jean Chesneaux, "The Federalist Movement in China, 1920–3," in Jack Gray (ed.), *Modern China's Search for a Political Form* (New York, 1969), p. 115.

8. British Minister (Peking) to Foreign Office, September 19, 1924 (FO 371/10244); and American Consul General (Nanking) to Secretary of State, November 1, 1924, in United States Department of State, *Records Relating to Internal Affairs of China, 1910–29* (hereafter cited as USDS), 893.00/5832.

9. United States Consul General (Shanghai) to Secretary of State, October 29, 1924, in USDS, 893.00/5801.

10. *North China Herald*, April 4, 1925, p. 2. Cunningham listed the leadership in his October 11 report of 1924, in USDS, 893.00/5720. Cf. *North China Herald*, October 18, 1924, p. 91.

11. *North China Daily News*, December 2, 1924; and *Shen-pao*, January 3, 1926.

12. United States Vice Consul (Nanking) to Minister MacMurray in Peking, October 21, 1925, in State Department, Diplomatic Post Records, Vol. 1237; and American Consul General (Nanking) to MacMurray, October 30, 1926, in USDS, 893.00/7913.

13. United States Consul General (Shanghai) to Secretary of State, January 26, 1926, in USDS, 893.00/7108.

14. For the text of the constitution, see *Tung-fang tsa-chih*, January 25, 1926.

15. *Tang-tai Chung-kuo ming-jen chih* (Shanghai, 1940), p. 365; and Cunningham's report of January 26, 1926, in USDS, 893.00/7108.

16. USDS, 893.00/7108.

17. *Hsin Chung-kuo jen-wu chih: Fen-sheng* (Hong Kong, 1930), p. 56; and *Shen-pao*, November 6, 1925.

18. *North China Herald*, June 5, 1926, p. 429.

19. United States Consul (Nanking) to Secretary of State, August 26, 1926, in USDS, 893.00/7715.

20. *Shen-pao*, January 26, 1926; June 14, 1926; and September 11, 1926.

21. Interview with Sun Fo in Yangmingshan, Taiwan, in 1966.

22. *Hong Kong Daily Press*, April 19 1926; and Ma, *Wo tsai liu-shih-sui i-ch'ien*, pp. 95–96.

23. State Department, Diplomatic Post Records, Group 84, Vol. 1237, Chekiang Civil War, 1925.

24. *Kuo-wen chou-pao*, September 19, 1926; *Hsin Chung-kuo jen-wu chih*, p. 272; and American Consul General in Nanking, October 30, 1926, in USDS, 893.00/7913.

25. *South China Morning Post*, September 10, 1926.

26. Report from Peking to Washington, April 7, 1926, in USDS, 893.00/7388;

and United States Consul General (Yünnan-fu) to Minister in Peking, September 8, 1926, *ibid.*, 893.00/7775.

27. *North China Herald*, October 23 and 30, 1926; *South China Morning Post*, October 21 and 28, 1926.
28. Report of American Consul General in Nanking to Secretary of State, October 15, 1926; and Ma, *Wo tsai liu-shih-sui i-ch'ien.* pp. 96–97, 110.
29. *Ti-i-tz'u kuo-nei ke-ming chan-cheng shih-ch'i te kung-jen yün-tung* (Peking, 1954), pp. 447–48; *South China Morning Post*, October 18 and 30, 1926; Cunningham to Secretary of State, October 21, 1926, USDS, 893.00/7835, and United States Consul in Nanking to the Peking Legation, October 25, 1926, *ibid.*, 893.00/7925.
30. *Shen-pao*, October 20, 1926.
31. *Ibid.*; and Kao Yin-tzu, *Chung-hua min-kuo ta-shih chi* (Taipei, 1957), p. 228.
32. Kao, *Chung-hua min-kuo ta-shih chi*, p. 228.
33. Cunningham to the Peking Legation, October 17, 1926, in USDS, 893.00/7755; Cunningham's report of October 21, 1926, *ibid.*, 893.00/7835; *Shen-pao*, October 20, 1926; *Min-kuo chün-fa ch'ü-hsien*, p. 199; and Boorman (ed.), *Biographical Dictionary of Republican China*, Vol. I, p. 252.
34. United States Consul (Nanking) to F. Mayer in the Legation, October 25, 1926, USDS, 893.00/7925.
35. *Hsien-tai shih-liao* (Shanghai, 1934), Vol. III, p. 172.
36. *Ibid.*; and British Consul in Shanghai to MacLeay in Peking, October 17, 1926 (FO 371/11660/425).
37. *Shen-pao*, October 22, 1926.
38. *Kuo-wen chou-pao*, October 31, 1926.
39. Cunningham to Secretary of State, October 21, 1926, in USDS, 893.00/7835.
40. *North China Daily News*, October 26, 1926; *Pei-fa chan-shih* (Taipei, 1959), Vol. II, pp. 597–98; and *Min-kuo chün-fa ch'ü-hsien*, pp. 201–202.
41. United States Consul General (Shanghai) to the Peking Legation, December 6, 1926, in State Department, Diplomatic Post Records, Group 84, Vol. 1237 (Chekiang).
42. *Kuo-wen chou-pao*, November 28, 1926.
43. *Ibid.*
44. *Shen-pao*, November 26, 1926.
45. *Kuo-wen chou-pao*, November 21, 1926.
46. *Shen-pao*, December 14, 1926.
47. *Kuo-wen chou-pao*, November 28, 1926; and United States Consul (Nanking) to Minister MacMurray, December 11, 1926, in USDS, 893.00/8032.
48. American Consul in Shanghai to Secretary of State, December 6, 1926, in USDS, 893.00/7990.
49. American Consul in Nanking to Minister MacMurray, December 15, 1926, *ibid.*, 893.00/8033.
50. *Kuo-wen chou-pao*, December 26, 1926; *North China Herald*, April 4, 1925.
51. *Kuo-wen chou-pao*, December 26, 1926.

52. *Ibid.*
53. Kao, *Chung-hua min-kuo ta-shih chi*, p. 236; United States Consul (Shanghai), December 6, 1926, in USDS, 893.00/7990.
54. Kao, *Chung-hua min-kuo ta-shih chi*, p. 236.
55. *Ibid.*, p. 237.
56. *North China Herald*, September 24, 1927, p. 520.
57. Ma, *Wo tsai liu-shih-sui i-ch'ien*, p. 111.
58. United States Navy Intelligence Report, August 19, 1927 (103-100.263), in USDS, 893.00/9522.
59. Lo Yü-t'ien, *Chün-fa i-wen* (Taipei, 1967).
60. Kao, *Chung-hua min-kuo ta-shih-chi*, p. 266.
61. *Pei-fa chan-shih*, Vol. III, p. 860.
62. *North China Herald*, September 24, 1927, p. 250.
63. *Ibid.*, September 24, 1927; October 15, 1927; December 17, 1927.
64. USDS, 893.00/7876.
65. Boorman (ed.), *Biographical Dictionary of Republican China*, Vol. I, p. 252.
66. Chesneaux, "The Federalist Movement in China," p. 134.
67. *Hsien-tai shih-liao*, Vol. III, pp. 26–28.

Chapter 8: Chiang Kai-shek's April 12th Coup of 1927

1. *Kuang-chou min-kuo jih-pao*, October 18, 1926.
2. In addition to Borodin, the group included Madame Sun Yat-sen, Eugene Ch'en, Sun Fo, T. V. Soong, and Hsü Ch'ien. They arrived in Nanchang on December 2. After a long talk between Chiang and Borodin three days later, a formal conference was held in Lushan on December 7. The group then proceeded to Wuhan and inaugurated the joint council on December 13. See Mao Ssu-ch'eng, *Min-kuo shih-wu-nien i-ch'ien chih Chiang Chieh-shih hsien-sheng* (n.p., n.d.; the editor's postscript is dated October 1936), Vol. XX, pp. 6–19; *Chiang Chieh-shih ch'uan-shu*, comp. by Tung-ya wu-wo-tzu (n.p., 1927), Pt. IV, pp. 36–37; and C. Martin Wilbur and Julie Lien-ying How (ed.), *Documents on Communism, Nationalism, and Soviet Advisers in China, 1918–1927* (New York, 1956), pp. 371–81.
3. The Chinese text of Chiang's interview with a reporter of the *Hankow Herald* in November 1926 appears in *Chiang Chieh-shih ch'uan-shu*, pp. 29–36.
4. See the essays by Tsou Ts'ui-fen and Yang Hsin-hua in *Hsien-tai shih-liao*, ed. by Hai-t'ien Publishing Company (Shanghai, 1934–1935), Vol. I, Pt. II, pp. 48–60. Li Tsung-jen claimed to have played a role in the mediation between Nanchang and Wuhan. See Yin-shih (pseud.), *Li-Chiang kuan-hsi yü Chung-kuo* (Hong Kong, 1954), pp. 25–26.
5. Chiang's speech on April 18, 1927, as quoted in Li Yün-han, *Ts'ung jung-Kung tao ch'ing-tang* (Taipei, 1966), Vol. II, pp. 536–37. Borodin delivered a speech in the April 18 banquet against personal dictatorship

and, by implication, Chiang. See "The Letter from Shanghai," by N. Nassonov, N. Fokine, and A. Albrecht, dated March 17, 1927, in Leon Trotsky, *Problems of the Chinese Revolution* (New York, 1932), pp. 397–432.

6. *Kuo-wen chou-pao*, Vol. IV, No. 16 (May 1, 1927), pp. 1–3; Lei Hsiao-ch'en, *Sa-nien tung-luan Chung-kuo* (Hong Kong, 1954), pp. 49—50.

7. According to Hollington Tong, Chiang's March 7 speech was his last effort to postpone the break with Wuhan. See Tong, *Chiang Kai-shek: Soldier and Statesman* (Shanghai, 1937), Vol. I, p. 145. For the Chinese text of the speech, see *Ch'ing-tang yün-tung*, ed. by Society for Advancement of Party Purification Movement (n.p., 1927), pp. 19–26. Ch'en Tu-hsiu responded in *Hsiang-tao chou-pao*, No. 192 (March 18, 1927) pp. 2073–75. Cf. *North China Herald*, April 2 and 9, 1927.

8. *Ch'en Kuo-fu hsien-sheng ch'uan-chi* (Hong Kong, 1952), Vol. V, pp. 70–75. Cf. Lei, *Sa-nien tung-luan Chung-kuo*, p. 64; and Chiang Yung-ching, *Bo-lo-t'ing yü Wu-han cheng-ch'uan* (Taipei, 1963), pp. 45–46.

9. Tien-wei Wu, "A Review of the Wuhan Debacle," *The Journal of Asian Studies*, Vol. XXIX, No. 1 (November 1969), p. 126.

10. "The Letter from Shanghai," p. 400; Lei Hsiao-ch'en's essay in *Hsien-tai shih-liao*, Vol. III, pp. 35–36; and Li Yün-han, *Ts'ung jung-Kung tao ch'ing-tang*, Vol. II, pp. 661–62. Cf. Chang Kuo-t'ao, "Wo ti hui-i," in *Ming-pao yüeh-k'an*, No. 20 (August 1967), p. 89; and Kuo Mo-jo, *Mo-jo wen-chi* (Peking, 1958), Vol. VIII, pp. 122–38.

11. For the opposition of the Soviet and Chinese Communists to Chiang's eastern campaign, see Wilbur and How (ed.), *Documents on Communism, Nationalism, and Soviet Advisers*, pp. 419 and 428; T. C. Woo, *The Kuomintang and the Future of the Chinese Revolution* (London, 1928), pp. 221–23; and *Ke-ming yü fan-ke-ming*, ed. by Lang Hsing-shih (Shanghai, 1928), p. 365.

12. In early March, two of Sun Ch'uan-fang's chief lieutenants, Ch'en T'iao-yüan and Wang P'u, defected to Chiang in Anhwei with their 40,000 men. This was followed by a change of flag of the navy of the Peking government in the Yangtze Valley under Yang Shu-chuang. For an American observation of the army of the northern warlords, see Barbara W. Tuchman, *Stilwell and the American Experience in China, 1911–45* (New York, 1971), pp. 107–10.

13. *Shen-pao* (Shanghai), April 17, 1927; Chiang, *Bo-lo-t'ing*, p. 115; and Li, *Ts'ung jung-Kung tao ch'ing-tang*, Vol. II, p. 500.

14. See Shih-ying's essays in *Hsiang-tao chou-pao*, No. 189 (February 28, 1927), pp. 2025–30, and No. 193 (April 6, 1927), pp. 2088–92; *Hsien-tai shih-liao*, Vol. III, Pt. II, pp. 170–86; *The China Press*, February 23, March 22 and 23, 1927; and *The New York Times*, March 23, 1927.

15. A Kuomintang Kiangsu Special Committee was established on September 4, 1926, with seven members: Ho Shao-ch'iu (Communist), Chang Jen-chieh (Kuomintang), Wu Chih-hui (Kuomintang), Ho Ch'eng-chun (military), Chu Chi-hsüan (Communist), Yeh Ch'u-ch'ang (Kuomintang), and Niu Yung-chien (Kuomintang). Among the Kuomintang members,

only Wu and Niu were responsible for the affairs in Shanghai. The strategy for the Communists to seize power in the city was based on Ch'u Ch'iu-pai's "Plan for the Shanghai Uprising." After the capture of the city, a convention of people's delegates was held to elect nineteen members for the reorganization of the provisional government of Shanghai. Among those elected, eight were Communists. The leading Kuomintang members, Pai Ch'ung-hsi and Niu Yung-chien, refused to participate. See *Hsiang-tao chou-pao*, No. 189 (February 28, 1927), pp. 2025–30; *Ch'ing-tang yün-tung*, pp. 252–69; Li, *Ts'ung jung-Kung tao ch'ing-tang*, Vol. II, p. 591; and Ch'u Ch'iu-pai, *Chung-kuo ke-ming chung chih cheng-lun wen-t'i* (n.p., 1928), pp. 197–200.

16. *Hsiang-tao chou-pao*, No. 189 (February 28, 1927), pp. 2025–30.

17. Great Britain, Public Record Office, F 653/F809/653/10; F 1809/F1908/156/10; and F 656/156/10.

18. *The China Press*, March 31, 1927; and *North China Herald*, April 2, 1927.

19. See the speeches delivered by Wang Shou-hua and Lo I-nung on April 6, 1927, in *Shen-pao*, April 7, 1927.

20. Pai, *Shih-liu nien ch'ing-tang te hui-ku* (n.p., 1932), p. 8; Yin-shih, *Li-Chiang kuan-hsi yü Chung-kuo*, p. 27.

21. *Ch'ing-tang shih-lu*, ed. by Chü Cheng (n.p., 1928), p. 383; and Li, *Ts'ung jung-Kung tao ch'ing-tang*, Vol. II, p. 612.

22. Huang Shao-hsiung, *Wu-shih hui-i* (Shanghai, 1945), Vol. I, pp. 175–77; and Pai Ch'ung-hsi, *Shih-liu nien ch'ing-tang te hui-ku*, p. 8. See also Ch'eng Ch'ien's report, as quoted in Chiang, *Bo-lo-t'ing*, p. 131; and Li, *Ts'ung jung-Kung tao ch'ing-tang*, Vol. II, p. 622.

23. The sum of 6 million yüan was reported in *Shen-pao*, April 16, 1927. According to *Hsiang-tao chou-pao*, No. 194 (May 1, 1927), a total of 15 million yüan was jointly provided by the imperialists and the Chinese bourgeoisie for the purpose of disarming the pickets of the workers (p. 2108). Cf. *China Weekly Review*, April 9, 1927; *The New York Times*, April 15, 1927; and Harold Isaacs, *The Tragedy of the Chinese Revolution* (Stanford, 1966), pp. 152–53, and 350. See also Great Britain, Public Record Office, F 4075/1530/10.

24. Shih-yi (pseud.), *Tu Yüeh-sheng wai-ch'uan* (Hong Kong, 1962), pp. 93–94; Y. C. Wang, "Tu Yüeh-sheng (1888–1915): A Tentative Political Biography," *The Journal of Asian Studies*, Vol. XXVI, No. 3 (May 1967), pp. 437–38; and Lu Ch'ung-p'eng's article on Yang Hu in *Ch'uan-chi wen-hsüeh*, Vol. XI, No. 4 (October 1967), p. 71.

25. J. Powell, *My Twenty-five Years in China* (New York, 1945), pp. 158–59; Chang Chün-ku, *Tu Yüeh-sheng ch'uan* (Taipei, 1967), Vol. I, pp. 332-33; and Pai, *Shih-liu nien ch'ing-tang te hui-ku*, p. 12.

26. *The New York Times*, March 30, 1927; Great Britain, Public Record Office, F 6378/210, and F 4013/F4051/1530/10. Cf. Akira Iriye, *After Imperialism: The Search for a New Order in the Far East, 1921–1931* (Cambridge, 1965), p. 139; and Russell D. Buhite, *Nelson T. Johnson and American Policy toward China, 1925–1941* (New York, 1968), pp. 31–32.

27. M. N. Roy, *Revolution and Counter-Revolution in China* (Calcutta, 1935), p. 520. See also Kuo Hua-lun, *Chung-kung shih-lun* (Taipei, 1969), Vol. I, p. 208. Chang Kuo-t'ao confirmed this in my interview with him on September 5, 1970.

28. Huang Hsu-ch'u's article in *Ch'un-ch'iu*, No. 253 (January 16, 1968), pp. 12–14; and Li, *Ts'ung jung-Kung tao ch'ing-tang*, Vol. II, pp. 615–16.

29. *Ke-ming wen-hsien*, comp. by Kuomintang Archives (Taipei, 1953–   ), Vol. XVII, pp. 3087–88; Chiang, *Bo-lo-t'ing*, p. 79.

30. *Kuo-wen chou-pao*, Vol. IV, No. 16 (May 1, 1927), p. 2; and *Ke-ming wen-hsien*, Vol. XVI, pp. 27–28. The English version appears in *The China Press*, April 5, 1927.

31. *Shen-pao*, April 6, 1927; *Ch'un-ch'iu*, January 16, 1968, p. 13; and *Kuo-wen chou-pao*, Vol. VI, No. 16 (May 1, 1927), pp. 23–28.

32. Quoted in *Ch'ing-tang yün-tung*, pp. 143–52.

33. Ch'en Tu-hsiu, "Kao ch'uan-tang t'ung-chih shu," dated December 10, 1929, on microfilm in the Hoover Institution at Stanford University.

34. Li, *Ts'ung jung-Kung tao ch'ing-tang*, Vol. II, p. 579; Chiang, *Bo-lo-t'ing*, p. 129; and Kuo, *Mo-jo wen-chi*, pp. 139, 150–51.

35. Chang Kuo-t'ao is the only source of this information. See *Ming-pao yüeh-k'an*, No. 22 (October 1967), p. 90. In his diatribe against Chang, Peng Shu-chih acquiesces in Chang's account, in *ibid.*, No. 30 (June 1968), pp. 13–22. The Soviet advisers then were reportedly plotting to murder Chiang. See *General Chiang Kai-shek and the Communist Crisis* (Shanghai, n.d.), p. 15. The rumor apparently originated from Captain Eugene Pick's *China in the Grip of the Red* (Shanghai, 1927). In my interview with Chang Kuo-t'ao on September 4, 1970, he rejected Pick's account as fabrication.

36. Li, *Ts'ung jung-Kung tao ch'ing-tang*, Vol. II, p. 624; and Chiang, *Bo-lo-t'ing*, p. 131.

37. *Shen-pao*, April 6, 1927; Chiang, *Bo-lo-t'ing*, pp. 131–32; and Li, *Ts'ung jung-Kung tao ch'ing-tang*, Vol. II, pp. 620 and 623.

38. *Ch'ing-tang yün-tung*, p. 204; and Li, *Ts'ung jung-Kung tao ch'ing-tang*, Vol. II, p. 593.

39. Benjamin I. Schwartz, *Chinese Communism and the Rise of Mao* (Cambridge, 1952), p. 60; and C. Martin Wilbur, "The Ashes of Defeat," *The China Quarterly*, No. 18 (April/June, 1964), p. 52.

40. *Shen-pao*, April 15, 1927; Li, *Ts'ung jung-Kung tao ch'ing-tang*, Vol. II, pp. 623–25; and Chiang, *Bo-lo-t'ing*, pp. 133–35.

41. *Shen-pao*, April 6 and 14, 1927; and Li, *Ts'ung jung-Kung tao ch'ing-tang*, Vol. II, pp. 648 and 654.

42. *Shen-pao*, April 6 and 15, 1927; Chang's memoirs in *Ming-pao yüeh-k'an* No. 20, p. 93.

43. *North China Herald*, April 9, 1927; Li, *Ts'ung jung-Kung tao ch'ing-tang*, Vol. II, p. 620; and Kuo, *Mo-jo wen-chi*, pp. 181, 184–85.

44. *Shen-pao*, April 14, 1927; and *Ke-ming wen-hsien*, Vol. XVI, pp. 2801–2806.

45. Chang, *Tu Yüeh-sheng ch'uan*, Vol. II, pp. 1–15; Shih-yi, *Tu Yüeh-sheng wai-ch'uan*, pp. 94–96; and Pai, *Shih-liu nien ch'ing-tang te hui-ku*, p. 12.

46. Sources vary as to the number of Tu Yüeh-sheng's workers who participated in the raids on April 12. See Chang, *Tu Yüeh-sheng ch'uan*, Vol. II, p. 25; and *North China Herald*, April 16, 1927.

47. *Shen-pao*, April 13, 1927; *North China Herald*, April 16, 1927; *Ti-i tz'u kuo-nei ke-ming chan-cheng shih-ch'i te kung-jen yün-tung* (Peking 1954), pp. 495–500; and Li Tien-min, *Chou En-lai* (Taipei, 1970), p. 86.

48. See Liu Ch'ih's memoirs in *Tzu-yu t'an*, Vol. XIII, No. 6 (June 1962), p. 43; and Pai, *Shih-liu nien ch'ing-tang te hui-ku*, p. 12. See also *Shen-pao*, April 13, 1927; and *North China Herald*, April 16, 1927.

49. *Shen-pao*, April 13, 1927; and *North China Herald*, April 16, 1927.

50. Pai, *Shih-liu nien ch'ing-tang te hui-ku*.

51. *Shen-pao*, April 13, 1927.

52. *Ibid.*

53. *Ti-i tz'u kuo-nei ke-ming chan-cheng*, p. 528.

54. *The China Press*, April 14, 1927. See also *Shen-pao*, April 14, 1927; and *Ti-i tz'u kuo-nei ke-ming chan-cheng*, p. 516.

55. *Ti-i tz'u Kuo-nei ke-ming chan-cheng*, pp. 521–22.

56. *Ibid.*, pp. 530–33.

57. Powell, *My Twenty-five Years in China*, p. 157. Cf. Harold R. Isaacs (ed.), *Five Years of Kuomintang Reaction* (Shanghai, 1932), p. 5.

58. Chiang, *Bo-lo-t'ing*, pp. 164–65; and Li, *Ts'ung jung-Kung tao ch'ing-tang*, Vol. II, pp. 658–59.

59. See, for example, Arno J. Mayer, *Dynamics of Counterrevolution in Europe, 1870–1956* (New York, 1971), p. 116.

60. *Izvestia* (Moscow), No. 91 (April 21, 1927).

61. Mao, *Selected Works* (Peking, 1965), Vol. I, p. 192; and Vol. II, p. 37.

62. Wang, "Tu Yüeh-sheng," p. 455.

63. Great Britain, Public Record Office, FO 371/12454.

64. *Ch'ing-tang yün-tung*, pp. 152—53.

65. *Ke-ming wen-hsien*, Vol. XVI, pp. 38ff; and *Ch'ing-tang yün-tung*, pp. 55–58.

Chapter 9: Japanese Response to Chinese Nationalism: Naitō (Ko'nan) Torajirō's Image of China in the 1920s

1. For example, Iriye, *After Imperialism: The Search for a New Order in the Far East, 1921–1931* (Cambridge, 1965); Nobuya Bamba, *Japanese Diplomacy in Dilemma: New Light on Japan's China Policy, 1924–1929* (Vancouver, 1972); William F. Morton, "Traditional Foreign Policy and National Revolution: The Tanaka Cabinet and China, 1927–1929" (unpublished Ph.D. dissertation, Columbia University, 1969); Usui Katsumi, *Nitchū gaikō shi: Hokubatsu no jidai* (Tōkyō, 1971); and Kamimura Shin'ichi, *Chūgoku nashionarizumu to Nikka kankei no tenkai*, Vol. XVII of *Nihon gaikō shi* (Tōkyō, 1971).

2. Naitō's works include: *Shinchō suibō ron*, *Shinchō shi tsūron*, *Tōyō bunka shi kenkyū*, and *Shina ron*. For his career and scholarship, see Hisayuki Miyakawa, "An outline of the Naitō Hypothesis and Its Effects on Japanese Studies of China," *Far Eastern Quarterly*, Vol. XIV, No. 4 (August 1955), pp. 533–52; Arthur F. Wright, "The Study of Chinese Civilization," *Journal of the History of Ideas*, Vol. XXI, No. 2 (April–June 1960), pp. 247–50; John King Fairbank, Masataka Banno, and Sumiko Yamamoto, *Japanese Studies of Modern China* (Cambridge, 1971); W. G. Beasley and E. G. Pulleyblank, *Historians of China and Japan* (London, 1961); Mitamura Taisuke, *Naitō Ko'nan* (Tōkyō, 1972); Ogawa Tamaki (ed.), *Naitō Ko'nan* (Tōkyō, 1971); and *Shinagaku*, Vol. VII, No. 3 (1934), pp. 1–96. Recently, Naitō's complete works have been compiled by his son: *Naitō Ko'nan zenshu*, 14 vols. (Tōkyō, 1969–   ), hereafter cited as NKZ.

3. "Shina kenkyū no hensen," NKZ, Vol. V, pp. 165–69; "Shina kyōiku dan," NKZ, pp. 105–106.

4. "Shin Shina ron," NKZ, p. 485.

5. *Ibid.*, p. 501.

6. "Shina ron," NKZ, p. 297.

7. "Shin Shina ron," p. 499.

8. "Shina kaikaku setsu no nijiki," NKZ, Vol. II, pp. 230–35.

9. "Shina ron," pp. 328–29; "Shinchō suibō ron," NKZ, Vol. V, p. 258; "Shina jikyoku to shin kyū shisō," NKZ, Vol. IV, p. 494.

10. "Shina ron," p. 294.

11. *Ibid.*, p. 296.

12. "Shina shōrai no tōchi," NKZ, Vol. IV, p. 541.

13. "Shina no genjō," NKZ, Vol. V, p. 25.

14. "Shina no seijiteki fukkatsu," NKZ, p. 51.

15. "Shina mondai," NKZ, Vol. IV, p. 582.

16. "Shina no genjō," p. 25.

17. "Santō mondai to hai-Nichi ron no kontei," quoted in Nomura Kōichi, "Tairiku mondai no imēji to jittai," in *Kindai Nihon seiji shisōshi* (Tōkyō, 1970), p. 65.

18. "Shina no kokusai kanri ron," NKZ, Vol. V, pp. 154 and 158.

19. "Shin Shina ron," p. 504; Ssu-yü Teng and John K. Fairbank, *China's Response to the West* (Cambridge, 1961), pp. 267–74.

20. "Shin Shina ron," pp. 493 and 520; "Shina mondai," p. 585.

21. "Ika ni shite Shina no sonritsu o hakaru beki ka," NKZ, Vol. V, p. 16.

22. "Shina ron," p. 381; "Shina shōrai no tōchi," p. 542.

23. "Shina kokuze no kompomgi," NKZ, Vol. IV, p. 532.

24. "Shin Shina ron," p. 528.

25. Nomura, "Tairiku mondai no imēji to jittai," p. 66.

26. "Shin Shina ron," p. 528; "Shina kokuze no kompomgi," p. 531.

27. "Shina ron," p. 398.

28. "Iwayuru Nihon no tenshoku," NKZ, Vol. II, p. 135.

29. "Shina ron," p. 514.

30. *Ibid.*, p. 514.

31. "Minami Manshū mondai," NKZ, Vol. IV, p. 495.

32. "Shina ron," p. 348.
33. "Nisshi kōshō o hyosu," NKZ, Vol. IV, pp. 511–15; "Nisshi kōshō ron," NKZ, pp. 516–22.
34. "Tai-Shi kōshō mondai," NKZ, pp. 505–10.
35. Ibid., p. 507.
36. "Waga memboku o ikan," NKZ, Vol. V, p. 56.
37. "Shina no genjō," p. 24.
38. "Shin Shina ron," p. 511.
39. Ibid., p. 514.
40. Ibid., p. 509.
41. Ibid., pp. 508–10.
42. Ibid., p. 504.
43. Ibid., p. 489.
44. Ibid., pp. 500–501.
45. Ibid., pp. 498 and 514.
46. "Shina to wa nan zoya," NKZ, Vol. V, pp. 159–64.
47. "Shin Shina ron," p. 506; "Shina ni okeru gaijin no kyōiku shisetsu," NKZ, Vol. V, p. 126.
48. "Shin Shina ron," pp. 489–98.
49. "Manshūkoku kongo no hōshin ni tsuite," NKZ, Vol. V, p. 184.
50. Fairbank, Banno, and Yamamoto, Japanese Studies of Modern China, p. 19.
51. For the signs of an emerging new China, see Mary Clabaugh Wright, "Introduction: The Rising Tide of Change," in Wright (ed.), China in Revolution: The First Phase, 1900–1913 (New Haven, 1968), pp. 1–63.

Chapter 10: In Search of Sovereignty: The Unequal Treaties in Sino-American Relations, 1925-1930

1. Charles Hodges, writing in China Weekly Review, hereafter cited as CWR, November 20, 1926, similarly categorized China's troubles (pp. 318–20). The theme appears recurrently in Mao Tse-tung, "On Contradiction" (August 1937); "On the Correct Handling of Contradictions among the People" (February 27, 1957); and in his "Report to the Second Plenary Session of the Seventh Central Committee of the Communist Party of China" (March 5, 1949).
2. The following discussion of extraterritoriality rests mainly on Wesley Fishel, The End of Extraterritoriality in China (Berkeley, 1952). Additional information and an interesting Chinese perspective comes from William L. Tung, China and the Foreign Powers (Dobbs Ferry, N.Y., 1970).
3. Stanley K. Hornbeck, a leading adviser on American policy, noted that the treaty system developed with cause and for good reasons, and that it rested upon law and contract. CWR, July 23, 1927, p. 196. That Chinese had freely granted extraterritoriality originally was commonly repeated in the mid-twenties. See, for instance, ibid., June 19, 1926, and the article by Charles Denby, "Extraterritoriality in China," in the American Journal of International Law, Vol. XVIII (October 1924), pp. 667–75.

4. The former Danish Minister to China, J. F. Oiesen, wrote that the treaty system had originated "due to the reluctance of the Chinese authorities to have anything to do with the troublesome and . . . often turbulent foreigners." CWR, November 13, 1926, pp. 289, 290.

5. "*Imperium in imperio*" was a popular phrase in the writings of the era. For a typical example, critical of the current situation, see M. T. Z. Tyau, "Extraterritoriality in China and the Question of Its Abolition," *British Yearbook of International Law* (1921–22), pp. 133–49.

6. An editorial in CWR, January 15, 1927, pp. 171, 172, argues that abuses brought the system into disrepute. Another aspect of growing dissatisfaction with the system was that the volume of trade and the number of foreigners in China had greatly increased since the original treaty eras, which brought the special privileges into wider and wider usage. *Ibid.*, June 19, 1926, pp. 9–11. Similar judgments appear in the article by Denby, "Extraterritoriality in China," p. 673, and in J. C. H. Wu and W. C. Dennis, "Problems of Extraterritoriality in China, with Discussion," American Society of International Law, *Proceedings* (1930), pp. 182–212.

7. "The Chinese people have groaned under the yoke of unequal treaties for nearly a century." Fang Lo-tien in CWR, November 17, 1928, p. 399. "Is China to remain for all time the victim of this anachronism?" *Ibid.*, June 19, 1926, p. 17. John Carter Vincent, veteran American diplomat, posed those questions sympathetically at the beginning of his monograph, *The Extraterritorial System in China* (Cambridge, 1970), pp. 3, 4.

8. Sao-ke Alfred Sze, Chinese Minister to the United States, said that for eighty years Chinese sovereignty had been violated by the west. He called for eradication of the whole treaty system and the erection of "a new international edifice" to be based on "justice and mutual interests." Reported in CWR, October 16, 1926, p. 180.

9. Chinese of the twenties believed that the system had been against the national interest, that it had placed Chinese traders and manufacturers at a disadvantage among other things. *Ibid.*, October 30, 1926, p. 232.

10. Sun in a 1925 statement said among other things that the Manchus, whom he had helped overthrow, had sold the freedom and equality of the Chinese to the various nations. Schurman to Secretary of State, January 2, 1925, *Foreign Relations of the United States*, 1925, Vol. I, p. 589. The most accessible information on the change in Sun's principles is in Li Chien-nung, *The Political History of China, 1840–1928*, trans. by Ssu-yü Teng and Jeremy Ingalls (Stanford, 1967), p. 443.

11. American diplomats saw such close connection between the Kuomintang and the Soviets in 1925 that they considered Kuomintang successes as Soviet triumphs. The Minister in China further reported that Sun Yat-sen, once in power, would denounce unequal treaties at least in part to please Karakhan, the Soviet adviser-ambassador to the Kuomintang. Schurman to Secretary of State, January 2, 1925, *Foreign Relations*, Vol. I, p. 589. Typical Kuomintang leaflets distributed in a riot on November 28, 1925, called for customs autonomy and cancellation of unequal treaties. MacMurray to Secretary of State, November 30, 1925, *ibid.*, p. 619.

12. Chiang Kai-shek favored immediate rather than graduate abolition of extraterritoriality, including parts relating to consular rights and practices. "This is a revolution, not an evolution." He believed the revolution would be incomplete until extraterritoriality had been abolished. CWR, December 4, 1926, pp. 2, 3.

13. The son of Chang Tso-lin, General Chang Hsüeh-liang, declared in the midst of conflict that "if foreign aggression in China continues, every Chinese, Northerner and Southerner, will rise together to defend the country." *Ibid.*, February 5, 1927, p. 249.

14. The standard and still unsurpassed work on American reaction to the Chinese revolution, including such outrages as the Nanking Incident, is Dorothy Borg, *American Policy and the Chinese Revolution, 1925–28* (New York, 1947). Vincent uses the word "berserk" in discussing the behavior of southern soldiers at Nanking in his *The Extraterritorial System*, p. 20.

15. The phrase was Charge Mayer's, in his message to the Secretary of State, July 10, 1925, *Foreign Relations*, 1925, Vol. I, p. 778.

16. "Sympathetic, thoughtful, and helpful cooperation with China is the wisest policy for the United States to pursue in the present crisis." Schurman to Secretary of State, March 29, 1925, *ibid.*, p. 604. "It is essential to placate the Chinese by making concessions that are just and desirable." Grew (Assistant Secretary of State, sometimes Acting Secretary of State) to Mayer, July 26, 1925, *ibid.*, p. 774. In typical and recurrent phraseology, Secretary of State Kellogg wrote Mayer that the current nationalist agitation provided occasion to "evidence to the Chinese our willingness to consider sympathetically and helpfully the modification of existing treaties in measure as the Chinese authorities demonstrate their willingness and ability to fulfill their obligations and to assume the protection of foreign rights and interests now safeguarded by the exceptional provisions of existing treaties." July 1, 1925, *ibid.*, p. 767. Americans proved their claim to friendliness among other things by recognizing the Chinese trademark law of May 3, 1923. "This appears to be the first practical step taken by any government toward the abolition of extraterritoriality." CWR, November 6, 1926, p. 264. On February 12, 1927, CWR reported a recent statement of Kellogg's: "This government wishes to deal with China in a most liberal spirit" (p. 273).

17. Senator Borah said that nationalism was the great factor in China's life and that it "must be reckoned with and respected." CWR, January 1, 1927, p. 120. On January 4, 1927, Congressman Porter of Pennsylvania, chairman of the House Foreign Affairs Committee, introduced a resolution to authorize the negotiation of new treaties with China on tariffs and extraterritoriality, and found much support for his proposal. *Ibid.*, January 22, 1927. Will Rogers wrote an exceedingly sympathetic essay on the subject and concluded that the United States had been in the wrong in the old treaty system. *Ibid.*, April 23, 1927, p. 201.

18. Senator Lodge even supported Porter's resolution, and favored American initiatives on treaty revision independent of the other powers. *Ibid.*,

March 5, 1927, pp. 9, 10. Senator Hiram Bingham gave an interview in which he declared the old days gone forever, and advocated immediate revision of treaties with China. *Ibid.*, July 9, 1927, pp. 134, 135.

19. Coolidge to Acting Secretary of State, July 10, 1925, *Foreign Relations,* 1925, Vol. I, p. 777. The Chinese Minister resented American and western demands for such accomplishments, especially since the powers had ended capitulations in Turkey before the Turks had met such conditions. CWR, January 29, 1927, pp. 223, 224. Perhaps it was more important for American policy that even in Turkey the powers had acted in concert, just as the British and Americans were currently doing in Persia, where disputes over capitulations similarly raged. United States Department of State, *Records Relating to Internal Affairs of China, 1910–29* (hereafter cited as USDS), 791.00/88a.

20. Americans feared Japan's attempts to win trade advantages out of the confusion. CWR, April 10, 1926, pp. 133–35. The United States preferred to follow rather than lead in giving up special privileges. Memo of December 4, 1928, USDS, 793.003/78.

21. CWR editorial of October 30, 1926, agreed that the Chinese had given the powers good reason to delay surrender of privileges (pp. 229, 230). The American Chamber of Commerce believed that "militarism, brigandage and Bolshevism have destroyed all semblance of law and order throughout China." *Ibid.*, May 7, 1927, pp. 248, 249.

22. There were many reports from China of the weak and ineffective central government. See, for instance, *ibid.*, March 27, 1926, pp. 84–86; August 21, 1926, pp. 291–94; October 2, 1926, pp. 118, 119.

23. The following discussion of American international law rests chiefly on the official treatment in Marjorie Whitman, *Digest of International Law* (Washington, D.C., 1963), Vol. I, pp. 233–82, especially pp. 237, 263, 265, 269, 271; and Vol. V (published 1965), pp. 134–53 and 216–18.

24. "China bases her case on the principle of the equality of the states before international law." Edward S. Corwin, a noted American jurist, in CWR, December 22, 1928, p. 156.

25. Hornbeck vigorously maintained that conditions in China did not permit relinquishment of rights in his pamphlet, *China Today: Political* (World Peace Foundation Pamphlets), Vol. X, No. 5 (Boston, 1927).

26. CWR, October 9, 1926, pp. 145, 146.

27. *Ibid.*, November 27, 1926, p. 343.

28. "There is no question but that the removal of extraterritoriality in China is a prerequisite to China's independence as a nation." Peter S. Jowe in *ibid.*, June 19, 1927, pp. 23, 24.

29. "We would be false to public trust should we surrender the privileges and immunities of our citizens without first assuring ourselves of the ability of the Chinese to carry out the burden of normal nationality." Mayer to Secretary of State, June 26, 1925, *Foreign Relations*, 1925, Vol. I, p. 766. ". . . thousands of Americans and foreigners have taken up their residence and carried on their business within that country [China]. The United States owes to them the duty of adequate protection." Kel-

logg to the American Bar Association, August 31, 1925, *ibid.*, p. 830. See also Thomas H. Etzold, "An American Jew in Germany: The Death of Helmut Hirsch," *Jewish Social Studies* (April 1973), pp. 125–40; and Etzold, "Politics or Protection? 'Pedicaris Alive or Raisuli Dead,' " *The Historian*, February 1975.

30. Fishel, *The End of Extraterritoriality*, p. 112.

31. "China must be impressed with the necessity of giving concrete evidence of its ability to suppress disorders and protect foreigners." A policy statement to the British Charge, repeated to all the Washington Powers, July 13, 1925, *Foreign Relations*, 1925, Vol. I, p. 780.

32. The department authorized the discontinuation of protest to Peking "if it will result in dividing responsibility or incurring ill will of so-called Nationalist authorities." January 19, 1927, USDS, 393.11/434.

33. Such warnings were frequent in 1927 and 1928. See, for instance, *ibid.*, 313.11/528, 538. Secretary of State to MacMurray, June 27, 1927, approved the submission to local authorities of claims for losses at nationalist hands. *Foreign Relations*, 1927, Vol. II, p. 138.

34. MacMurray to Secretary of State, August 14, 1926, asking for decision on whom to recognize now that Peking government was disintegrating. Secretary of State replied: "It would not be wise for the United States to take the lead . . . in giving public notice to China that she has no government." *Foreign Relations*, 1926, Vol. I, pp. 671–79 and p. 682 respectively. Officially the United States did not recognize any government in China after the fall of the Tuan administration in April 1926. Secretary of State to MacMurray, April 14, 1928, *ibid.*, Vol. II, p. 179. Lee's credentials refused: memo of conversation between Lee and Nelson T. Johnson, Assistant Secretary of State, November 17, 1927, USDS, 893.00/9609.

35. CWR, July 14, 1928, pp. 232, 233. In MacMurray to Secretary of State, December 5, 1928, there is evidence of how unforthcoming the Chinese were becoming in one important case. *Foreign Relations*, 1928, Vol. II, p. 290.

36. Minister Schurman noted the unanimity of Chinese support for abrogation of treaties in his message to the Secretary of State on January 12, 1925, *Foreign Relations*, 1925, Vol. I, p. 722.

37. The doctrine appears implicitly in a Chinese note transmitted by Mayer on June 24, 1925, *ibid.*, p. 763. The actual phrase appeared in elaborate arguments Chinese representatives presented to the Commission on Extraterritoriality. Fishel, *The End of Extraterritoriality*, p. 114.

38. A CWR editorial saw abrogation of the Belgian treaty as a sign of China's growing diplomatic strength. November 13, 1926, pp. 285, 286.

39. "Unless lives of American citizens are actually in danger, the Department would disapprove the use of force." Grew to MacMurray, December 24, 1925, *Foreign Relations*, 1925, Vol. I, p. 626.

40. Frequent references to American governmental and popular opposition to intervention or the use of force appear in CWR, May 14, 1927, pp. 275–77; May 21, 1927, pp. 307–10; June 11, 1927, pp. 28, 29; June 25, 1927, pp. 80–82; May 11, 1929, p. 443. Vincent, *Extraterritorial System*, pp. 19–21, 83 ff.

41. CWR noted that Americans were losing their leadership influence in nationalist circles. March 31, 1928, pp. 129, 130. The periodical also predicted that China was certain to succeed in asserting its sovereignty. March 2, 1929, pp. 2, 3.

42. Silas H. Strawn, the American delegate to the commissions on treaty revision, wrote that intervention would be ineffective because at the least it would result in guerrilla warfare. *Ibid.*, September 3, 1927, pp. 1, 2.

43. "Use of diplomatic pressure to prevent hostilities [in China] would be intervention and would inflame anti-foreignism." Secretary of State to the British ambassador, April 2, 1925, *Foreign Relations*, 1925, Vol. I, p. 618.

44. Schurman had described American policy in 1925 as one of "masterly inactivity." Schurman to Secretary of State, March 29. 1925, *ibid.*, p. 604. Hornbeck wrote that further treaties [revisions] only await China's stabilization. Reported in CWR, August 25, 1928, pp. 421–23, 426. CWR anticipated that if China did not agree to gradual rather than immediate abolition of extraterritoriality, the powers would probably not do anything. December 7, 1929, p. 2.

45. CWR, October 27, 1928, pp. 275, 276; May 4, 1929, pp. 397, 398.

46. Johnson memorandum of conversation with Minister Wu who said that the Chinese were expecting a great deal from the United States in the matter of relinquishment of extraterritoriality. July 2, 1929, USDS, 711.933/74. Consul Jenkins in Canton reported that *China Truth*, a semi-official paper, had called on the United States to take the first step to abolish extraterritoriality, and that if it did not, its "traditional policy of friendly cooperation with China is meaningless." July 20, 1929, *ibid.*, 711.933/107.

47. An article in CWR argued that unilateral abrogation of the treaties would be necessary and lawful. November 17, 1928, p. 399. Curiously, Hornbeck and Frank Lee agreed on August 3, 1928, that discussions of extraterritoriality should wait till China was less occupied with "other matters." USDS, 711.933/14.

48. C. C. Wu, Minister to the United States, remarked: "China should not be compelled to alter her basic institutions so that they will be entirely to the liking of guests who may choose to reside within her boundaries." This spunky statement was reported in CWR, May 11, 1929, pp. 443, 444. Nationalist leaders apparently expected no stiff United States reaction or refusal to cooperate in the unilateral abolition of extraterritoriality. Dispatches of December 28 and December 30, 1929, from Shanghai legation, in USDS, 793.003/233.

49. Ambiguities noted in *New Republic*, and reprinted in CWR, February 15, 1930, p. 377.

50. CWR, January 25, 1930, p. 279.

Selected Bibliography

Amann, Gustav. *The Legacy of Sun Yat-sen: A History of the Chinese Revolution*, trans. by Frederick Philip Grove (New York: Louis Carrier & Co., 1929).

Bamba, Nobuya. *Japanese Diplomacy in Dilemma: New Light on Japan's China Policy, 1924–1929* (Vancouver: University of British Columbia Press, 1972).

Borg, Dorothy. *American Policy and the Chinese Revolution, 1925–1928* (New York: Macmillan Co., 1947).

Brandt, Conrad. *Stalin's Failure in China, 1924–1927* (Cambridge: Harvard University Press, 1958).

Chang Kuo-t'ao. *The Rise of the Chinese Communist Party, 1921–1927: Volume One of the Autobiography of Chang Kuo-t'ao* (Lawrence: University Press of Kansas, 1971).

Ch'en, Joseph T. *The May Fourth Movement in Shanghai: The Making of a Social Movement in Modern China* (Leiden: E. J. Brill, 1971).

Ch'en Kung-po. *The Communist Movement in China*, ed. with an introduction by C. Martin Wilbur (New York: Octagon Books, 1966).

Chesneaux, Jean. *The Chinese Labor Movement, 1919–1927*, trans. by H. M. Wright (Stanford: Stanford University Press, 1968).

Chow Tse-tsung. *The May Fourth Movement: Intellectual Revolution in Modern China* (Cambridge: Harvard University Press, 1960).

Eudin, Xenia Joukoff and Robert C. North. *Soviet Russia and the East, 1920–1927: A Documentary Survey* (Stanford: Stanford University Press, 1957).

Fuse Katsuji. *Soviet Policy in the Orient* (East Peking: Enjinsha, 1927).

Grieder, Jerome B. *Hu Shih and the Chinese Renaissance: Liberalism in the Chinese Revolution, 1917–1937* (Cambridge: Harvard University Press, 1970).

Hu Shih. *The Chinese Renaissance* (New York: Paragon Book Gallery, Ltd., 1964).

Iriye, Akira. *After Imperialism: The Search for a New Order in the Far East, 1921–1931* (Cambridge: Harvard University Press, 1965).

Isaacs, Harold R. *The Tragedy of the Chinese Revolution* (Stanford: Stanford University Press, 1961).

Leng Shao Chuan and Norman D. Palmer. *Sun Yat-sen and Communism* (London: Thames and Hudson, 1961).

Linebarger, Paul Myron Anthony. *The Political Doctrines of Sun Yat-sen: An Exposition of the San Min Chu I* (Baltimore: Johns Hopkins Press, 1937).

Loh, Pichon P. Y. *The Early Chiang Kai-shek: A Study of His Personality and Politics, 1887–1924* (New York: Columbia University Press, 1971).

Louis, William R. *British Strategy in the Far East, 1919–1939* (New York: Oxford University Press, 1971).

MacNair, Harley Farnsworth. *China in Revolution: An Analysis of Politics and Militarism under the Republic* (New York: Howard Fertig, 1968).

Meisner, Maurice. *Li Ta-chao and the Origins of Chinese Marxism* (Cambridge: Harvard University Press, 1967).

Mitarevsky, N. *World-wide Soviet Plots, as Disclosed by Hitherto Unpublished Documents Seized at the USSR Embassy in Peking* (Tientsin: Tientsin Press, Ltd., n.d.).

North, Robert C. *Kuomintang and Chinese Communist Elites* (Stanford: Stanford University Press, 1952).

Pollard, Robert T. *China's Foreign Relations, 1917–1931* (New York: Macmillan Co., 1933).

Pye, Lucian W. *Warlord Politics: Conflict and Coalition in the Modernization of Republican China* (New York: Praeger Publishers, 1971).

Roy, M. N. *Revolution and Counter-Revolution in China* (Calcutta: Renaissance Publishers, 1946).

Schwartz, Benjamin I. *Chinese Communism and the Rise of Mao* (paperback edition; New York: Harper & Row, Publishers, 1967).

———— (ed.). *Reflections on the May Fourth Movement: A Symposium* (Cambridge: Harvard University Press, 1972).

Sharman, Lyon. *Sun Yat-sen, His Life and Its Meaning: A Critical Biography* (Hamden: Archon Books, 1965).

Sheridan, James E. *Chinese Warlord: The Career of Feng Yü-hsiang* (Stanford: Stanford University Press, 1966).

Sokolsky, George E. *The Tinder Box of Asia* (New York: Doubleday, Doran & Co., Inc., 1932).

T'ang Leang-li. *The Inner History of the Chinese Revolution* (New York: Dutton, 1930).

Tong, Hollington K. *Chiang Kai-shek: Soldier and Statesman,* 2 volumes (Shanghai: China Publishing Co., 1937).

Vishnyakova-Akimova, Vera Vladimirovna. *Two Years in Revolutionary China*, trans. by Steven I. Levine (Cambridge: Harvard University Press, 1971).

Whiting, Allen S. *Soviet Policies in China, 1917–1924* (New York: Columbia University Press, 1954).

Wilbur, C. Martin and Julie Lien-ying How (ed.). *Documents on Communism, Nationalism, and Soviet Advisers in China, 1918–1927* (New York: Columbia University Press, 1956).

Woo, T. C. *The Kuomintang and the Future of the Chinese Revolution* (London: George Allen & Unwin, Ltd., 1928).

Yü, George T. *Party Politics in Republican China: The Kuomintang, 1912–1924* (Berkeley: University of California Press, 1966).

CONTRIBUTORS

F. Gilbert Chan is associate professor of history at Miami University. With a Ph.D. from Columbia University, he has published articles on revolution and warlordism in twentieth-century China. He is the editor of two forthcoming books, *China at the Crossroads, 1927–1949: Republicanism versus Communism* and *China under Communism: Revolution and Diplomacy, 1949–1975*, both to be published by New Viewpoints. He is currently completing a study on Liao Chung-k'ai and the Chinese revolution.

Thomas H. Etzold, associate professor of strategy at the United States Naval War College, studied with Robert H. Ferrell at Indiana University and with Gaddis Smith at Yale University. He is co-author and editor of *Pacific Empires: Aspects of Sino-American Relations, 1784–1975,* and author of *The Conduct of American Foreign Relations,* both forthcoming from New Viewpoints.

Dan N. Jacobs is professor of political science at Miami University. He specializes in Soviet politics and Russo-Chinese relations since 1917 and has published in both areas. He has recently written a biography of M. M. Borodin.

Donald A. Jordan is associate professor of history at Ohio University. He received a Ph.D. from University of Wisconsin and is the author of *The Northern Expedition: China's National Revolution of 1926–1928,* published by the University Press of Hawaii. His current research interest centers on the origins of the Japanese military intervention in Shanghai, 1931–1932.

Richard C. Kagan received his Ph.D. from University of Pennsylvania and has a joint appointment with Leigh Kagan as assistant professor of history at Hamline University. He is the editor of *The China Lobby in American Politics* (Harper & Row, 1974).

Richard B. Landis is professor of history at Montana State University. After being its president, he is at present the secretary-treasurer of the Montana Association for International Studies, as well as its delegate to the Council on Intercultural Studies and Programs.

Shumpei Okamoto is associate professor of history at Temple University. With a Ph.D. from Columbia University, he specializes in the political and diplomatic history of modern Japan. He is the author of *The Japanese Oligarchy and the Russo-Japanese War* (Columbia University Press, 1970) and the coeditor of *Pearl Harbor as History: Japanese-American Relations, 1931–1941* (Columbia University Press, 1973).

Ssu-yü Teng is University Professor of Indiana University. His many publications include *Chang Hsi and the Treaty of Nanking, 1842* (University of Chicago Press, 1944), *New Light on the History of the Taiping Rebellion* (Harvard University Press, 1950), *China's Response to the West: A Documentary Survey, 1839–1923* (with John K. Fairbank; Harvard University Press, 1954), *The Nien Army and Their Guerrilla Warfare, 1851–1868* (Mouton & Co., 1961), *Japanese Studies on Japan and the Far East: A Short Biographical and Bibliographical Introduction* (Hong Kong University Press, 1961), *Historiography of the Taiping Rebellion* (Harvard University Press, 1962), and *The Taiping Rebellion and the Western Powers: A Comprehensive Survey* (Clarendon Press, 1971).

C. Martin Wilbur is George Sansom Professor of Chinese History at Columbia University. In 1971–1972 he was president of the Association for Asian Studies. He is the author of many publications, including *Slavery in China during the Former Han Dynasty* (Field Museum Press, 1943), coeditor of *Documents on Communism, Nationalism, and Soviet Advisers in China 1918–1927* (Columbia University Press, 1956), and editor of *The Communist Movement in China: An Essay Written in 1924 by Ch'en Kung-po* (reprint; Octagon Books, Inc., 1966). He has just completed a biographical study of Sun Yat-sen, to be published by Columbia University Press.

Odoric Y. K. Wou is associate professor of history at Rutgers University at Newark. He has published on warlordism in twentieth-century China and is the author of a forthcoming book, *Militarism in Modern China: As Exemplified in the Career of Wu P'ei-fu*, to be published by Wm. Dawson & Sons Ltd.

Tien-wei Wu received his Ph.D. from University of Maryland and, in recent years, taught at Southern Illinois University at Carbondale and University of Victoria in Canada. He is the author of *Mao Tse-tung and the Tsunyi Conference: An Annotated Bibliography* (Center for Chinese Research Materials, 1974).

Ka-che Yip is assistant professor of history at University of Maryland at Baltimore County. With a Ph.D. from Columbia University, he specializes in the anti-Christian movement in modern China and has published on the subject.

Index

All-Chekiang Society, 134–135,
136
Anhwei College of Law, 97
Anti-Christian Federation, 105
Anti-imperialism: and Kuomintang, ix, 47, 51, 106; and Chinese Communists, ix, 63, 67–
70; and influence of Russia,
x; and Britain, 9; and Sun Yat-
sen, 26; and May Fourth intellectuals, 36; and Comintern, 64–65; and Ch'en Tu-
hsiu, 71; and student activism,
103–104; and warlords, 128
April 12 coup (1927), xii, 7, 13,
53, 147, 156–157, 159
Austria, 3
Autumn Harvest Uprising, 7

Belgium, 9, 193

Blyukher, V., 11
Borodin, Mikhail, xii, 5, 11, 43,
72, 79, 148, 154, 220; as political adviser of Kuomintang,
44–54
Boxer uprising: Ch'en Tu-hsiu's
views on, 71–72; and anti-
foreignism, 111
Britain, 8, 9, 10, 30, 31, 179, 183,
189, 195; and May Thirtieth
Incident, 6, 47, 69, 103; and
Borodin, 43; and Wu P'ei-fu,
68, 104; and Canton–Hong
Kong strike, 69; and San-yüan-
li, 111; and Opium War, 120,
178; and extraterritoriality,
177, 196
Bubnov, A. S., 49, 50, 89

Canada, 30

Canton—Hong Kong strike, 48, 69

Chang Chi, 35, 203

Chang Chih-tung, 112, 123

Chang Ch'iu-pai, 31, 203

Chang Chün, 148

Chang Hsiao-lin, 152, 156

Chang Hsüeh-liang, 228

Chang Hsün, 1

Chang Jen-chieh, 142—143, 148, 151, 221

Chang Kuo-t'ao, 33

Chang Ping-lin: and traditional nationalism, 112

Chang Po-ch'i, 155

Chang Shao-tseng, 119

Chang T'ai-lei, 30, 35

Chang T'ao-fan: and Sun Yat-sen, 19

Chang Tsai-yang, 141

Chang Tso-lin, 3—4, 5, 131, 228; and raid of Soviet Embassy, 8—9; and Sun Yat-sen, 23, 33; and Japan, 68, 104; and National Pacification Army, 115, 138; and Wu P'ei-fu, 121; and Sun Ch'uan-fang, 133, 135, 137

Chang Tsung-ch'ang, 138, 139, 150

Chang Yüan-chi, 161

Chao Heng-t'i, 4, 23, 29

Chekiang-Kiangsu War (1924), 131

Chekiang Military Academy, 128, 130, 135, 141

Ch'en Chiung-ming, 5, 33, 92; and Sun Yat-sen, 4, 16, 20—26, 36; and Soviet Russia, 28—30; and June 16 coup (1922), 25—26, 34, 200, 201, 204; and federalism, 117; and Revolutionary Alliance, 199

Ch'en Chuo, 144

Ch'en, Eugene, 32, 220

Ch'en Kung-po: and Chinese Communist Party, 34, 204

Ch'en Kuo-fu, 149

Ch'en T'iao-yüan, 221

Ch'en Tu-hsiu, xii, 11, 28, 96, 154; and May Fourth intellectuals, 17—18; and Sun Yat-sen, 18, 33; and Marxism, 26; and Maring, 29; and Chinese Communism, 34, 55—56; and Kuomintang, 35; and iconoclasm, 56-59, 63-64; and anti-statist movement, 61—63, 64; and national movement of anti-imperialism, 64—66, 69—72; and Communist nationalism, 114; and April 5 manifesto (1927), 152—153

Ch'en Yi: Chekiang provincialism, 130—133, 135—138, 140—142, 145

Ch'eng Ch'ien, 150, 151, 154

Ch'i Chi-kuang, 11, 85, 87, 116

Chiang Hsien-yün, 149

Chiang Kai-shek, xi, xii, 4, 49, 130, 134—135, 136, 138, 139, 140—141, 142, 144, 145, 177, 220, 221; and Northern Expedition, 5, 51, 115, 127; and April 12 coup (1927), 7, 13, 147, 156—157; and Whampoa Military Academy, 11—12, 77, 78—80; and Sun Yat-sen, 24,

25, 27, 32, 33; and March 20 coup (1926), 50; and conflict with Chinese Communists, 52–54, 148–159; on unified spirit and organization, 80–85; on organizational weakness, 85–89; on military knowledge imparted at Whampoa Military Academy, 89–91; and his military political analysis, 91–93; and his resignation, 143

Chiang Meng-lin, 19, 100

Chiang, Monlin: see Chiang Meng-lin

Chiang Tsung-kuei, 134, 140, 141

Chicherin, 28, 29, 32

Chien-she tsa-chih: see *Reconstruction Magazine*

Chihli-Anfu War (1920), 118

Chihli-Fengtien Wars (1922 and 1924), 3, 121

Chin dynasty, 124

Ch'in dynasty, 124

China Mutual Advancement Society, 152, 155–156

China's Youth, 99

Chinese Communist Party, ix, 73, 95, 126, 146, 204, 207, 208; and Sun Yat-sen, xi, 11, 15–16, 35, 37, 205; and Ch'en Tu-hsiu, xii, 55–56, 62–64; and labor, 6; and raid of Soviet Embassy, 8–9; and Kuomintang, 10, 33, 34, 48, 72, 147; and Whampoa Military Academy, 12, 78; and Chiang Kai-shek, 13, 50–52, 83, 91, 92, 149–159; and founding of, 26, 36; and Voitinsky,

28–29; and Maring, 29, 35; and Russia, 41, 54; and Borodin, 44; and anti-imperialism, 66–70; and student movement, 102, 104–105; and Wu P'ei-fu, 202

Chinese Eastern Railroad, 32, 66, 69

Chinese Revolutionary Party, 15, 16, 20, 33, 60

Chinese Tramcar Company, 156

Ch'ing dynasty, 112, 128, 165, 168, 176, 180; and last Manchu emperor (Hsüan-t'ung), 1, 3; and anti-Manchu movement, 18, 58, 60, 109; fall of, 39; and Boxer uprising, 71; and 1911 revolution, 92, 111; and Chinese nationalism, 108

Ch'ing-nien tsa-chih: see *Youth Magazine*

Chou En-lai, 151

Chou Feng-ch'i: and Chekiang provincialism, 130–133, 135–146; and Chiang Kai-shek, and suppression of workers, 155–156

Chu Chi-hsüan, 221

Chu Chih-hsin, 20

Ch'u Fu-ch'eng, 131, 134–135, 140, 142, 146

Chu Ho-chung, 30, 31, 32

Chu P'ei-te, 153–154

Ch'uan-Che kung-hui: see All-Chekiang Society

Chung-hua ke-ming-tang: see Chinese Revolutionary Party

Chung-kuo ch'ing-nien: see *China's Youth*

Chung-kuo kung-chin hui: *see* China Mutual Advancement Society

Chung-kuo kuo-min-tang: *see* Kuomintang

Comintern, 40–41, 42, 70; and Sun Yat-sen, 28–29, 31; and Chinese Communists, 35, 67; and Ch'en Tu-hsiu, 56, 66; and anti-imperialism, 64–65

Commercial Press (Shanghai), 97, 156

Communist Youth Corps, 105

Confucianism: and anti-Confucian movement, 2, 7, 17, 55; and Wu P'ei-fu, 12, 115–116, 123–125, 125–126; and Ch'en Tu-hsiu, 57–58, 63, 71; and Chiang Kai-shek, 86; and traditional nationalism, 112

Congress of the Toilers of the Far East (1922), 31

"Constitution protection movement," xi, 15, 21, 36, 110

Coolidge, Calvin, 184

Dalin, S. A., 31–32, 34–35, 37

Darwin, Charles, 99

Dewey, John, 1, 17, 19, 99

Eastern Expeditions, 77; First Eastern Expedition, 80, 84, 89, 90, 91, 92; Second Eastern Expedition, 80, 89, 93

Extraterritoriality, 103, 179; Extraterritorial Commission, 8, 189–190; abrogation of, 9, 177, 228; and United States, 178, 184–185, 187, 191, 193,

195–196; and Chinese nationalism, 180

Federation of Canton-Hankow Railway Workers Unions, 6

Federation of Han-yeh-p'ing Labor Unions, 6

Feng Kuo-chang, 2–3

Feng Yü-hsiang, 3–4, 53–54, 115, 125, 146

Fessenden, Stirling, 152

First National Labor Congress (1922), 6

France, 27, 71, 155, 183, 193

Fu Ssu-nien, 2, 18

Fukien rebellion, 11, 69–70

Galen: *see* Blyukher, V.

Gandhi, Mohandas K., 1

General Labor Union (Shanghai), 150, 155, 156, 157

Germany, 18, 30, 31, 32, 43, 61, 65, 79, 189, 191

Green Gang, 152

Guide Weekly, 71

Han dynasty, 13, 124, 162, 171

Harding, Warren G., 27

Ho Ch'eng-chun, 221

Ho Shao-ch'iu, 221

Ho Ying-ch'in, 143–144

Hsia Ch'ao, 128, 130, 139, 141, 145, 146; and Sun Ch'uan-fang, 131, 132–133, 136, 137; and Kuomintang, 134, 135; execution of, 138, 142

Hsiang-tao chou-pao: *see Guide Weekly*

Hsin-ch'ao: *see New Tide*

Hsin ch'ing-nien: see *New Youth*

Hsing-ch'i p'ing-lun: see *Weekly Review*

Hsiung-nu, 124

Hsü Ch'ien, 220

Hsü Shih-ch'ang, 3, 16, 24

Hsüeh-sheng tsa-chih: see *Student Magazine*

Hsüeh Yüeh, 155

Hu Han-min, 33, 61, 93

Hu Shih, 96; and "Chinese Renaissance," 16–17; and literary revolution, 17; and his education in United States, 18 199; on foreign powers, 68, 71; and student movement, 97; and liberal nationalism, 113

Huang Chin-yung, 152, 156

Huang Fu, 141, 148

Hungary, 3, 65

Intellectual revolution: see May Fourth Movement

Ishibashi Tanzan, 168

Japan, 3, 9, 36, 130, 135, 150, 215; and China, xii–xiii, 160, 162, 163, 164, 165–166, 167–175, 181, 189, 195, 196; and Twenty-one Demands, 1; and Chang Tso-lin, 4, 104; and May Fourth Incident (1919), 6, 68, 198; and anti-Japanese movement in China, 13, 34, 69, 147; and anti-Manchu movement, 18, 58; and war with Russia (1904–1905), 26; and Korean

independence movement, 61; and invasion of Manchuria, 70; and May Thirtieth Incident (1925), 103; and Wu P'ei-fu, 115, 118, 120, 121, 122

Japan-Manchukuo Culture Association, 161

Joffe, Adolph, 11, 26; and Sun Yat-sen, 4–5, 33, 35–36, 41–42; and Liao Chung-k'ai, 36, 74

June 16 coup (1922), 32, 34, 36, 201

Kan Nai-kuang, 154

K'ang Yu-wei, 163; and Ch'en Tu-hsiu, 58; and traditional nationalism, 112

Karakhan, L. M., 42, 44, 47, 227

Karakhan manifesto, 26, 36, 42, 201

Kommunisticheskii Internatsional, 28

Komoto Daisaku, 4

Komura Jutarō, 161, 167

Koo, V. K. Wellington, 3

Korea, 61–62, 124, 171

Kropotkin, 99

Ku Chieh-kang, 2

Ku Shun-chang, 151

Ku Ying-fen, 151

Kuan Yü, 116

Kuibyshev, N. V., 50

Kuibyshev, V. V., 50

Kuo Mo-jo, 149

Kuo Sung-ling, 4

Kuomintang, xi, 21, 23, 24, 39, 48, 49, 64, 73, 79, 85, 91, 93, 109, 127, 130, 131, 148, 150, 151, 152,

153, 154, 155, 177, 203; and Chinese Communist Party, ix, 33–35, 37; and party reorganization, xii, 11, 15, 20, 33, 43, 45, 54, 74, 80, 88, 95, 102, 173; and Russia, 5, 10, 28–37, 51, 66, 69, 148–149, 227; and Sun Yat-sen, 25–26, 46, 86, 87; and Borodin, 43, 44–45, 46, 47; and March 20 coup (1926), 50; and Chinese Communist Party, 52, 54, 55, 56–57, 67, 68, 70, 72, 83, 92, 104, 105, 126, 147, 158, 205; and Northern Expedition, 61, 190; and Ch'en Tu-hsiu, 62; and Whampoa Military Academy, 76, 77, 78, 81, 89; and anti-imperialism, 106; and Chekiang provincialism, 134, 136–137, 139, 141, 142, 144, 145, 146; and Chiang Kai-shek, 157, 159; and unequal treaties, 181–182, 195; and United States, 183, 184, 191, 192

Kyōtō Imperial University, 161, 167–168

Labor movement, 95; and May Fourth Incident, 5–6, 94; and Kuomintang, 29, 148; and May Thirtieth Incident (1925), 47; and Wuhan government, 53; and Maoist education, 107; and Chiang Kai-shek, 149, 154; and Chinese Communist Party, 150; and April 12 coup (1927), 156

Lafayette, Marquis de, 27, 39, 45

Lee, Frank, 191

Leng Hsin, 84

Lenin, V. I., 39, 40–41, 49, 52, 63, 64; and Leninism, 27, 31, 37, 69, 95, 99, 104, 111, 114; and Sun Yat-sen, 32; and anti-imperialism, 36, 67, 103; and Borodin, 43, 45; and M. N. Roy, 65

Li Chi-shen, 151, 157

Li Hung-chang, 163, 165

Li Lieh-chün, 149

Li Shih-tseng, 151, 157

Li Ta-chao, 9, 26, 35, 114

Li Tsung-jen, 153, 154

Li Yüan-hung, 2–3, 110, 119

Liang Ch'i-ch'ao, 109, 163; and Ch'en Tu-hsiu, 58; and traditional nationalism, 112

Liao Chung-k'ai, 11, 93; and Joffe, 5, 36, 74; and Ch'en Chiung-ming, 21, 25, 204; and Yeh Chü, 24; and Sun Yat-sen, 28, 29, 30, 31; and death of, 49; and Whampoa Military Academy, 77, 78–79, 83

Lin Shu: and traditional nationalism, 112

Lin Tse-hsü: Wu Pei-fu on, 120–121

Lin Tsu-han: and Sun Yat-sen, 33

Literary revolution: see May Fourth Movement

Liu Ch'ih, 155

Lo Chia-lun: and May Fourth Movement, 18

Lu Hsiang-t'ing, 132–133, 138

Lu Hsün: and liberal nationalism, 113

Lu Jung-t'ing, 4

Lu Yung-hsiang, 3, 131

Ma Hsü-lun, 134, 136, 142–143, 144
Ma Soo: see Ma Su
Ma Su, 27
Manchu dynasty: see Ch'ing dynasty
Manchukuo, 161, 173
Mao Tse-tung, 70, 158, 177; and Autumn Harvest Uprising, 7; and mass mobilization, 54; and Chinese Communist Party, 67; and Maoism, 107
March 20 coup (1926), 50, 52
Maring, G., and Chinese Communist Party, 26, 205; and Sun Yat-sen, 29–30, 32–33, 35, 37, 203; and Wu P'ei-fu, 202
Marx, Karl, 9; and May Fourth Movement, 26; and Sun Yat-sen, 28, 30, 31, 37; and Marxism, 40, 47, 49, 55, 56, 63, 64, 65, 66, 70, 95, 104, 114; and Ch'en Tu-hsiu, 62, 72; and student movement, 93, 103; and Chinese nationalism, 111
May Fourth Incident (1919), 2, 10, 17, 181; and student movement, 6, 94, 101; and Sun Yat-sen, 20; and United States, 198
May Fourth Movement, 1, 7, 8, 16–18, 36, 72, 104, 121, 126; and Sun Yat-sen, 18–20, 37; and Marxism, 26; and Chinese Communist Party, 34, 55, 62; and literary revolution, 59; and imperialism, 68; failure of, 94–95, 96; and student

movement, 101; and Naitō Torajirō, 164
May Thirtieth Incident (1925), 6, 47, 69, 103, 106
Mencius: on democracy, 124
Meng Chao-yüeh, 142
Mexico: and extraterritoriality, 9; and Borodin, 43
Miyazaki Torazō: and Sun Yat-sen, 27
Morocco, 189
Moslem rebellions, 7

Naitō Torajirō, xiii, 13, 161, 174, 175; on Chinese society, 162–163; on China's political capabilities, 163–166; on Sino-Japanese relations, 166–173
Nanchang Uprising, 7
Nanking Incident (1927), 182, 228
National Pacification Army, 115, 138, 143, 144
National Protection Army, 110
National Protection Movement, 110
National Revolutionary Army, 84; and Northern Expedition, 51, 134, 145; and Chiang Kai-shek, 115, 127; and Chekiang provincialism, 128, 135–136, 138–143, 146
National Student Association, 105
National University of Peking, 17, 162; and Chinese Communist Party, 62; and student activism, 96
Nationalism, ix, xii, 1, 9–10, 11,

12, 13, 101, 127; definition of, 10, 55, 108–115; and Kuomintang, 36; Chinese nationalism, 38, 45, 46, 48, 54, 103, 160, 172, 174; and Chiang Kai-shek, 53; and Chinese Communist Party, 56, 67; and student movement, 96, 98; and Wu P'ei-fu, 115–126; and provincial militarism, 128, 133, 135, 143, 146; and unequal treaties, 178, 180

Nationalist Army, 115

New Education Movement, 100

New Tide, 18, 19

New Youth, 17, 18, 19, 26, 59, 99

Nien rebellions, 7

Nihonjin, 161

Nikolsky, M., 26

Niu Yung-chien, 221, 222

Nixon, Richard M., 176

Northern Expedition, 51, 127, 173; and Chekiang provincialism, xii, 13, 128, 134, 142, 145; and Chiang Kai-shek, 5, 115, 159; and Whampoa Military Academy, 11, 102; and Ch'en Tu-hsiu, 61; Third Northern Expedition, 73, 76, 78, 93; Second Northern Expedition, 77, 80; and anti-foreignism, 182, 190; and unequal treaties, 193; and Sun Yat-sen, 198

Okano Masujirō, 119

Open Door policy, 184

Opium Wars, 8

Ōsaka asahi shimbun, 161

Ou-yang Hsiu, 60

Pai Ch'ung-hsi, 143, 144, 150, 151, 155, 222; and April 12 coup (1927), 156–157

Paoting Military Academy, 116

Paris Peace Conference (1919), 38; and May Fourth Movement, 8, 18, 181; and Chang Kuo-t'ao, 33; and anti-foreignism, 111

Peasant movement, ix, 5, 6–7, 53, 95; Maring on, 29; and Ch'en Tu-hsiu, 71; and Maoist education, 107; and Chiang Kai-shek, 149, 158

Peita: see National University of Peking

Peiyang Army, 116, 117

Persia, 189

Pi Shu-ch'eng, 150

Po Wen-wei, 61

Price, Ernest B., 200

Reconstruction Magazine, 19

Red command schools, 11, 74–76

Reinsch, Paul, S., 198–199

Revolution of 1911, 18, 73; and Sun Yat-sen, xi; failure of, 38; and Ch'en Tu-hsiu, 72; and Chiang Kai-shek, 92; and student movement, 96; and nationalism, 108, 109; and anti-Manchuism, 111; and Chekiang provincialism, 128, 130; and Naitō Torajirō on, 163

Revolutionary Alliance, 18; and Ch'en Tu-hsiu, 61, 62, 199; and Sun Yat-sen, 79

Roosevelt, Theodore, 188–189

Roy, M. N., 65

Russell, Bertrand, 1; and Sun Yat-sen, 19

Russia, xii, 1, 11, 155; influence on Kuomintang, ix–x, xi, 10, 155, 227; and Sun Yat-sen, 5, 15–16, 26–37, 38–39, 182–183; and Chang Tso-lin, 8–9; and Lenin, 39–41; and Joffe, 41–42; and Borodin, 43, 45–54, 79–80; and anti-imperialism, 64–66; and Ch'en Tu-hsiu, 69–70; and influence on Whampoa Military Academy, 74–78, 89; and Chiang Kai-shek, 85, 88, 91–93, 148–149, 159; and student movement, 94, 103; and Wang Ching-wei, 152; and Manchuria, 168; and Japan, 169

Russo-Japanese War, 120, 167, 169

Seamen's Labor Union, 156

Self-strengthening Movement, 112

Shakee Incident (1925), 47, 48

Shantung Question, 198

Shen Ting-yi, 19

Shidehara Kijūrō, xiii, 160

Shikan Gakkō, 130, 133, 134, 135, 138, 140, 141, 145

Sino-Japanese War (1894–1895), 116; and Wu P'ei-fu, 119; and Naitō Torajirō, 167

Sneevliet, H.: see Maring, G.

Snow, Edgar, 157

Soong Mei-ling, 5

Soong, T. V., 5, 152, 154, 220

Stalin: and Borodin, 43; and Chinese revolution, 49, 50, 51, 54; and Chinese Communist Party, 64; and Wang Ching-wei, 152; and Chiang Kai-shek, 158

Student Magazine, 99

Student movement, xii, 12, 38, 94; and May Fourth Movement, 10, 20, 34; and Maring, 29; and growth of radicalism, 95–98; and student subculture, 98–99; and education system, 99–101; and anti-militarism, 101–102; and anti-imperialism, 102–104; and revolutionary parties, 104–106

Suehiro Shigeo, 167

Sun Ch'uan-fang, 5, 221; and Chekiang provincialism, 128, 130–145

Sun Fo, 220

Sun-Joffe manifesto (1923), 5, 15, 36–37, 42, 74

Sun Yat-sen, 52, 111, 126, 198, 201, 227; and Russia, ix, xi, xii, 4–5, 11, 15, 26–37, 41–46, 74, 182–183, 203, 205; and northern campaigns, 10; and May Fourth Movement, 18–20; and Ch'en Chiung-ming, 20–26, 200; and Chinese revolution, 38–39, 60; and Borodin, 43–46, 50, 79; death of, 49; and Three Principles of the People, 81, 153; and Chiang Kai-shek, 83, 86, 87, 88, 91, 92, 93, 149, 158; and "constitution protection movement," 110;

and liberal nationalism, 113; and Wu P'ei-fu, 124; and Kuomintang, 177; and anti-imperialism, 181
Sung dynasty, 120, 124

Tagore, Rabindranath, 1
Tai Chi-t'ao, 19, 33
Taiping rebellion, 7, 73, 176
T'an Yen-k'ai, 76, 148, 149
Tanaka Giichi, xiii, 160
T'ang Chi-yao, 4, 109
T'ang dynasty, 124
T'ang Shao-yi, 21, 22
T'ang Sheng-chih, 4, 146
Tariff Conference, 8
Teng K'eng, 23
Terauchi Masatake, 161
Three Principles of the People: and influence of Russia, 45–46; and Whampoa Military Academy, 78, 81, 82, 86, 91, 92, 93; and Wu P'ei-fu, 124; and Ch'en Tu-hsiu, 153; and Chinese revolution, 158; and foreign powers, 181
Tōyō keizai shimpo, 168
Treaty of Portsmouth, 169
Treaty of Wanghsia, 178, 179
Trotsky, Leon, 62, 63, 64; and Trotskyites, 53; and Trotskyite theory, 54; and Chinese Trotskyist Party, 69; and red command schools, 74, 75, 77
Ts'ai Ao, 109–110
Ts'ai Ho-sen, 35, 126
Ts'ai Yüan-p'ei: and May Fourth Movement, 17; and Sun Yat-sen, 18, 25; and Che-

kiang provincialism, 139, 141, 142; and Chiang Kai-shek, 151; and April 12 coup (1927), 157
Ts'ao Ju-lin, 199
Ts'ao K'un, 3, 110
Tseng Kuo-fan, 11, 112, 165
Tsou Lu, 61
Tu Yüeh-sheng, 152, 155, 156, 158
Tuan Ch'i-jui, 2–3, 5, 23, 110, 121
T'ung-meng-hui: see Revolutionary Alliance
Turkey, 189
Twenty-one Demands, 1, 8, 13, 18, 27, 111, 168, 170

Unequal treaties: and anti-foreignism, 8, 67, 180, 181, 182; and student movement, 103; and Sino-American relations, 176–182, 185; and Sun Yat-sen, 227
United States: and China, xii, 94, 167, 169, 176–179, 183–196; and Sun Yat-sen, 23, 25, 27, 30, 39; and Borodin, 43; and Chinese Communists, 68–69; and Chiang Kai-shek, 152; and studies of China, 162

Versailles: see Paris Peace Conference (1919)
Voitinsky, G. N., 28–29, 41
Von Hintze, Paul, 31, 32

Wang, C. T., 139
Wang Ching-wei: and Ch'en Chiung-ming, 21; and Maring, 29; and Ch'en Tu-hsiu, 33,

152–153; and Kuomintang leadership, 49–50, 93; and Chiang Kai-shek, 51, 159; and Chinese Communists, 155, 156
Wang Ch'ung-hui, 202
Wang Po-ling, 152
Wang P'u, 221
Wang Shou-hua, 155
Washington, George, 39
Washington Conference, 8, 27, 68, 121, 172, 181, 184, 189
Weekly Review, 19
Wei dynasty, 124
Wen T'ing-shih, 161
Whampoa Military Academy, 11–12, 46–47, 136, 144; and Sun Yat-sen, 5; and Russia, 54; training and indoctrination, 73–93; and students, 102
Wilson, Woodrow, 18, 33, 191
Wu Chih-hui, 105, 151, 152, 155, 157
Wu P'ei-fu, xii, 3, 5, 12, 13, 110, 135; and suppression of rail-way workers, 6; and Ch'en Chiung-ming, 23; and Russia, 28–30; and Sun Yat-sen, 33; and Britain, 68, 104; and Chinese nationalism, 115–126
Wu T'ing-fang, 21, 22
Wu Yü, 2, 113
Wuchang uprising (1911), 18, 39

Yeh Chien-ying, 149
Yeh Chü, 24, 25
Yeh Ch'u-ch'ang, 221
Yen Fu, 112, 161
Yen Hsi-shan, 146
Yenching University, 9, 12
Yorozu chōhō, 161
Youth Magazine, 17, 59
Yü (ancient king), 2
Yüan dynasty, 124
Yüan Shih-k'ai, 1, 3, 60, 109, 130; and anti-Yüan campaigns, xi; death of, 2, 110, 115; and Pei-yang Army, 116–117; and Naitō Torajirō, 164, 165
Yüeh Fei, 116, 120